A Prince Among Them

OTHER BOOKS BY AL AND JOANNA LACY

Hannah of Fort Bridger series:
Under the Distant Sky (Book One)
Consider the Lilies (Book Two)
No Place for Fear (Book Three)
Pillow of Stone (Book Four)
The Perfect Gift (Book Five)
Touch of Compassion (Book Six)
Beyond the Valley (Book Seven)
Damascus Journey (Book Eight)

Mail Order Bride series:
Secrets of the Heart (Book One)
A Time to Love (Book Two)
Tender Flame (Book Three)
Blessed Are the Merciful (Book Four)
Ransom of Love (Book Five)
Until the Daybreak (Book Six)
Sincerely Yours (Book Seven)
A Measure of Grace (Book Eight)

Shadow of Liberty series:
Let Freedom Ring (Book One)
The Secret Place (Book Two)

Shadow of *Liberty*

BOOK THREE

A Prince Among Them

AL&JOANNA LACY

Multnomah® Publishers *Sisters, Oregon*

A PRINCE AMONG THEM
published by Multnomah Publishers, Inc.

© 2001 by AlJo Productions, Inc.

International Standard Book Number: 1-57673-880-9

Cover image by Aleta Rafton
Background cover image by Tony Stone Images
Design by Chris Gilbert/Uttley DouPonce DesignWorks

Scripture quotations are from:
The Holy Bible, King James Version

Multnomah is a trademark of Multnomah Publishers, Inc.,
and is registered in the U.S. Patent and Trademark Office.
The colophon is a trademark of Multnomah Publishers, Inc.

Printed in the United States of America

For information:

MULTNOMAH PUBLISHERS, INC.•POST OFFICE BOX 1720•SISTERS, OREGON 97759

Library of Congress Cataloging-in-Publication Data

Lacy, Al.
   A prince among them / by Al and JoAnna Lacy.   p. cm. -- (Shadow of liberty ; bk. 3)
   ISBN 1-57673-880-9 (pbk.) 1. Great Britain--History--Victoria, 1837-1901--Fiction.
   2. Windsor, Edward, Duke of, 1894-1972--Fiction. 3. British Americans--Fiction.
   4. Kidnapping--Fiction. I. Lacy, JoAnna. II. Title.
PS3562.A256 P75 2002 813'.54--dc21   2001005804

02 03 04 05 06—10 9 8 7 6 5 4 3 2 1 0

With deep affection we dedicate this book to
Jennifer Curley
in appreciation for her excellent editing work on our novels.
May the Lord bless you, Jennifer. We love you!

1 THESSALONIANS 5:28

And I the LORD will be their God,
and my servant David a prince among them;
I the LORD have spoken it.

EZEKIEL 34:24

*I*n the 1870s a group of French citizens celebrated the centennial of the American Revolution by commissioning the construction of a statue of "Liberty Enlightening the World." The statue was to be presented to the people of the United States to demonstrate the harmonious relationship between the two countries.

The statue, monumental in size, would be the creation of the talented French sculptor, Frédèric Auguste Bartholdi, whose dream was to build a monument honoring the American spirit of freedom that had inspired the world.

In the United States, government leaders were pleased with the kind gesture and set about raising the $300,000 needed to build a pedestal for the huge French statue, which would be erected on Bedloe's Island in New York Harbor. Promotional tours and contests were organized to raise the money. During these fund-raising campaigns, American poet Emma Lazarus—the daughter of a prominent Jewish family in New York City—wrote the poem "The New Colossus" which was inscribed on the pedestal just prior to the statue's dedication by President Grover Cleveland on October 28, 1886.

Emma Lazarus's immortal words transformed the French statue of Liberty Enlightening the World into the American Statue of Liberty, welcoming the oppressed of the world within its borders to have opportunity to make their dreams come true.

"The New Colossus" on Miss Liberty's pedestal reads:

Give me your tired, your poor;
Your huddled masses yearning to breathe free,
The wretched refuse of your teeming shore.
Send these, the homeless, the tempest-tossed to me,
I lift up my lamp beside the golden door!

Castle Island in New York Harbor served as the chief entry station for immigrants between 1855 and 1891, though it was diminutive in size. In order to enlarge the facilities for processing immigrants, New York authorities began considering another site in the harbor. Eyes shifted to Governor's Island, but that was already occupied by the United States Coast Guard. Attention turned to a larger island just a few hundred yards north of Bedloe's Island, where Lady Liberty held high her torch. (Bedloe's Island was later named Liberty Island.)

The choice island was originally called Kioshk, or Gull Island, by Native Americans in the 1600s; Gibbet Island in the early 1700s when criminals were hanged there from a gibbet, or gallows tree; later it was Oyster Island because of its abundant population of shellfish. In the early 1780s, the island was purchased by wealthy merchant Samuel Ellis, from whom it derived its present name. New York state bought Ellis Island in 1808, and used it as an ammunition dump until June 15, 1882, when the immigration facility—built at a cost of $500,000—officially opened its doors. From that time, Ellis Island was the lone entry station for immigrants, and remained so until 1943.

The hopeful message on the Statue of Liberty's pedestal has greeted millions of immigrants from countries across the seas who left their homelands behind in search of a better life in the United States of America.

According to the Statue of Liberty–Ellis Island Foundation, today more than a hundred million Americans can trace their roots to ancestors who came into this country through Ellis Island. This means that approximately half of today's Americans are the offspring of pioneering ancestors who registered into the country through that immigration station which stands virtually in the shadow of the Statue of Liberty.

Martin W. Sandler, author of the book *Immigrants,* says, "Our culture diversity is our greatest strength, for we are more than a nation. Thanks to those who dared to be immigrants, we are a *nation* of nations. It is a heritage of which we should all be proud."

American historian Oscar Handlin said, "Once I thought to write the story of the immigrants in America. Then I realized that the immigrants *were* America's story."

They came from many countries across the Atlantic Ocean. For many, the journey was treacherous, and the good life they came for was just a dream. For others, the sailing was smooth, and they prospered in the new land. Both kinds of people created the rich and diverse country in which we live today.

They heard talk about a place where all men were free, a place of compassion. But what about the cost? Not just money for the passage, but the emotional toll. For most immigrants, grandparents, aunts, uncles, cousins, and friends would be left behind. The same was often true of wives and children. The men would have to go alone and send for their families later. Many of the children, who came with their mothers later on, would see their fathers for the first time in months—sometimes years—in the shadow of the Statue of Liberty.

The immigrants were driven by pain and fear and hopelessness; by poverty and hunger; by religious persecution; or by the simple need to survive. They came with nothing but the clothes on their backs, a pocketful of dreams, possibly a flimsy suitcase, trunk, or lidded woven basket, and some crumpled bills carefully stashed in pockets or purses. There are countless stories of new friendships and relationships that were begun while aboard ship or while waiting at the process station to be approved by physicians and government officials to enter the country.

None who entered this new land and found their place within its borders did so without having their lives changed forever.

A Note from the Authors

It is with great pleasure that we present this series of novels about America's immigrants. We have walked the grounds of both Liberty and Ellis Islands and caught the spirit of those men, women, and children who left their homes in faraway countries, traversed the oceans, and came to the Land of the Free.

Passing through the same buildings on Ellis Island where they took their medical examinations and their verbal tests in hope of entering this country, we could almost hear the shuffle of their weary feet, the murmur of voices, the laughter of children, and the crying of babies.

The walls of the buildings are covered with photographs of the immigrants, their faces displaying the intimidation they felt, yet a light in their eyes that showed the hope that lay within them for a better life in America.

We have purchased many historical books that have been written about the immigrants. Some tell us of statements that were made by them during and after their arrival in New York Harbor. A Slovenian immigrant told of when he first entered New York City as a boy. The skyscrapers at that time were an amazing ten, eleven, or twelve stories in height. "The city dazzled us," he said. "We had never seen such buildings, such people, such activity. Maybe the stories were true. Maybe everything *was* possible in America!"

Those readers who know our other fictional series are fully aware that our stories are filled with romance, adventure, and intriguing plots designed to make the books hard to lay down. They are interlaced with Scripture that will strengthen and encourage Christians, and as always, the Lord Jesus Christ is honored and His gospel made clear.

Since the books in this series are about the people of Europe, which is comprised of many countries and tongues, and because a great number of them spoke several languages, we will not weary the reader by continuously pointing out what language they were speaking. We will simply give it to you in English. Since this third volume in the series takes place in Great Britain and the United States, the language spoken is English, making this particular novel an easy one.

It is our desire that the reader will feel as we did when we walked those hallowed halls, deeply impressed with the courage of those people who helped settle this land we call home.

Introduction

*I*n British history, the longest reigning monarch was Queen Victoria, who reigned from 1837 to 1901—a period of sixty-four years.

Alexandrina Victoria, the daughter of Edward and Mary Louise Victoire, Duke and Duchess of Kent, was born May 24, 1819, and was called "Drina" as a child. She became queen of England at eighteen years of age upon the death of her uncle, King William IV, on June 20, 1837.

Victoria's father died when she was eight months old, and as she grew older, she faced many emotional trials with a domineering mother, who was her regent, and a tyrannical household controller who had plans to educe a financial fortune for himself when Drina became queen.

When Victoria ascended the throne, the people of Great Britain were in doubt of her ability to successfully lead the nation with all of its problems. She surprised them all. Her painful early life had shaped and toughened her. In her formative years, she learned to overcome severe emotional deprivation and adversity, so that when she became England's reigning monarch, she brought to her role extraordinary strength, determination, and resilience.

Diminutive in form, yet strong in spirit, Victoria emerged as the defining symbol of her day. While the forces of social, economic, and religious change swirled around her, she stood her ground for what was right, armed with her own fortitude.

Today, we still hear much about the Victorian era, with its high moral standards and ingrained respect for God and His Word. This is the legacy Queen Victoria left behind. History has not recorded for us the exact time in Victoria's life when she opened her heart to the Lord Jesus Christ as her own personal Saviour, but there is plenty of irrefutable evidence recorded, which leaves us with no doubt that she was a true Christian.

John Townsend, a British physicist and professor of experimental physics at Oxford University—and a devout Christian—wanted to hear it from the queen herself. He wrote her a letter, putting in several Scriptures on salvation, and told her if she was not sure that she was going to heaven, she needed to heed those Scriptures and put her faith in Jesus Christ to save her.

In her letter of reply, Victoria said, "Your letter of recent date received. I appreciate your concern, and want you to know that I have carefully and prayerfully read the portions of Scripture referred to. I want you to know that I believe in the finished work of Christ at Calvary for me, and trust by God's grace to meet you in that Home of which Jesus said, 'I go to prepare a place for you.'"

During her reign, Queen Victoria often attended Christian musical concerts, and especially loved composer George Frideric Handel's Christ-honoring oratorio, "Messiah." The story is told that upon hearing Handel's "Messiah" for the third time in her life, Victoria was overwhelmed with the way it glorified the Saviour, and when the majestic oratorio built to a crescendo, with tears streaming down her cheeks, she rose to her feet. The entire audience of thousands saw the queen rise and instantly did the same. From that moment, audiences always rise to their feet when the oratorio reaches the Hallelujah Chorus.

In February 1840, when she was twenty years of age, Victoria married Prince Albert of Saxe-Coburg-Gotha. In the following seventeen years, she bore him nine children. Albert died of typhoid fever in December 1861, leaving Victoria to enjoy her many grandchildren and great-grandchildren without him. She grew especially close to her first great-grandson, Prince Edward Albert, who was born in June 1894. In the confusing Windsor tradition of rarely calling family members by their real names, he was nicknamed "David." He would one day become King Edward VIII. Victoria doted on him. To Victoria, David stood out in the royal family, and was truly "a prince among them."

During her long reign as Queen of England, Victoria saw many victories for truth and righteousness, which brought her much joy, but there were also many national crises through which she suffered, in addition to a half-dozen attempts to assassinate her. There were also many tragedies within the family—beyond Albert's early death—as some of Victoria's children and grandchildren died with various diseases.

On September 23, 1896, Victoria had reached a milestone. She wrote in her journal, "Today is the day on which I have reigned longer, by a day, than any English sovereign. God has guided in the midst of terrible trials, sorrows, and anxieties, and has wonderfully protected me."

Queen Victoria died on January 22, 1901, at the age of eighty-one, after a brief illness. Her death caused consternation among nearly all her subjects, as no one under the age of seventy could remember living under another monarch.

Today, on the grounds of Buckingham Palace—the London residence of the British sovereign in the city of Westminster—there stands in the eastern gardens a memorial to one British monarch: Queen Victoria.

One

It was a gloomy, fog-enshrouded Monday morning in late December 1819. An icy rain was falling steadily in downtown London, England, and Londoners were hurrying along the boardwalks, some with hats pulled low and heads bent into the strong northerly wind. Others were holding onto umbrellas that were buffeted about by the powerful gusts.

At Physicians' Clinic, bookkeeper Esther Knowles, a fifty-year-old spinster, stepped out into the driving wind, holding an umbrella in one hand, and a leather portfolio in the other. Bracing herself for the two-block walk to Barings Bank, she paused, stuck the portfolio under her arm, and used her free hand to secure her hat and tighten the scarf that encircled her neck. Then with the valise in hand again, she headed down the street.

The relentless wind flung prickling ice crystals in her face, making her gasp and suck the ice-cold air into her lungs, but she pressed on. The deposits had to be made, and she had another errand to tend to at the bank.

Inside Barings Bank, twenty-eight-year-old loan officer Gordon Whitaker sat at his desk, protected from the inclement weather except for the cold gusts of wind that swept his way from across the lobby when customers came and went through the bank's double doors. From time to time, Whitaker looked up from his paperwork to smile and speak to customers who moved past the area where he sat among other bank officers.

When Esther Knowles approached the bank's double doors, a man was coming out and held the door open for her. She thanked him and moved inside. The sudden warmth of the bank's interior made her face tingle. Esther stepped aside, shook the moisture from her black umbrella, and placed it in a stand which the bank provided for its customers. She was using her coat sleeve to wipe the portfolio dry when her eyes strayed across the lobby, and she saw Gordon Whitaker looking at her.

Gordon smiled and waved. Esther nodded, smiled rather grimly, and headed toward the tellers' counter to make the deposits. She was opening the portfolio as she stepped up behind a man who was having several bills of currency counted out to him by the teller.

A minute passed.

"'Tis a right blustery day out there, isn't it, Miss Knowles?" said the dapper young teller, who looked at her over his half-moon spectacles.

Esther was deep in her own thoughts, eyes on the papers inside the portfolio, and hadn't realized that the man in front of her had gone.

"Ah…yes, Reginald," she said, stepping up to the counter and laying the first deposit in front of him. "It's about the worst weather day we've had so far this winter. It's nice and warm in here, though."

Reginald grinned sheepishly as he began flipping through the stack of checks, checking for endorsements. "I'm glad to say I have a job inside, rather than out in the weather like some poor blokes have."

"For sure, Reginald," said Esther as she prepared to hand him the next deposit when he was ready.

While making a receipt, Reginald said, "When I was in to see Dr. Paulsen a few days ago, I noticed that a fifth doctor has been added to the clinic staff."

"Yes. We're getting more and more patients all the time. I've been with Dr. Paulsen since he first opened the clinic almost eight years ago, and it's been a steady growth ever since."

Handing her the receipt, Reginald took the next deposit and said, "I suppose most of the patients who have been with Dr. Paulsen since way back are like me. They still want to see him when they come in."

"Yes, they do. But the work has to be spread out, so one of the other doctors usually gets them."

"I know it has to be that way, but I was in my midteens when our family started going to Dr. Paulsen, and even though I know the other doctors no doubt are good, I still like to be taken care of by him when I'm sick."

"I understand," said Esther. "We get attached to a doctor, and we like to stay with him."

When the deposits had been made and Reginald handed Esther the last receipt, she thanked him, placed it with the others in the portfolio, and started to turn away.

"I hope you have a good day in spite of the weather," said Reginald.

Esther paused and managed a small smile. "Thank you."

The smile faded as she made her way toward the area that was closed in by a balustrade. Gordon Whitaker was not one of Esther's favorite patients, and she would rather not have to talk to him, but Dr. Paulsen expected her to inform him about the duke's sudden turn for the worse. Gordon was a very demanding person and Esther was quite uncomfortable around him, as she also was around Alice, his snooty wife.

Gordon had a customer at his desk as Esther moved through the small gate. Looking up, he smiled. "Did you need to see me, Esther?"

"Yes, sir," she said.

"I'll be through here in just a moment," said Gordon. He

pointed to a small row of chairs just inside the gate. "Have a seat right there."

The moment turned into almost twenty minutes, and a fidgety Esther Knowles arose from her chair as the man walked past her and Gordon motioned for her to come to him.

Gordon was on his feet behind the desk as Esther drew up. He bid her sit down on the chair in front of the desk, then sat down, himself. "What did you need to see me about?"

In a solemn tone, Esther said, "Dr. Paulsen was called to Kensington Palace almost an hour ago. Your friend, the Duke of Kent, has taken a turn for the worse. Just before he left the clinic, Dr. Paulsen told me to let you know about it when I came in to make the deposits. He said as close friends as you and Edward are, you would want to know. I'm afraid this relapse could mean the thing the royal family has dreaded is going to happen. Edward may not have long to live."

Gordon Whitaker's features stiffened. "Oh my. This indeed is bad news, Esther. But I thank you for letting me know. I can't get away quite yet, but I'll head for the palace as soon as possible."

"I'm sure the doctor will be with Edward for quite a while, Mr. Whitaker," said Esther, noting the deep frown on his brow while rising to her feet.

As Esther made her way to the small gate, passed through, and headed across the lobby, the frown on Gordon's brow disappeared and an evil smile curved his lips. "Thanks for the good news, Esther," he whispered, chuckling. "Thank you very much."

Esther made her way to the stand where her umbrella waited for her, paused, wrapped the scarf tightly around her neck, and secured her hat carefully on her head. She picked up the dripping umbrella and pushed her way out the ornate door into the wintry day.

People were passing by the enclosed area near Gordon's desk as he watched Esther move outside. There was a wicked gleam in his eyes as he rubbed his palms together. Hurriedly, he completed the paperwork before him, then made his way to the desk of the small, bald, bespectacled man who was secretary to the officers in that section. "Wilfred, I see that Mr. Brookman's office door is closed.

When he's free, will you tell him I had to leave because a friend of mine has become seriously ill?"

"Of course, Mr. Whitaker," said the man.

"I'll be back as soon as I can," said Gordon, and, putting on his hat and coat, left by the back door.

Alice Whitaker was ironing one of her husband's shirts in the kitchen when she heard the front door of the house open and close. She instantly recognized Gordon's footsteps, and as he entered the kitchen, she set the iron back on the stove to heat up again. "Gordon, what are you doing home at this hour? Are you ill?"

A grin spread from ear to ear as he moved up to her, cupped her face in his hands, and kissed her. "Sweetheart, I've never felt better in my entire life!"

Eyeing him quizzically, Alice said, "Well, tell me why you're home in the middle of the morning, then."

Looking around, Gordon asked, "The children anywhere near?"

"No. They're playing in the spare room upstairs. Why?"

"I have something to tell you, and I don't want little ears hearing it."

"All right. What is it?"

Quickly, Gordon told Alice what he had learned from Esther Knowles when she came into the bank to make a deposit.

Elation lit up Alice's eyes. "Oh, do you suppose—"

"Yes! From what Esther said, it looks like it! Maybe Edward is about to leave this world…and we're taking a giant step closer to the riches we've been talking about."

Alice took a deep breath and smiled. "Well, get over there to the palace before Dr. Paulsen leaves!"

Lamps were lit throughout the sprawling old brick mansion known as Kensington Palace—on the north bank of the river Thames—in an attempt to ward off the gloom of the day.

The weathered bricks around the front door on the outside had a mellow hue where two large lamps burned, their flames flickering from the boisterous wind. The dual glow helped adorn it some, but the aged structure had never been an imposing one, and on this raw December day it seemed to huddle close to the ground as if seeking warmth and comfort.

Inside the mansion, in the hallway outside the master bedroom on the third floor, Mary Louise Victoire, Duchess of Kent, sat on a long padded bench, holding her seven-month-old daughter, Alexandrina Victoria. Sitting next to her was the baby's governess, Louise Lehzen.

Mary's lips quivered as she looked at Louise through a mist of tears and said, "Oh, Louise, I'm afraid Edward is going to die. He will miss watching little Drina grow up, and she will have no memories of him."

Patting Mary's hand, Louise said, "Now, dear, let's not give up. Maybe Dr. Paulsen will come out of there with good news. He might be able to tell us that this relapse isn't as bad as it seems."

"Oh, Louise, you are such a help to me," said Mary, gripping the hand that was patting her. "I don't know what I would do without you."

Louise was about to comment when Meredith Palmer, the palace's maid and cook, topped the stairs and headed toward them. Meredith said, "Madam Mary Louise, Mr. Gordon Whitaker is here and asked if he might wait and see the duke after Dr. Paulsen has gone."

"Of course," said Mary. "Dr. Paulsen told me he had sent word about Edward to Mr. Whitaker this morning. I was sure he would come soon. Please bring him in."

Meredith headed back down the stairs.

Louise said, "I believe we would have to say that Mr. Whitaker is the duke's best friend, wouldn't we?"

"Yes," said Mary, brushing the blond hair of her baby girl from her eyes. "Without a doubt. Gordon has shown himself to be so."

Little Alexandrina, who was enjoying a full stomach, cooed contentedly, for which Mary was thankful. If she became fussy, Louise would take her to the nursery a little farther down the hall, and right now, Mary needed Louise with her.

Gordon Whitaker came up the stairs at a fast pace, and when he reached the top, he hurried toward the women. He stood two inches under six feet, and his sand-colored hair was already beginning to thin on the back of his head. Most women did not think of him as handsome.

"I came as soon as I could, Mary. Dr. Paulsen's bookkeeper told me about Edward when she came into the bank. He wanted me to know about Edward being sick again."

"Thank you for coming," Mary said, thumbing a tear from her eye. "Dr. Paulsen wasn't encouraging at all before he went in there. I'm afraid Edward isn't going to live much longer."

Gordon looked at the governess. "I'm glad Mary has you, Louise. I know you are a comfort to her."

"I try to be," said Louise.

Bending over the duchess, Gordon embraced her in a brotherly fashion. "Of course I want Edward to live a long life, Mary, but if this is his time to go, I want you to know that I'll be here at your side to help in any way I can."

Dabbing at her tears with a hanky, Mary said, "Thank you, Gordon. You are such a true friend. I can't tell you what it means to know—"

They heard footsteps coming toward the door of the bedroom.

"—to know you will be here to help me," Mary finished.

The door came open and Dr. Ralph Paulsen stepped into the hall, black medical bag in hand. He closed the door quietly behind him. His face was dismal and gray. Nodding at Gordon, he said, "I'm glad Esther got the message to you, Gordon." Then to the duchess: "Mary…I…I can't give you any hope. Edward isn't going to get better. He has at best a week or maybe two. I haven't told him this, but I'm sure he knows his time is short."

As Mary burst into tears, little Drina started to cry. Louise said, "I'll take her, Mary," and gently lifted the baby from her mother's arms, held her close, and patted her back, whispering to her in a soothing tone.

Meredith topped the stairs, worry showing on her face as she headed toward them.

Gordon stepped toward Meredith and whispered, "Dr. Paulsen just gave us the bad news. Edward is going to die."

Meredith's face pinched. "Oh, no."

As Mary sobbed, the kindly physician laid a hand on her shoulder and spoke in soft tones, trying to comfort her, but for the moment it was as if he wasn't even there.

While the sobbing went on, Dr. Paulsen opened his medical bag, took out a paper packet, handed it to Meredith, and said, "Mix this with a strong cup of tea, please. Get it down her as quickly as you can. It will help calm her. I wish I could stay longer, but I have surgery scheduled this afternoon, and I must get back to the clinic."

"Of course, Doctor," said Meredith, clutching the small packet in her work-roughened hand. "I'll walk you down to the door."

Paulsen nodded and turned back to Mary. Patting her shoulder, he said above her loud sobs, "I'll be back tomorrow, Mary."

She looked up through her tears, drew a shuddering breath and sniffed. "Th-thank you…for coming, Doctor. See you…tomorrow."

To Louise, the doctor said, "If I'm needed before tomorrow, please send for me."

"I will."

Paulsen nodded at Gordon, the look in his eyes showing that he appreciated his presence, and followed Meredith toward the stairs.

Mary choked on her tears, pressed her hanky to her mouth momentarily, then stood up on shaky legs. "Gordon, I want to go in and see Edward for a few minutes. Then you can spend some time with him. All right?"

"Of course," said Whitaker. "I understand. I'll be glad to wait."

Mary stepped to Louise, caressed her baby's chubby cheeks lovingly, then squeezed Louise's shoulder and said, "You're such a dear."

Louise, who was fighting tears herself, managed a thin smile.

Mary moved up to the bedroom door. Taking a shaky breath, she got a tight grip on her emotions, dabbed the tears from her cheeks, opened the door, and stepped in. Closing the door behind her, she leaned against it and stood there for a brief moment, observing her beloved husband in the bed across the room. Tears surfaced once again as she gazed at his thin, emaciated form, which once wore the uniform of the British army and fought tenaciously in many a battle.

Quickly dashing the tears from her eyes, she made her way quietly up to the side of the bed, admonishing herself to be strong for Edward's sake.

Edward lay perfectly still, his eyes closed, laboring for every breath. His face was pallid and drawn.

Mary cautiously lowered herself onto the straight-backed wooden chair beside the bed. She looked longingly at the dear face of the one who had captured her heart when first they met. Slowly she reached out a trembling hand and caressed his sunken cheek.

It seems like only yesterday, she thought, *that he was a healthy, robust man. How could he deteriorate so rapidly?*

Feeling Mary's soft hand on his cheek, Edward opened his pain-filled eyes and looked tenderly at his love.

Mary pressed a smile on her stiff lips, and, still caressing his cheek, uttered words of encouragement that neither one believed but both hoped for deep in their hearts.

After spending some twenty minutes with him, Mary said, "Darling, Dr. Paulsen sent word to Gordon at the bank, to tell him of your setback. He's out in the hall and wants to see you. I'll step out so the two of you can be alone."

Edward licked his dry lips, managed a weak smile, and said softly, "Please send him in."

Two

When Gordon Whitaker entered the room, he noted quickly that Edward's features were pale, but as he moved up to the bed, the ailing duke did his best to smile as he drew a shuddering breath. "Hello, Gordon. I appreciate your coming to see me."

Sitting down on the chair beside the bed, Gordon faked a worried look and said, "The minute Dr. Paulsen's bookkeeper told me that you were feeling worse, I began making arrangements so I could get away from the bank long enough to spend some time with you. I hope you're feeling better soon."

Edward ran a dry tongue over equally dry lips. "Gordon, you're the best friend I have. I can level with you."

"Of course."

"Dr. Paulsen tried to show optimism about my condition, but Gordon, I'm not going to get better. I know my time is short."

Deepening the false look of sadness on his features, Gordon said, "I hope you're wrong and the doctor's right, Edward, but...well, if you're right, I remind you of the suggestion I made when you first took sick and it appeared that you might not live much longer. With you gone, Mary and the baby are going to be worse off financially."

Edward swallowed with difficulty and nodded. "I've been thinking about your suggestion a lot since I've been ill. It's best for Mary, Gordon."

The two men discussed the fact that even though the duke and duchess were allowed by the king to live in the aging Kensington Palace, they were given no income from the royal family. Edward's sickness had cost them a great deal, and though he had a small pension because he had served in the British army, because of their debts it would barely be enough to live on when he died.

Edward said, "Gordon, if you tell me you will help Mary by becoming controller in the household and guide her in the management of her funds, as you suggested, I can die with peace about the situation."

With a secret warm feeling inside him, Gordon laid a hand on Edward's arm. "I'll be glad to shoulder this responsibility. It's the least I can do."

Edward managed another weak smile. "Thank you. Would...would you bring Mary Louise in so I can explain it to her?"

"Of course."

Gordon opened the door, told Mary that Edward wanted to explain something to her, and as she moved past him, he closed the door and followed her to Edward's bedside. Mary sat down on the chair and took the shaky hand her husband offered. With Gordon standing beside her, Edward explained to Mary what Gordon had offered when he first became ill. He told her that they had just discussed it, then because his breathing was becoming more labored, he asked Gordon to explain to her exactly what he would do to help her manage her money so she and Drina would be comfortable financially.

While dabbing at her tears with a hanky, Mary looked up at Gordon and said, "I can't tell you how much I appreciate your willingness to take over this responsibility, Gordon. I know so little about managing money. Thank you."

"I'm glad I can be here for you and Drina," said Whitaker. "I've promised Edward I will see that you and that sweet baby are taken care of." He leaned down and laid a hand on Edward's shoulder. "I'll leave you two alone. I must get back to the bank. I'll check on you real soon."

When Gordon was gone, Mary broke down and sobbed, clinging to Edward's hand. After a few minutes, she gained control of herself, and said, "I'm sorry, darling. This is just…just so hard."

"I know," he said, barely above a whisper. "But, sweetheart, at least I can die peacefully, knowing you and Drina will have Gordon to look out for you. And—" He gasped for breath. "And even if at times you don't understand the decisions Gordon makes concerning the finances, please do whatever he says. He's a banker. He knows what he's doing."

Wiping tears, she said, "I will, darling. I'll do whatever he says."

Gordon Whitaker left the palace with a secret smile on his face, climbed into his carriage, and headed for home.

While guiding the horse along the narrow streets, Gordon thought about the royal family, and the opportunity that Edward's death was going to give him to take a huge step toward the riches he and Alice had been dreaming about. He pondered little Alexandrina Victoria's right to the throne. She was the only living grandchild of King George III, who was elderly and in poor health.

"Ol' George won't live much longer," he said aloud to himself. "And then there's his oldest son, George IV. The hopeless alcoholic. Hmpf! When he becomes king, he won't last long. At fifty-seven, he's not married. No heirs to the throne from him."

Gordon heard someone on the boardwalk call his name. He looked up to see one of his bank customers and called out, "Hello, Charles! How are you?"

"Fine!" said Charles.

By this time, the carriage had passed him. Twisting on the seat, Gordon smiled and waved. He squared himself on the seat, and immediately his mind went back to the royal family.

"Yeah, George," he chuckled. "With your liver problems, you aren't going to last long. And then there's your brother, William. He's two years younger than you, but like you, he has no children to follow him to the throne. And even if he lives to the ripe old age of seventy-five, Drina will be twenty years old when she becomes queen. Alice and I will still be in our forties. We'll have plenty of time to enjoy the wealth."

When Gordon arrived home, he put the horse and carriage in the small corral behind the house, and as he stepped up on the back porch, he saw the eager face of Alice looking at him through the window. When he reached for the doorknob, the door flew open, and Alice said, "Tell me! Tell me!"

Closing the door, he looked around. "Where are the children?"

"Upstairs again. Tell me!"

Taking both her hands in his, Gordon said with elation, "Doc Paulsen says Edward doesn't have more than two weeks! Edward knows he's dying. He and I talked alone, and I brought up my suggestion. He thanked me for offering, agreed to it, then had Mary come in so we could explain it to her. She went for it, too!"

"Wonderful! So just like we planned…when the day comes that Drina becomes queen and all that wealth is showered on her, she'll be so grateful for what you did for her and her mother, she'll share the riches with you."

"That's it. In the meantime, I'll work on Mary so she'll feel so obligated to me, that she'll influence Drina's thinking in my favor."

"Oh, it'll work. I'm sure of it!" Alice kissed him, looked deep into his eyes and said, "I'm proud of you for so cleverly working your way into the position to lay hold on the royal money. It'll be worth waiting for."

Edward, Duke of Kent, died in January 1820. Shortly thereafter, King George III died, and his son George IV ascended the throne. He reigned for ten years and died in 1830. The aging William IV became king in his brother's place.

During the decade since Edward's death, Gordon Whitaker had served the Duchess of Kent as her financial controller, even putting up his own property and possessions as collateral at times in order to guarantee her loans until she could pay them off with her meager pension.

Early in the decade, a bargain was sealed between Whitaker and the duchess—the bargain he had planned on. She agreed if he continued to pledge his collateral, and to handle her finances in such a way as to keep her creditors at bay, she would repay him handsomely once her daughter ascended the throne. Mary vowed to herself that she would always give Drina reason to trust her, so when Drina became queen, Mary Louise would be endowed with her own riches. And Drina would honor her mother's promise to Gordon.

There were times when Mary had cause to wonder about some of Gordon's financial dealings. On occasion, she cautiously questioned him, and he soothed her fears, reminding her that it was Edward's dying wish that he handle her affairs. Feeling guilty for doubting Gordon and questioning Edward's judgment, from then on she submitted to Gordon's decisions, keeping any adverse thoughts to herself. As time went by, Mary was less and less involved in any decision making and yielded all financial control to Gordon. She told herself he had been a kind and patient friend and had been willing to mortgage possessions and property to keep her solvent. She owed him the trust Edward had asked her to give him.

While growing older, Princess Victoria became aware of Whitaker seeking her trust, and at times he and her mother seemed to be vying for influence over her, each seeking to gain the upper hand over the other to gain her favor. This pressure was clouding Drina's childhood and making her dislike Whitaker.

As the years passed, the princess saw Whitaker gaining more and more control over her mother. Because he was seeing to it that Mary Louise's creditors were happy, she was allowing him to take more and more control of her life, which the child resented. Drina was finding Gordon Whitaker more and more loathsome.

On June 26, 1830, when word had come to Kensington Palace that King George IV had died, Mary Louise sat her daughter down and said, "Honey, with your Uncle William now king of England, this puts you next in line for the throne, even though you are very young. We've talked about this many times before."

The eleven-year-old, eyes still red and swollen from weeping over the news of her Uncle George's death, said, "Yes, Mother. I'm the Princess of Wales now, and it frightens me."

Mary patted her hand. "You have royal blood in your veins, sweetheart. I've noticed of late that you are already showing the poise and dignity befitting a queen."

Drina's features tinted.

"And this brings up something I've been thinking about the past few weeks with Uncle George being so sick," said Mary. "Since you are now Princess of Wales, you will no longer be called Drina, but Victoria. It sounds more dignified."

"Whatever you say, Mother. I want to please you in every way."

Mary smiled. "I knew you wouldn't object, honey. Now that you have this new importance, I'm going to begin giving grand dinners here at the palace in your honor. I'll invite King William, as well as other members of the extensive royal family, and of course, we'll have nobles and ambassadors so everyone possible can get to know England's Princess of Wales."

"I appreciate what you want to do, Mother," said Victoria, "but all of these grand dinners will cost money. You will have to hire chefs, waiters, and servants."

"Yes, as well as additional dressmakers and milliners," said Mary.

The princess frowned. "But how will you pay for it?"

"Gordon will make it possible. I've already talked to him about it. He agrees that it should be done."

Victoria did not show it, but the mention of Gordon made her stomach turn sour. This would be something else that would make her mother beholden to him.

At each grand dinner, the princess appeared before the guests, scrubbed and polished until she shone. Her darkening blond hair had been curled charmingly around her face each time by Louise Lehzen, who had dressed her in stiff organdy gowns, wide satin sashes, and lace-trimmed pantalets.

After one dinner, Mary overheard some of her foreign guests

discussing how short the princess was for an eleven-year-old. Before the next dinner, Mary had begun training her daughter to hold herself well by pinning holly under her chin as an adornment, but in actuality, it was so if her head drooped, the sharp thorns pricked her neck.

Victoria's polished manners were noted and approved by the dinner guests time after time. She was quite able when called upon to recite French and German poetry, being adept in both languages. She also pleased the guests when she sat down at the piano and played "There's No Place Like Home" or "The Battle of Prague," and they showed it with enthusiastic applause.

There was, however, one continual unpleasant note in Princess Victoria's life. She detested Gordon Whitaker the more as it became apparent that he was now in firm command of the household, and her mother was simply beaten down, convinced of the wisdom of her financial controller.

Whitaker now made all decisions—both financial and personal—for Mary and her daughter, and he ruled Victoria with an iron hand. He was subtle in his approach. Though his orders were actually delivered to Victoria through the duchess, the child knew what was going on and despised him for it.

One night in September, after a grand dinner and concert, Mary walked into Victoria's room as the child was putting on her nightgown in preparation for bed.

"Honey," said Mary, "I want to talk to you about the way you've been acting at the dinners. You seem so solemn and grim. What's the matter?"

Buttoning her nightgown, Victoria said, "I…I've tried to keep it inside me without it showing, Mother. But I guess the last few days I haven't done so well at it."

"Well, what is it?"

A stony look captured her eyes. "It's Gordon. Why do you let him control you? And why does he have any say in my life?"

Mary set affectionate eyes on her daughter. Victoria was a loving and obedient child, and she was exceptionally bright. It was time to tell her. "Sweetheart, there's something I need to explain to you. Let's sit down here on the bed so we can talk."

They sat down together. Mary put an arm around Victoria, and told her about the promise she had made to Gordon of a generous financial remuneration when Victoria one day became queen.

The child's flawless brow took on a deep frown. "Why did you promise him that, Mother?"

"Because I knew I needed his help with my finances. Your father always handled the money in this household, dear. I just don't know that much about it. But Gordon is a banker. He knows how to handle money." Mary pulled the little princess tight against her side. "Honey, the promise I made Gordon has paid off. He has kept us solvent all of these years. Without him, we would have lost everything. I owe it to him to let him control the household. And I certainly owe him a financial reward."

Victoria's troubled eyes darkened. She took a deep breath, feeling nerves twitching throughout her small body. "As far back as I can remember, Mother, I have never trusted him. I don't like his having this control over us, and I don't like *him*. I want you to send him away. We can make it without him."

Mary was frowning. "No, we can't. We have to have his help."

"No, we don't, Mother. He is a wicked, greedy man, and I don't want him to ever get any of our money when I become queen."

Mary stood up, put hands on hips, scowled, and snapped, "You have a bad attitude, young lady! The reason you think we can make it without Gordon's help is because you're too young to understand. I've noticed that you haven't been very nice to Gordon lately, and I want this to change."

Victoria started to speak, but Mary cut her off by saying, "I want you to promise me that you'll be nice to Gordon from now on."

Victoria bit her lower lip. "But—"

"But nothing! Gordon has gone out of his way many times to help us, Victoria. Promise me you'll be nice to him from now on."

The child sighed, looked at the floor, then raised her eyes to meet her mother's gaze. "All right. I'll be nice to him."

"Thank you," said Mary. She bent down and kissed Victoria's forehead. "Good night. See you in the morning."

"Good night, Mother," Victoria said softly.

When Mary moved into the hallway and closed the door behind her, Victoria jumped off the bed and began pacing the floor. Fury toward Gordon Whitaker boiled inside her. Breathing hotly, she said through clenched teeth, "When I become queen, Gordon, you won't get any money, and you will no longer have a place in my life nor my mother's life!"

In the afternoon of the next day, Victoria was with her mother and her governess in the library where she was playing a new piece she had learned on the piano.

Just as she finished, Maude Erlinger, the new cook and maid, entered the room and said to Mary, "Mr. Gordon Whitaker is here, madam, and wishes to see you."

"Of course," said Mary. "Send him in."

Victoria left the piano bench, bracing herself.

When Gordon stepped into the library, he smiled and said, "Good afternoon, ladies."

All three greeted him. Mary noted with pleasure that her daughter was smiling at Gordon.

Looking at Mary, Gordon said, "I would like to talk to you alone."

"Certainly," Mary replied pleasantly. "Louise, you and Victoria talked earlier about taking a walk. Now would be a good time for it."

"Yes," said Louise. "Let's go, Victoria."

As child and governess were heading for the door, Gordon cleared his throat. "Louise, don't take Victoria off the palace grounds. You can walk around the perimeter of the house. I don't want Victoria out on the streets."

A distasteful look captured Louise's features as she followed Victoria out the door and closed it.

As Mary and Gordon sat down in worn-out chairs, facing each other, he said, "We must protect Victoria in every way. If something happened to her, neither one of us would come into the wealth we are both planning on."

"I want my child protected, of course, Gordon, but I'm quite satisfied with the protection I have always given her."

"Yes, but she wasn't Princess of Wales then," argued Gordon. "We must tighten security on her a great deal more. You and your servants must follow the rules I am about to lay down, and after she becomes queen."

Mary listened as Gordon laid down the rules, which she could see were designed to keep the princess in a safe but stifling cocoon. Victoria must be kept in isolation from other children, except Gordon's children. She was not to leave the palace grounds except on carefully chaperoned excursions.

"And another thing," said Gordon. "Victoria has been taken to church regularly since she was eight years old when Louise became one of those 'born-again' Christians. Victoria is no longer to attend church. There are too many people there. She isn't safe in a crowd. And besides, she is doing too much Bible reading on her own, as well as being taught from it daily by Louise. This has got to stop."

Mary—who never went to church herself—said, "Gordon, I won't let Victoria go to church anymore, since you feel it compromises her safety. But I can't take the Bible reading and lessons from her. She loves it too much."

Whitaker shrugged. "All right. But another thing that worries me is the affection she has for Louise. If she gets too attached to Louise, I want the woman dismissed. And I don't want Louise being given any money by Victoria when she becomes queen. Maude, either, for that matter."

Mary pulled her lips into a thin line and nodded. As time had passed, she had found it more and more difficult to give in to his demands. By now, she was so deeply indebted to him she could see no way out.

Gordon listed more rules, making sure that Mary understood.

"Something else," Gordon said levelly. "If Victoria shows me contempt over these rules—as she has been known to do—she is to be disciplined. Understand?"

"I've already talked to her about her attitude toward you. It will be all right now."

"Good!" said Gordon, rising to his feet. "Well, I'll be on my way."

Mary walked to the front door with Gordon and watched him drive away in his carriage. She found herself wishing Gordon's rules didn't have to be so strict and confining to her daughter. But she told herself it would be worth it in the long run. When Victoria was older, she would know it was all for her own good. When Victoria became queen, she would need Gordon as her financial advisor even as King William had Baron Robert Quinton as his financial advisor. By then, Victoria would appreciate Gordon's care over her and have the confidence in him to make him her personal financial controller.

When Gordon's carriage passed from view, Mary turned and headed for the winding staircase. As she climbed slowly, she told herself Victoria did need the best of protection. After all, she was heir to the throne.

All of Great Britain would one day be under her rule. They would need her to guide the country to even better things than they had now.

"And I need you, precious daughter," Mary said as she topped the stairs of the second floor and began mounting those to the third floor.

"As mother of the queen, I'm looking forward to living in luxury…something I have never known, even as a duchess. Whatever would happen to me, Victoria, if your life were cut short? I am far too beholden to Gordon to ever have any kind of life of my own."

That evening, when Mary, Victoria, and Louise went together to the library after dinner, Mary said to her daughter, "Honey, I have something very important to talk to you about, and I want Louise to stay and listen too."

They sat down together, then Mary laid down Gordon's new rules carefully and explicitly.

"Mother," said Victoria, "I've tried to be obedient to you, but I do not have to be obedient to Gordon. I don't like his rules."

"Mary," said Louise, "the rules are far too strict. It will almost be like the child is in prison."

The duchess's features stiffened. "It's all for her own good, Louise. Gordon is just wanting to protect her from all possible harm and danger. He doesn't want her in crowds, where some dissident person would be in a position to hurt her. So…" Mary took a deep breath and cleared her throat. "So…Victoria will no longer be allowed to go to church with you."

Silence fell over the room like a dark, settling dust.

Louise could only stare mutely at her mistress.

Victoria's face was white. Her arms and legs felt leaden. The pulse on the sides of her neck raced as tears welled up in her eyes. "Mother, as you have listed all of these rules, I have thought to myself that at least I still had one bright spot. And that was going to church on Sundays with Louise. But this too is being taken away from me."

Her own heart pounding, Mary said, "I just told you that Gordon says crowds can be dangerous for you. There's no way to know who might want to kill you because of who you are. They can blend into a crowd and do their damage without anyone suspecting them until it's too late. Gordon is right. His rule is now *my* rule, Victoria."

The princess pulled a hankie from her sleeve, wiped the tears from her cheeks, and for a moment, could not speak. Louise looked at her with compassion.

Swallowing hard, Victoria choked once as she tried to speak, swallowed again, and with sadness in her eyes, said softly, "Mother, I will do as you say because God's Word tells me to. In Colossians 3:20, it says, 'Children, obey your parents in all things: for this is well pleasing unto the Lord.' I never want to be disrespectful to you. At least I can still read my Bible and have Louise teach me here at home."

"Yes," said Mary. "You can do that."

"And I can still pray, can't I?"

"Of course."

"That's good, because I've been praying for you, Mother, that you will open your heart to Jesus and let Him be your Saviour. And I will keep praying till you do."

"And so will I," said Louise.

"Oh, pshaw," Mary spurted out, rising to her feet. "What has your God ever done for me? He took my beloved husband, and left us destitute." She headed for the door. "Without Gordon's help, we would be in the poorhouse right now."

With that, Mary was gone.

With tears flowing again, the child stood up and looked to her friend and governess. Louise was out of her chair instantly, and folded Victoria in her arms.

"Don't cry, sweetheart. You and I will keep praying for your mother. We're both God's children because we've been born again, and He will be with us every moment of our lives. He cares about us, and He wants your mother to be saved. We must make sure that we have surrendered our all to Him, so He can use us to be witnesses to her."

Dabbing at her eyes with the hankie again, Victoria gave her governess a watery smile. "I have so much to learn, Louise. Thank you for helping me. You have taught me so much, and I want you to teach me lots more. I'm going to need God's wisdom more and more as I grow older."

The door opened, and Mary came back in. "There are some other changes I need to tell you about, Victoria," she said, moving up to them. "First, Gordon says since Kensington Palace doesn't have armed guards like Buckingham Palace does, he doesn't want you sleeping in a room by yourself. We'll put a cot in my room, and you can sleep there."

"How long will I have to do this?" asked the princess.

"Till Gordon says differently. Secondly, when you go up or down the stairs in this house, Louise or some other person must walk with you and hold your hand lest you trip and fall. And when you go outside and walk around the grounds, you are always to have someone with you."

"Mary," said Louise, "you know I love my position here as

Victoria's governess, and I don't want my job terminated, but this hovering over the child is going to smother her. Surely you can ease up a bit."

Mary looked at her affectionately. "Louise, you'd really have to do something terrible for me to terminate your job. I understand your wanting Victoria to feel she has some freedom, but all of this is for her own good."

"Mother," said the princess, "I don't mean to seem rebellious toward you, but I have to say that Gordon's rules are not for my own good. They're really for Gordon's good. He figures if something happens to me, he'd lose out on that money you promised him."

Louise frowned, looking puzzled, but said nothing.

Ignoring her daughter's words, Mary said, "The final change I want to tell you about is that when you sit down to a meal, the food set before you must be sampled first by Maude. Gordon fears that Maude might be bribed by some enemy of the throne to poison you. So she has to sample the food that goes on your plate. This rule, like all the others, will be obeyed and followed to the letter. I've already told Maude about it."

It was all Louise could do to keep her mouth shut, but she knew even if she spoke up, it would be of no use. Gordon Whitaker had a hold on the duchess which seemed unbreakable.

Three

On Christmas day, 1830, Princess Victoria awakened on the cot next to her mother's bed, hearing the rustling sounds the duchess was making as she was dressing near the closet.

Victoria yawned and stretched her arms.

"Merry Christmas, sweetheart," she heard her mother say.

Victoria rolled over, smiled, and said, "Merry Christmas to you, too, Mother."

Mary moved up to the bed while buttoning the last button on her blouse, bent down, hugged her, and kissed her cheek. "Have you looked out the windows?"

Victoria sat up and swung her gaze toward the bedroom's two large windows. "Oh! It's snowing! We're going to have a white Christmas!"

"Yes! We need to get this day started. I'm going downstairs. You'd better get dressed. I'll let Louise know you're up, so she can come in and fix your hair all nice and pretty. Breakfast should be ready in about an hour."

With that, Mary hastened from the room, closing the door behind her.

Victoria jumped off the cot and hurried to the window. She smiled when she saw that there was already about an inch of snow on the ground.

Excitement filled her heart. Christmas had always been a joyous holiday at Kensington Palace. Although funds were scarce, love abounded. Not only did Victoria have the love of her mother, but there was also the love of Louise Lehzen, her faithful governess and friend.

While watching the snow fall in big fat flakes, Victoria thought of Meredith Palmer. Meredith had gone to America to live with relatives almost two years ago. Her letters conveyed the happiness she had found there. Victoria was glad Meredith was happy, but she still missed her, and the love Meredith always showed her. However, she and Maude Erlinger were enjoying a sweet relationship, and the love between them was growing.

Almost putting her nose on the window, the princess looked toward the heavy sky and said, "Happy birthday, Lord Jesus. I've always loved Christmas, but I love it even more now that I'm a Christian and truly understand the miracle of Your birth."

Rubbing her arms from the slight chill that was in the room, Victoria went to a nearby chair, picked up her wrapper, put it on, then sat down on the chair and slid her feet into her felt slippers. A tempting aroma was making its way into the room, causing her mouth to water. Maude was working her magic down in the kitchen, and the princess was eager to get a taste of it.

Just as she stepped out into the hall, she saw Louise come out of her room, tying the belt on her robe. Rushing to her, Victoria wished her Merry Christmas, and they embraced as Louise returned the greeting.

"You ready for me to fix your hair?" asked Louise.

"Not quite. I want to go down and see if I can get a sample of that sweet-smelling coffee cake Maude's making. It'll only take a few minutes. I need to wash my face before you fix my hair. I'll tap on your door when I'm ready."

"All right, honey," said Louise. "You do that."

Victoria hurried down the back stairs and headed for the kitchen.

She paused at the kitchen door, and looked toward the front of the house. It was a beautiful sight. Victoria had been allowed to help her mother, Louise, and Maude decorate the drafty old mansion with small pine trees in pots, adorned with holly red ribbons to brighten them. Small tables in all the rooms on the main floor were decorated with colored wax candles. There was a festive aura in the air.

Entering the kitchen, Victoria found Maude taking a fragrant coffee cake from the oven, and the air was redolent with the aroma of cinnamon.

Maude's back was toward her, and she was unaware of her presence until she heard her say, "Mmm-mmm! That smells so good. Could I sneak a little piece?"

Maude chuckled. "This is for dinner later on, sweet stuff. Breakfast will be on the table in the dining room in about forty minutes."

Victoria looked at the coffee cake, ran her tongue over her lips, and said, "Just a teeny-weeny piece?"

Setting the tray down, Maude dropped the pot holders and hugged the child. "Oh, all right. You want some hot chocolate to go with it?"

Beaming, the princess said, "Oh yes! You're the best cook in all the world, Maude."

Maude laughed. "That kind of talk will get you anything! Sit down. I'll fix you right up."

Victoria sat down at the round oak table and rested her chin in her hands while watching Maude cut a piece of the coffee cake and pour her a mug of hot chocolate.

When it was set before her, Maude said, "Now I have to take a bite of the coffee cake and a sip of the hot chocolate to prove I didn't put poison in it."

Victoria stood up, kissed Maude's cheek, and said, "You don't have to do that. I know you're not going to poison me. Mother won't know, and neither will Gordon."

Maude smiled. "All right. Enjoy it."

The princess hugged her and said, "By the way…Merry Christmas!"

Maude hugged her again and said, "Merry Christmas to *you*, my little friend."

Less than ten minutes later, Victoria swallowed the last bite of the cake, finished the mug of hot chocolate, and wiped the sticky sweetness from her mouth with a napkin. Thanking Maude for letting her sneak the piece of cake, she hurried up the back stairs, tapped on Louise's door to let her know she would be ready for her hair to be fixed in a few minutes, then hurried down the hall and entered her own bedroom.

Pausing for a moment, she looked around the room lovingly. She missed sleeping there, but at least she still got to use the room to wash up, dress, and get her hair done. The face of Gordon Whitaker came to mind, and shaking her head to make it go away, she went to the closet where her clothes were kept and opened the ornate door. She mused for a moment, then took a green velvet dress from a hanger and laid it on the bed.

After washing her face in the icy water from the enameled pitcher, she dried off briskly. Knowing her mother expected her to be prompt in the dining room for breakfast, she hurriedly slipped the soft velvet dress over her head. The creamy lace collar added a glow to her face.

She fastened the row of buttons down the bodice and was tying the wide sash in back when there was a light tap on the door and Louise came in.

"My, don't you look nice!" Louise said, giving her a hug.

Victoria looked her governess over, and said, "You look nice, yourself."

The lovely woman's face tinted. "It's sweet of you to say that, honey."

Victoria giggled. "I only say it because it's true."

Louise guided her to the dresser, where she sat down on the stool and looked at herself in the mirror. Louise picked up a hairbrush, and brushed the princess's hair briskly. Then she picked up a comb and worked at it until the hair shone in curly ringlets around her face.

"How's that, honey?" asked Louise.

Victoria looked at herself in the mirror. "Just fine, like it always is when you do it."

Louise bent down, kissed the top of her head, and said, "What would I do without you to bolster my ego?"

Victoria slipped into her favorite pair of shiny black shoes, and together, governess and princess headed downstairs.

When they entered the dining room, Maude was placing steaming bowls of oat cereal on the table as Mary stood by and watched. Louise greeted the duchess and the cook with a Merry Christmas wish, and Maude joined them as they sat down to eat.

Leaning toward Victoria, Maude said, "All right, sweet stuff, I'll take a bite of the cereal and a sip of the milk I just poured for you."

Smiling at her, the princess watched her mother from the corner of her eye and said, "You don't have to do that, Maude."

"Oh, but she does," said Mary. "Not that I distrust Maude in the least, but Gordon made the rule and we must abide by it."

The cereal and the milk were sampled by Maude, Louise prayed over the food as usual, and they began to eat.

Victoria's appetite had been satisfied with the piece of coffee cake earlier, but knowing her mother might disapprove of the snack she had appropriated from Maude, she forced herself to down the cereal.

When they were finishing their breakfast, Victoria looked at her elders and said, "We're going to have a happy day, aren't we?"

Louise and Maude exchanged fretful glances, which did not go unnoticed by the princess.

Victoria looked at her mother, who suddenly seemed a bit nervous. "What's wrong, Mother?"

Mary cleared her throat. "Nothing's wrong at all, dear. I…uh…I haven't told you, but we're having guests today. I…I've invited the Whitakers to come at eleven o'clock and spend the rest of the day with us."

Victoria felt as if a battering ram had hit her in the chest. "Oh," she said as her countenance fell.

Mary reached across the corner of the table and took hold of her daughter's hand. "Now, honey, we owe Gordon more than we could ever repay him for what he has done for us all these years. I felt it was only right that we share Christmas day with him and his family."

Victoria ran her gaze to Louise, who had been showing her Scriptures concerning how Christians should maintain their testimony before lost people. When the governess met her gaze, she smiled and gave the princess a look that said, *Here's your opportunity to put your spiritual depth to a test.*

It was difficult, but Victoria made a smile and nodded.

At precisely eleven o'clock that morning, Gordon and Alice Whitaker arrived at Kensington Palace with their three children, Marianne, Lorene, and Edgar—fourteen, thirteen, and five years of age respectively.

Mary gave them a warm welcome, then turned her attention to her daughter.

Doing her best to conduct herself appropriately for the mother and her children, Victoria curtsied before Alice. "How nice to see you, Mrs. Whitaker. Merry Christmas."

"And Merry Christmas to you, too, dear," said Alice.

Ignoring Gordon, Victoria stepped up to the three children and smiled. "Hello, Marianne, Lorene, Edgar. Merry Christmas."

The Whitaker sisters responded by curtsying, and both wishing the princess Merry Christmas.

Alice looked down at her son, frowned, and said, "Edgar, Princess Victoria wished you Merry Christmas. Can't you wish her Merry Christmas, too?"

Edgar ducked his head momentarily, then slowly raised his eyes to meet those of the princess. "Merry Twis'mas, Pwincess Bictoria."

Edgar's sisters laughed, and Marianne said, "You'll have to excuse our little brother, Princess Victoria. He's only five years old."

Victoria smiled and patted the boy's head. "That's all right. You're a good boy, Edgar."

Mary laid a hand on Victoria's shoulder. "Ah…haven't you forgotten someone?"

It seemed like cold waves were lashing at the edge of Victoria's mind as she looked up at Gordon and said in a dull tone, "Merry Christmas, Mr. Whitaker."

Gordon felt the full impact of Victoria's attitude toward him, but decided to disregard it. Doing a slight bow, he said in a cheerful tone, "And a very Merry Christmas to you, Princess."

Mary invited the Whitakers into the large drawing room, where Alice commented on the potted pine trees and the colored wax candles. There was idle chit-chat among the adults for some time, then Louise appeared and offered to take the children on a tour of the mansion with Princess Victoria at her side. When this was over, Louise and Victoria took the children into the parlor and played games with them.

Thus the day wore on.

The unwelcome presence of Gordon Whitaker in the house on Christmas Day galled Victoria. Having to share her holiday with the man she detested was a bitter reminder to the young princess of her awkward, painful situation with no father.

When the day was over, Victoria and Louise had their usual Bible study and prayer time in the bedroom the princess used to occupy until Gordon Whitaker's mandate took it from her.

As soon as they sat down, Victoria shared her feelings with her governess. Louise read Scripture to her to comfort her and to instruct her on how a Christian should react to her situation. Louise commended her for the way she acted toward Mrs. Whitaker and the children, but told her she could have been more hospitable toward Gordon for her mother's sake.

Victoria said she would try harder next time. They prayed together, and when they finished, Victoria hugged Louise. "Thank you for being so patient with me."

Louise gave her one of her magnetic smiles. "I love you, honey. The Lord is patient with me because He loves me, so it's only right that I show you the same courtesy."

"Thank you, too, for not only being my faithful governess, but for being my true friend."

∞

That night, Victoria lay quietly on the cot next to her mother's bed. She could tell by her mother's deep, even breathing that she was asleep.

Barely moving her lips in a soft whisper, the princess said, "Dear Lord, why does my life have to be like this? Everything would be wonderful if it weren't for Gordon Whitaker. Something has to be done about him and the control he has over Mother."

Tears surfaced. Her lower lip quivered. "Lord Jesus, I've prayed ever since I got saved that You would do something to remove Gordon from our lives. I'm trying hard to live for You and to please You. I want to go to church, but because of him, I can't do that. He has Mother dangling on a string like a puppet. I'm sure my father never meant for this to happen when he told Mother to let Gordon handle our money. Mother won't admit it, but she's unhappy with things like they are. And…Lord, he is making my life so miserable. You have the whole world in Your hand. You can do something about Gordon. I don't understand why he's still here. Please. Please get him out of our lives."

When Victoria had said her amen and was mopping tears with the sheet, she remembered something Louise had told her a few weeks ago about prayer. *Victoria, honey, God always answers the prayers of His born-again children if their hearts are right with Him, but the answer isn't always an immediate yes. Sometimes it is a clear and emphatic no…but usually it is wait.*

As time passed, a prospect of misery, not delight, seemed to stretch before the unhappy Princess of Wales, who was increasingly hemmed in by the inescapable fact of her personal significance. Upon entering her teen years, her life became even more confined and regimented than ever, and she knew the despicable Gordon Whitaker was behind it. In spite of trying to take a different attitude because she was a Christian, Gordon's control of her life served only to deepen the repulsion she felt toward him.

On Victoria's sixteenth birthday, May 24, 1835, King William IV had a birthday party for her at Buckingham Palace. The men of Parliament were there as well as a great number of dignitaries. The king had invited Gordon Whitaker and his wife as a favor to the Duchess of Kent. The Whitakers were seated next to Mary, who was seated next to the king.

While Victoria was fulfilling the request of her uncle to play a tune on the piano for the crowd, William leaned over to Mary and said, "Now that Victoria is sixteen and coming of age, it is expected by the people of Great Britain that she put in public appearances all over the country, since one day she will be their queen. I suggest you make plans to do this."

Overhearing the king's words, Gordon smiled at him. "Your Majesty, I was telling some of my coworkers at the bank this very thing a couple of days ago. I think it is imperative that the public appearances be made. The people of our country have heard a lot about Princess Victoria, but few have laid eyes on her. I believe I can get off from the bank to do the first tour. I could take my whole family."

"Really?" said William. "That would be wonderful. I'm sure that would make Mary happy."

"Why, of course," said Mary, already dreading to tell her daughter that the Whitakers would be going along on the first trip.

To Mary, William said, "They should be lengthy trips during spring, summer, and early fall, so the populace of Great Britain can get to know her. Since spring is on us, the first trip should be to Wales."

"I agree," said Mary. "I'll tell Victoria about it this evening, and we'll begin making plans. We should be ready in a few days."

"Good," said William. "I will provide a comfortable barouche for Victoria, you, and her governess to travel in. And as a precaution, I will send a dozen armed guards on horseback to accompany you."

"I appreciate that, Your Majesty," spoke up Whitaker. "We can't be too careful with the future queen's life."

That evening, Mary told her daughter in the presence of Louise Lehzen about the tours her uncle William had suggested, and Victoria was thrilled at the prospect of them. She was especially excited about going to Wales until her mother announced that Gordon Whitaker and his family would be going along on the first tour. This made Victoria angry, but she did not show it.

The entourage pulled out of London on Monday, June 1, 1835. Word had been spread to every town and village along the way that the Princess of Wales would be passing through. Great crowds appeared on the streets by a populace that accorded her the welcome owed to their future ruler.

They were delighted to see her, and many commented how glad they were that the princess was quite ordinary in her physical appearance, though quite small. It was a comfort to them for it made her seem familiar, as one of themselves. She was dressed simply and sensibly—as guided by Louise—with a touch of primness to her dresses. Flat shoes and a straw hat, adorned with a red ribbon, worn straight across her guileless brow, completed her costume.

As the princess rode in the barouche between her mother and her governess, she smiled and waved with white-gloved hands at the crowds, and periodically picked up a comment about her small stature.

Though Victoria knew at sixteen she no doubt had reached her full height—which was four feet, eleven inches—she had accepted her diminutive size gracefully. With the cloud Gordon Whitaker had brought into her life, her stature was a minor thing. Knowing that he was in the carriage just behind the barouche kept her uneasy. The princess's posture was perfect, and she had learned with the help of her governess to hold herself erect without seeming to be stiff, and according to Louise this gave the illusion that she was a little taller than she actually was.

As the royal entourage entered each town and village through specially erected arches garlanded with flowers, the people cheered her, calling out her name. Victoria was encouraged, and she smiled broadly, waving to them. A deep love and respect for her future subjects was taking root in her heart. With it came a strong determination to do her best, with God's help, to be a fair and just ruler. There was both delight and trepidation in her heart as she pondered her future as England's queen.

In some towns, choirs sang and bands played in homage to the princess. In others, cannons were fired in her honor and dignitaries made speeches.

They arrived in Cardiff, Wales, on Thursday, June 4. Cardiff was known for its equestrian lifestyle. Victoria had ridden horses a few times under careful supervision and loved it. For at least five miles before they arrived, she commented on the horse farms and public riding stables along the way.

When the entourage pulled to a halt at the town square, the people cheered the princess, and the town band played. Mayor Donald Redding gave a rousing speech, saying to Victoria in front of the crowd that he hoped King William would live a long life, but when the king's time came to leave this world, he was going to be very pleased to have the daughter of the late Duke of Kent as his queen.

While the crowd was applauding, Redding approached the royal party, who were seated in a shady spot near the podium. "I have a close friend who owns a riding stable just out of town a few miles. I would like to invite the princess, her mother, and her governess, and the others in the party to spend the afternoon horseback riding."

Victoria clapped her gloved hands together joyfully. "Oh, I'd love it!"

The duchess, Louise Lehzen, and the Whitakers all politely declined, but Mary looked at her daughter. "Honey, I'll let you go if Mayor Redding will assure me that you will be in good hands."

"She'll be in the best of hands, ma'am," said the mayor. "The stables are owned by my friend Hugh Barlow, and he will see that the princess is escorted properly on her ride. The rest of you will be given rooms in our finest hotel."

As Victoria rode away in her barouche with the mayor's carriage following and the dozen guards flanking them, Gordon stepped to Mary and said in a subdued voice, "You shouldn't have let her go riding. It's too dangerous."

"She's been riding before," Mary said, meeting his stern gaze. "You know that. She loves it."

"I was never in favor of it, even though she had proper accompaniment," Gordon said. "You shouldn't have been so quick to take the mayor's word concerning her safety."

Louise was standing close by. "Gordon," she said in a tone he had never heard her use, "Victoria's life is already too confining. She needs to do something now and then that gives her some freedom and enjoyment."

Giving her a disgusted frown, Gordon glanced at his wife and children and shook his head. Taking Mary by the arm gently, he guided her away from the others till they were out of earshot. "I don't like the tone Louise just used on me. I want you to fire her, and I mean as soon as we return to London."

Mary looked at him askance. "I will not fire Louise. She means too much to Victoria. It would totally crush her if Louise was taken from her."

Gordon took a deep breath and let it out slowly through his nostrils. "I'll let it go this time, but if that woman ever crosses me again, I want her fired. Understand?"

Mary turned away without comment.

When the barouche neared the Barlow's Stables in the lush countryside, Victoria could hardly contain her excitement.

The mayor's carriage was directly behind her. Victoria turned and called out, "Mr. Mayor, it's beautiful!"

Redding smiled.

As the vehicles and the twelve mounted guards reined to a halt at the large white barn and white-fenced corral, they saw a stout man and a slender, handsome teenage boy who resembled him smiling at them. Other men could be seen moving about the corral and the grounds.

The mayor jumped out of his carriage and rushed up to the pair. "Hugh, only one person in the entourage wanted to go riding and it's the princess! Come. Let me introduce you."

Victoria remained in the barouche, observing the mayor, and smiled as the man and the teenage boy followed him. When they drew up, Redding said, "Princess Victoria, I want you to meet my friend Hugh Barlow, owner of the stables, and his son, John."

Both Barlows smiled, bowed, and told the princess they were glad to meet her.

"And I am glad to meet both of you," she said in her engaging manner.

John whispered something to his father, and when Hugh nodded and whispered his reply, John stepped up to the side of the barouche. "Princess Victoria, may I help you down?"

The handsome young man could be no more than eighteen. Victoria's eyes sparkled as she said, "Of course. Thank you."

When Victoria's feet touched ground, John—who stood two inches under six feet—was amazed at how small she was. "My father and I are deeply honored to have you here."

Warming him with a smile, she said, "Thank you, John."

"Are you going to ride, Donald?" asked Hugh.

"No. I need to get back to town," said Redding. He gestured toward the dozen mounted guards. "These gentlemen will ride along with the princess."

"Of course," said Hugh. "Would it be all right if John goes, too? As you know, it is customary for an employee to accompany the riders. And John asked me a moment ago to let him be the one."

"That would be fine," said the mayor.

Victoria and John smiled at each other. She found him quite charming, and sensed that he felt the same way toward her.

"It will be my pleasure to accompany you, Princess Victoria,"

John said, his face beaming. "Have you ridden before?"

"Oh yes. And I love it."

"You would like a sidesaddle?"

"Yes."

"You wait right here. I'll saddle your horse and mine, and I'll be right back."

When John returned, leading both horses, the mayor's carriage was already rolling up the lane, heading for the road. The guards looked on with amusement as young Barlow—obviously taken with the princess's loveliness—let go of the reins. "May I help you mount up, ma'am?"

"Why, yes. Thank you," Victoria said, warming him once again with a smile.

Four

As John Barlow guided Princess Victoria past the white-fenced corral toward the open grassy fields on the family property with the guards following, her attention was drawn to a large flower garden.

"Oh, John! What beautiful flowers."

"That's Mom's hobby, Princess," said John. "She's quite the flower lover. She planted everything you see there. I wish you could meet her, but she's in Birmingham, visiting a longtime friend who recently had surgery."

"I see," said Victoria, her eyes glued to the magnificent garden. "I'm a flower lover myself, but I've never planted any. I—" She drew a sharp breath and pointed at a certain section. "What kind of flowers are those? The real bright ones with so much color? I've never seen any like that before."

"Let's stop a minute," said John, pulling rein.

Victoria halted her horse, and the guards did likewise.

While Victoria gazed at the colorful flowers waving in the slight breeze, John said, "Those are petunias, Princess."

"Petunias? It seems I have heard of them, but like I said, I've never seen any before."

"Well, the petunia is an annual herb of the nightshade family, but the reason you've never seen any in England, or anywhere in Europe for that matter, is because they are native to the Americas. My parents have a friend who works aboard a British transport ship that makes regular journeys to the east coast of the United States. Three years ago, he brought Mom a box of planted petunias from somewhere in New Jersey. He watered them and took care of them all the way across the Atlantic. She planted them here in the garden, and you can see how they've reproduced themselves into that large patch."

"I'll say. They're magnificent, John. Well, I guess we'd better get on with our ride."

Soon they were trotting across rolling green fields. During the ride, the guards stayed close behind their princess and her guide. John made the ride very enjoyable by saying funny things and making Victoria and the guards laugh.

After two hours, they were returning to the corral and barn. When they passed the flower garden, Victoria commented another time on the exquisite beauty of the petunias.

When they drew up to the barn where her driver and Hugh Barlow were sitting on a bench in the shade, John slid from the saddle and helped the princess down.

"Princess Victoria," he said, looking deeply into her eyes, "will you wait a few minutes before you head back to Cardiff, please? There's something I would like to do for you. I'll be back shortly."

"All right, John," she said, puzzlement showing on her features.

Hugh and the driver heard what John said, and both rose to their feet.

"Come sit here with us, Princess," said Hugh. Then he said to the guards, "You gentlemen may dismount. I'm sure you'd like to stretch your legs a bit."

"That we would, sir," said the leader of the guards.

Some fifteen minutes had passed when Victoria saw John coming from the backside of the corral, carrying a lovely bouquet of petunias. Jumping to her feet, she smiled at him as he drew up.

Blushing a bit, John said, "Princess Victoria, I cut these especially for you."

Victoria sighed. "Oh, thank you, John!" she said, taking the bouquet from him. "Thank you very much! They're so beautiful."

"Just like you, if I may say so," John said.

"Oh, aren't you the kind one?" said Victoria, lifting the flowers to her nose and inhaling their sweet aroma.

John helped the princess into the barouche. Holding the bouquet as she settled on the seat, she thanked him again for the flowers, and for escorting her on the ride. She smiled and waved as the driver put the vehicle in motion.

Hugh stepped up beside his son as the boy watched the barouche and the guards heading up the lane toward the road. Victoria turned and waved, and John waved back.

John took a deep breath. "What a lovely young lady she is, Dad."

"That she is, son," agreed the father.

John looked at his father. "I wish I could see her often and get to know her."

Hugh laid a hand on John's shoulder. "Son, I see stars in your eyes. It wouldn't do any good for you to try to build a romance with her. People in the royal family always marry royalty, usually distant cousins, or someone from another royal family. We're just ordinary people."

John sighed again, and set his gaze on the girl in the barouche. "I know, Dad, but it still doesn't keep me from dreaming."

Arriving back in Cardiff, Victoria's driver let her off in front of the Wellington Hotel, and accompanied by two guards, she headed for the lobby, carrying the bouquet of petunias. One of the guards hurried ahead of her. Before he reached the door, a well-dressed man came out, smiling, and said, "Princess Victoria, we've been expecting you. I'm Walter Moore, the manager. Welcome to the Wellington. We are more than honored to have you staying with us. I am to take you to your mother's suite."

"Thank you, Mr. Moore," said the princess, and followed him

toward the wide staircase, her guards flanking her.

Employees of the hotel and guests looked on in curiosity as the princess and her guards passed through the lobby.

Mary opened the door quickly in response to the manager's knock, and smiled as she looked at her daughter. "Well, honey, did you have a nice ride?"

"The best in my whole life, Mother!" came the jubilant reply.

"Well, I'm glad." Mary's eyes widened. "What beautiful flowers! Where did you get those?"

"John Barlow gave them to me. Do you know what kind they are?"

"No. But they sure are lovely. So bright and colorful."

"They're petunias—from America."

"Oh, really?"

"Mm-hmm. John's mother had a friend bring her some from America, and she planted them in her flower garden. I just love them."

"That was sweet of John to give the bouquet to you."

"Duchess," said the manager, "I'll be going now. I've ordered some tea and crumpets sent up to you. They will be here shortly."

"Thank you, Mr. Moore," Mary said, flashing him a warm smile.

As the manager walked back toward the stairs, the two guards took their places, one on each side of the door. Mary knew there would always a pair of guards there as they had been in the other hotels on the journey.

She closed the door and said, "There's an empty vase in one of the cupboards, honey. Let's put them in it and water them."

The petunias were placed in the vase, and as Victoria was pouring in water, Mary said, "I gather that John Barlow is a fine young man."

"He certainly is, Mother." She finished pouring in the water and set the pitcher down. "I hope one day I can marry a young man like John."

Mary frowned. "You must remember, dear, you can only marry within the realm of royalty. Someone like John would be out of the question."

Victoria chuckled. "I know, Mother. I simply meant that I hope to find a young man with the kind of personality and character that John has among the royal prospects." She paused, then with a pensive look capturing her eyes, said, "I've been thinking about—"

A knock at the door cut off Victoria's words.

Mary went to the door, opened it, and a silver-haired man in a white jacket with black ascot stood between the guards, holding a tray.

"Your tea and crumpets, Duchess."

That evening, in Cardiff's music hall, an impromptu musicale was held in Victoria's honor, followed by a reception.

During the reception, which included all of the princess's entourage and many of the town's leading citizens, Mayor Donald Redding stood before the crowd and told of meeting both King George IV and the present king, William IV.

While the mayor was giving some personal experiences with the last two kings, Gordon Whitaker sat next to his wife, musing about the present king. He wished something would happen to William IV that would take his life very, very soon. *In fact,* he thought, *I wish there was something I could do to hasten William's demise…but it would be foolish to try. I'll just have to be patient.*

Gordon's attention returned to Mayor Redding, who was telling of the time he had spent with Princess Victoria earlier in the day.

"Our Princess of Wales is quite the young lady," said Redding. "For a sixteen-year-old, she is very mature. And upon getting to know her a little, I was impressed with her unaffected dignity, her strong sense of herself, and her self-command. She truly is of royal blood."

Redding's words brought applause first, then as it grew louder, the crowd was on its feet, cheering the young lady they knew would one day be their queen.

As the months passed in 1835, the trips went on—without the presence of the Whitakers—until late October when the cold weather began to come. Winter brought a respite for Victoria from the fatigues and pressures of appearing in public.

When spring was coming on in 1836, King William IV was having health problems, and was now staying in beautiful Windsor Castle, a second home for the British sovereign, besides the newly renovated Buckingham Palace. Windsor Castle was much smaller, and in a country setting in Berkshire County, a few miles from London, away from the hustle and bustle of the city.

Mary and Victoria visited the king in early May, just before starting out on their first tour, and went to see him each time they were home during the summer. In mid-September, they embarked on the last trip scheduled for that year.

In early October, while making a short stop in a village in northern England, one of the guards rode up to the royal barouche holding a rolled-up newspaper in his hand. "Duchess," he said, "some people over there across the street were waving this at me. I took a look at it, and I knew you would want to see it."

Mary took it and saw that it was a copy of the *London Times,* which had come off the press two days earlier. When she opened it and saw the front page, her mouth dropped open. Looking on as she sat beside her, Victoria asked, "What is it, Mother?"

"It's about Uncle William, honey," Mary said, her eyes scanning the headlines then the text of the article.

Leaning close, the princess read the lines for herself. The article told that King William's health was deteriorating quickly, and at seventy-one years of age he was now barely able to keep up with his royal duties. His doctors had been interviewed by a *Times* reporter on the Windsor Palace grounds the day before the article was published, and the doctors had revealed that they had strongly advised the king to step down and abdicate the throne for health reasons. William, however, had stated that he must carry on for the sake of Great Britain, no matter how difficult it might be for him.

Mary folded the paper and looked at her daughter with worried eyes. "Honey, we're cutting this trip short. We've got to go home."

King William had just awakened from his afternoon nap on Wednesday, October 12, when he heard the bedroom door open softly and turned to see his nurse, Thelma Carter, come in.

"Did you get a good nap, Your Majesty?" asked Thelma as she moved toward the bed.

"Yes, I did, thank you," said William rising to a sitting position and glancing at the grandfather clock in the corner. "It's almost four o'clock. Is Lord Chamberlain here?"

"No, sir. He sent a messenger about an hour ago to let you know that he can't be here today for his meeting with you. He will come tomorrow and explain."

"That's fine. I know he'd be here if it wasn't something extremely important."

"Yes, sir. But there is someone here to see you. The Duchess of Kent and Princess Victoria."

William's bushy eyebrows arched. "Oh? I wasn't expecting them to return to London for another couple of weeks. Please send them in."

It was almost time for the evening meal when Mary and Victoria arrived back at Kensington Palace. Louise had seen the carriage pull up, and opened the door for them as they crossed the wide porch. "So how did you find him?" she asked.

"Oh, Louise," said Mary, "he's not good. I'm so worried about him."

"You can give us the details over dinner," said Louise. "Maude has it just about ready."

"All right, we'll both freshen up and be right there."

"Ah…Mary…"

"Yes?"

"Mr. Whitaker was here while you were at Windsor Castle."

"Mm-hmm."

Victoria felt a cold ball settle in her stomach.

"He wants to see you, Mary," said Louise. "He said to tell you he will be back this evening after supper."

At precisely eight-thirty, Mary, Victoria, and Louise were in the library when Maude stepped in and said, "Ma'am, Mr. Whitaker is here."

The words had barely come from Maude's lips when Gordon brushed past her, carrying a bouquet of fall flowers.

"Hello, ladies," he said, rushing up to Victoria. He extended the bouquet to her, smiling. "Princess, these are for you."

Victoria wanted to throw them in his face, but caught the look in her mother's eye and curtsied. "Thank you."

This was the fourth time since spring that Gordon had given Victoria flowers when they had come home from one of their journeys. His nice little deeds did not fool her at all. She knew he had an ulterior motive.

Gordon then looked at Mary and said, "I need to have a private conversation with you."

"Victoria and I will go upstairs," Louise said, taking the princess by the arm.

Maude had already disappeared.

When Victoria and Louise were gone, Mary invited Gordon to sit down. As soon as they were comfortable, he said, "So how long do you think William will last?"

"It's hard to tell," she replied, "but he is awfully weak."

"Good. Then maybe the moment of our glory is drawing close."

A slight frown penciled itself across the duchess's brow. "Gordon, I very much want to come into the royal wealth myself. But I can't wish King William dead. I want him to live as long as possible."

Gordon bit his tongue, wanting to lash out at her for being so foolish. But he refrained. "Well, if his doctors are trying to get him to abdicate the throne because of his health, he's got to be in pretty bad shape."

"They won't say how long they think he'll live, Gordon, but they are trying to prolong his life by getting him to step down."

Gordon rose to his feet. "Well, maybe it's best that he just stay on the throne. Hopefully that'll make him die sooner. I'll see you in a day or two."

❦

When Gordon arrived home, Alice was at the door to meet him.

"Well, tell me," she said. "Does Mary think William will live much longer?"

Gordon looked around for the presence of any of the children.

"They're upstairs," Alice said quickly. "Come on, out with it."

"She told me his doctors won't commit themselves as to how long they think he'll live, but I told her if they are trying to get him to abdicate the throne for health reasons, he's got to be in pretty bad shape."

"I certainly agree with that."

Gordon laughed lightly. "When I said maybe the moment of our glory is drawing close, she admitted that she wants to come into the royal wealth herself, but said she can't wish King William dead. She wants him to live as long as possible. Well, she can wish all she wants, but William isn't going to live much longer. I've got to work harder than ever to ensure that when Victoria becomes queen, my own status and influence will rise with hers."

"I think you're doing fine, dear," said Alice. "Did Victoria like the flowers?"

"Hard to tell. She did thank me for them, but there was no bubbly elation."

"Women like flowers. It's making an impression on her, believe me."

"Whether it makes the impression I intended, it is impressing Mary. Mary is the one who will handle my becoming Victoria's personal controller. She promised. I'll be Victoria's primary manager of finances when she becomes queen, as I have been Mary's for seventeen years. I haven't told you this, honey, but I'm planning on quitting the bank once I come into the big money Mary has promised as soon as Victoria is queen."

Alice looked surprised. "Gordon, you'd better make sure it's all going to work out the way Mary has promised before you quit your job."

"I will, but I can't see it not going as Mary and I have planned.

Victoria is a young woman, and upon ascending the throne, she'll need a man to handle her business. I'm sure with her mother's influence and the nice little things I'll keep doing, I'll become Victoria's personal controller. And from what Mary has promised, this will mean more money for us than my bank job can provide."

Alice threw her arms around his neck and squeezed tight. "Oh, darling, I'm so excited! Our big dream is coming closer every day as William's health deteriorates! I wish we could tell the children what's coming, but like we've agreed, we'll have to hold off telling them until it actually happens."

As time went on, Gordon was at Kensington Palace four or five times a week, paving his way with Mary, so she would be sure to keep her promises. He continued to do nice things for the princess, doing his best to gain her favor. However, resentment toward him continued to fester within Victoria.

As November came, King William's health was getting worse. Realizing that he would live only a few more months, Mary decided she needed to better prepare Victoria for her pending reign.

One morning at breakfast, Mary looked across the table at her daughter and said, "Victoria, I want to talk to you when we're done."

"Louise and I were going to take our walk immediately after breakfast, Mother. Could it wait till we get back, or is it urgent?"

Mary flicked a glance at Louise, then said, "It's important, honey, but not urgent. It can wait till you get back from your walk. I'll be in the library."

It was going on ten o'clock when Mary glanced up from her chair in the library to see her daughter come in. Victoria looked refreshed after having been out in the crisp November air. Her cheeks were rosy and her eyes had a sparkle.

Sitting down in a chair so she could face her mother, Victoria said, "What did you want to talk to me about?"

Mary laid aside the book she had been reading. "We both know that your Uncle William's health is continuing to fail, dear. It is quite evident that he isn't going to get any better."

Victoria nodded, her face showing the sadness she felt. "Yes, Mother."

"Victoria, you need to be thinking about marriage. It doesn't have to happen before you become queen, but you need to have the right man in mind so you can marry within a reasonable time thereafter. As you know, you must choose a husband within the ranks of royalty. You have several distant cousins you can consider."

Having been groomed most of her life to become Great Britain's sovereign, Victoria knew she had little hope of marrying for love. Yet deep in her heart of hearts, this was her fondest desire, and she had prayed much about it. There was one slim chance. "Mother," she said, adjusting her position on the chair, "do you remember that day at the Wellington Hotel in Cardiff when I had been given the bouquet of petunias by John Barlow?"

"Yes."

"And I said I hoped that one day I could marry a man like John."

"Yes, and I—"

"You reminded me that I have to marry in the realm of royalty."

"Mm-hmm."

"And I said I simply meant that I hoped to find a young man with the kind of personality and character that John has among the royal prospects. Do you remember…I started to tell you that I had been thinking about someone, then I was interrupted when the man with the tea knocked on the door?"

"Yes, I do. I was going to ask you about that, then it slipped my mind. Are you saying that you have had someone in mind?"

"There is one prospect among my cousins that interests me very much. And I think he may be interested in me."

"Who, honey?"

"Prince Albert."

Mary's eyebrows arched, and a smile creased her face. Victoria's distant cousin Prince Albert was the son of Ernest I, duke of the state of Saxe-Coburg-Gotha in Germany. Victoria had met Prince Albert for the first time when he and his father had come to London to visit King William IV just that past May, a week before Victoria's birthday.

"Oh…Albert, eh? Such a pleasant young man. A gentleman in every sense of the word, and quite handsome, I might add."

"He is all of that, Mother, but more, too. When he and I got to talking and I found out he was a born-again child of God, I really felt an attraction for him. He was very pleased to find out that I am a Christian, and before he and his father left to return to Germany, Albert kissed my hand, then held it while he looked into my eyes and told me how glad he was to finally meet me, and to learn that I am a Christian. He—well, he also told me I am the most beautiful girl he has ever seen."

Mary was not impressed with the Christian aspect of what her daughter had seen in Albert, but she was pleased to learn of the attraction they had for each other.

"Of course, it is wonderful that Albert is so good looking, too, Mother," Victoria said with a lilt in her voice. "Those large blue eyes, that beautiful nose, and his sweet mouth with such perfect teeth. And he has such a warm personality, not to mention his air of dignity and his regal demeanor. He really is quite the young man."

Mary chuckled. "I'm surprised you haven't brought him up to me before now."

Victoria blushed. "I have to admit that he has been on my mind daily. Other than when I started to mention him that day in Cardiff, I've just kept it to myself. I sure would love to see him again."

The next day, while Victoria and her governess were taking their walk, they saw Mary riding in the family carriage as it pulled through the gate and rolled down the street.

Some three hours later, Victoria and Louise were together in the library. Victoria was playing the piano when the door opened and Mary came in. The princess stopped in the middle of her tune when Mary rushed up to her and said, "Honey, I've got some good news!"

"Maude told us you were going to Windsor Castle," Victoria said, leaving the piano bench. "Is Uncle William getting better?"

"No, he's not, honey. I wish that was part of my good news, but let me tell you the good part. I talked to your Uncle William about how you feel toward Albert. I told him that it seems Albert feels the same way toward you. It made your uncle so happy to think that something could develop between the two of you, so he is sending an invitation to Prince Albert to come and visit him at Windsor Castle. He will arrange it so you and Albert can spend time together."

Victoria was delighted with her mother's news. She happily clapped her hands, hugged Mary, thanked her for talking to Uncle William about it, hugged Louise, then hurried out the door, dashed up the stairs, ran down the hall and into her room.

She threw open the double doors of her closet and ran her eyes over the clothes on hangers. "Oh, my. My wardrobe is sadly lacking. This is going to take some ingenious planning. I want to look my very best when Prince Albert comes."

Darting back into the hall, she rushed down the stairs, looking for Louise. She found her in the kitchen with Maude. They were sitting at the work table, sipping hot tea and chatting.

"Louise, I need your help," she said, catching her breath.

"Of course, honey," said Louise. "What is it? I was just telling Maude about Prince Albert's upcoming visit."

"Are you all right, honey?" asked Maude.

"Oh yes! I'm happier than I've been in a long time! Finally, some good news has reached my ears. It's just that—well, it's my wardrobe. Most of my real fancy clothes are so old and worn. These tours I've been doing have taken their toll on them. I want to look good for Albert when he comes."

Louise smiled. "Well, Victoria, we can't let you miss out on the opportunity to marry the prince if this is what the Lord wants. Your mother is running low on money, I know. But I have a little stashed away for a rainy day, and it looks like the rainy day has come. We can't have you in tatters, can we?"

"I have a little stashed away, too," said Maude. "We'll get you fixed up."

Tears misted Victoria's eyes. "Oh, bless you both!"

"Let's go up to your room and see what's there, so we'll know what we have to do," said Louise.

"I'll go with you," said Maude.

The three women mounted the stairs, Victoria in the lead, a new purpose in her life.

Three weeks later, Prince Albert of Saxe-Coburg-Gotha arrived at Windsor Castle. Given immediate audience with the ailing king, he was told that Princess Victoria wanted to see him again and spend some time with him.

Albert was pleased, for he had found a strong fascination for his distant cousin Victoria when they had met in May. He climbed in a royal carriage and headed for London.

Five

At Kensington Palace, Maude Erlinger was busy with a feather duster in the drawing room when she heard the metal knocker make its familiar clattering sound at the front door.

Laying the duster on a small table, she hurried to the door, opened it, and took in the tall, slender form that stood before her.

"Good morning, ma'am," the handsome young man said almost in a melody. "I'm Prince Albert of Saxe-Coburg-Gotha. I believe Princess Victoria is expecting me."

"Oh yes, sir," said Maude, swinging the door wider. "Please come in. She most certainly is expecting you. My name is Maude Erlinger. I'm the cook and maid."

Removing his hat and coat as he stepped inside, Albert said, "I am very happy to meet you, ma'am."

At that moment, Mary and Louise appeared, having heard the knock.

Smiling broadly, Mary said, "Prince Albert! Welcome! We thought it might be you. You remember Louise Lehzen, Victoria's governess."

"Of course," said Albert, doing a courteous bow. "It is nice to see you again, Miss Lehzen."

"Since you did not come to Kensington Palace when you were here in May," said Mary, "you did not meet our maid and cook. But I assume Maude introduced herself to you."

"Yes, she did."

"I'll go tell Victoria the prince is here, Mary," said Louise.

Mary called after her, "Prince Albert and I will be in the drawing room."

Louise looked back over her shoulder and nodded.

Not realizing Albert would arrive at Kensington Palace quite so early, Princess Victoria was in her room looking over the new dresses that Louise and Maude had provided for her, trying to decide which one to wear. She had them laid out on the bed.

There was a tap on the door, followed by the muffled sound of Louise's voice, saying, "Victoria, may I come in?"

"Yes, of course," the princess called.

When Louise entered the room, her eyes were sparkling. "He's here, honey!"

"Already?" said Victoria, her hand going to her mouth. "Oh, my! I've got to get dressed in a hurry."

"I'll help you," said Louise.

Unbuttoning her robe, Victoria said, "I think I'll wear the blue dress today."

Moments later, when Victoria was in the blue dress and Louise had fluffed the skirt to make it look just right over the petticoats, she went to the mirror and touched up her hair, making herself fully presentable. "How do I look?"

Louise giggled. "You look gorgeous, dear. Come on. Let's give Albert an eyeful."

"Oh, Louise!" Victoria said in a shaky voice as they stepped out the door and headed down the hall toward the stairs. "I'm so nervous!"

"You'll get over it when you see how pleased Albert is with the way you look."

"I...I sure hope so!"

When they stepped into the drawing room, Albert jumped to his feet and a smile worked its way across his handsome face. "Hello, Princess. My, how lovely you look."

"Thank you, Cousin Albert," said Victoria. "And welcome! It's so nice to see you!"

As she spoke, she extended her hand. Albert took it gently into his own, bowed, clicked his heels, and softly kissed it.

"Come, sit down, dear," said Mary. "I want to talk to you and Albert for a few minutes. Louise, you may stay."

When all four were seated, Mary said, "Albert, we are all so happy that you could come at King William's invitation."

"The pleasure is mine, Duchess," said Albert.

"You understand that King William invited you basically because Victoria wanted to spend some time with you and get to know you better," said Mary.

"Yes, ma'am. King William explained that in his invitation. And may I say, Princess, that I am flattered and pleased that you wanted me to come."

Victoria flashed him a smile.

"I wanted to talk to the two of you together," said Mary, "so we would all understand the proper etiquette for conduct during Albert's visit. He will, of course, be sleeping at Windsor Castle."

Victoria and Albert both nodded.

"And it is only proper, Albert," said Mary, "that you and Victoria be chaperoned while you are here."

"Of course," Albert replied softly.

"Louise will be your chaperone. I want you to spend all the time together that you can, and while you are doing so, Louise will be close by, keeping you in sight, but out of earshot in order to give the two of you a degree of privacy."

"I understand, Duchess," said Albert, "and I am in full agreement with your rules."

Knowing this was normal royal protocol, Victoria said, "I am in full agreement, too, Mother."

"Well!" said Louise. "Since Albert has never been here to the palace, how about a nice walk around the grounds? It's a bit chilly outside, but we'll be comfortable in our coats."

The walk lasted until almost noon, with Louise staying far enough behind the couple to give them privacy to talk. Maude had a delicious lunch prepared for them.

After lunch, Albert requested a concert by his cousin, saying he had been told that she was quite the pianist and had a lovely voice. So the foursome went to the library and Victoria played for him on the piano and sang a few.

After each, Albert vigorously applauded, complimenting Victoria on her talent.

This pleased her immensely.

By midafternoon, the unusual warmth of the sun made the day quite comfortable for late November, and Victoria suggested that she and Albert go outside and sit on the veranda.

Victoria and her guest found a spot at the front of the mansion, near the door, and sat down for a chat. Louise placed herself near the corner of the veranda, several yards away. She had brought a book and concentrated on reading except to look up once in a while and glance at the young couple.

Albert and Victoria told each other things about their childhood, and often laughed together over past incidents.

It was almost four o'clock when Victoria noticed a familiar carriage coming up the lane. Her stomach cramped.

As Gordon Whitaker pulled rein in front of the mansion, he saw the pair sitting near the door on the veranda. From his viewpoint as he stepped out of the carriage, he couldn't see Louise, who was blocked by a large bush that grew close to the veranda railing. He wondered why Mary was allowing her daughter to see a young man alone. He was about to say something about it to Victoria, but while mounting the steps, his eye caught sight of Louise, sitting nearby.

Louise had already noticed the frustration on Victoria's face. The princess obviously was uncomfortable because she would be expected to introduce Albert to Whitaker. Louise jumped from her chair and hurried to the rescue.

Relief came over Victoria's features when Louise introduced

Prince Albert to Gordon, explaining that he was a banker and also Mary's personal financial controller. Albert was very polite, and Gordon put on as if he was glad to meet the prince, but both Victoria and Louise knew better.

To Louise, Gordon said, "I would like to see Mary."

"I'll go announce your presence," said Louise. "You wait here with Victoria and Albert."

While Louise was gone, Albert showed polite interest in Gordon, asking what bank he worked for and then asked pertinent questions about the banking business.

Soon Louise returned and said, "Mr. Whitaker, the duchess will see you in the parlor."

Mary was adjusting the chimney on a lamp when Gordon entered the parlor, a deep frown on his face. "Gordon, what's wrong?"

"Why are you allowing Victoria to see this prince from Germany?" he asked, crisply.

"Hold on, now. Calm down. I'm more than allowing it. I made it happen."

"You what?"

"Didn't they tell you that Albert is Victoria's cousin? Distant, of course."

"No. Louise simply introduced him as Prince Albert, the son of Ernest I, duke of a state in Germany."

"All right, but now you know he's her cousin. I had King William bring him here for a good reason. Victoria will soon be queen, Gordon. She needs to marry within at least two to three years after she ascends the throne. This will be expected by the British people, and it wouldn't look good for Victoria to remain single as queen. You know that."

"Well, I…uh—"

"Albert was here in London last May, Gordon. He and Victoria took a liking to each other. I wanted to help their friendship along, hoping a romance would develop, so I asked William to bring him here as his guest, but especially to spend time with Victoria."

Embarrassment flushed Whitaker's face. "Oh. Well, I…I'm sorry,

Mary. I guess I wasn't thinking too clearly. I didn't realize…that is to say, I—well, I see the good sense in it. You did the right thing."

"I'm glad you see that. I went back to see King William a few days ago, and he has some plans to help things along between Victoria and Albert. Although he's confined to his bed much of the time, he has had his personal aid planning several activities for Victoria and Albert. The big thing is the concert that he has planned for tomorrow night at Buckingham Palace in their honor. The London Symphony Orchestra will be giving the concert."

Gordon's eyebrows raised. "Hmm. Well, I guess he is going all out, isn't he? I imagine Victoria was thrilled when she heard about it."

"She doesn't know yet. I've kept it a secret so it will be a surprise to them. All she knows is that she and Albert, along with Louise and I, are to be at Buckingham Palace at eight o'clock tomorrow night as guests of her Uncle William."

"She didn't ask why the king would be at Buckingham instead of Windsor?"

"No. She was happy to know that he could make the short trip from Windsor to the palace, but she didn't ask any questions. I really doubt the king will be able to attend, but there isn't room to host such an event at Windsor Castle."

"So who's invited?"

"All of Parliament and a host of other government officials, including London's police chief and the head inspector of Scotland Yard."

"Should be a huge crowd."

"Prime Minister William Melbourne is the master of ceremonies. I can't wait to see Victoria's face when she hears him announce that the concert is in honor of herself and Prince Albert."

During the next day, Buckingham Palace was abuzz with more activity than it had seen in a long time. Happy smiles wreathed the faces of the king's staff as they prepared the palace for the concert. They dearly loved the princess, and every effort was put forth to make the concert a joyful occasion for her and Prince Albert.

That evening, when the guests began to arrive, Buckingham Palace was dressed in all of its finery. The members of the London Symphony Orchestra were in their places on the wide platform in the great room.

Lantern light spilled from the palace's numerous high windows as carriage after carriage arrived and rolled to a halt in front of the ornate double doors. People were dressed in silk, satin, and velvet, and the ladies were adorned with an awesome array of jewelry as they alighted from the carriages.

It was already a magical night for Victoria as Prince Albert stepped out of the royal carriage and helped her down. Their eyes met and held for a moment as he squeezed her hand. She smiled at him coyly, and he warmed her with a smile of his own.

Mary and Louise followed the young couple as they moved inside the main foyer. The foursome was flanked by six guards who had ridden beside the royal carriage on horseback.

The princess had prepared herself all day for the evening. Louise had done Victoria's hair in an elaborate upsweep, with long curls descending down her back. Her dress was a gossamer dream of deep lavender. A high ruffled snowy collar caressed her neck. Tiny seed pearl buttons marched down the back of the bodice, ending at the waist. A multitude of crinoline petticoats held the dress out and rustled with each step Victoria took. Her cheeks were rosy and her eyes were bright with excitement as she took Albert's arm and he guided her into the great room.

Victoria, Albert, Mary, and Louise were seated in a special section reserved for the royal party and the half-dozen guards. The great room was full to capacity, and everyone was anticipating the concert.

The conductor picked up his baton, took his place before the orchestra, then looked off to the side of the platform and nodded. Immediately, Prime Minister William Melbourne moved toward the center of the platform and after shaking hands with the conductor, turned to face the audience.

"Ladies and gentlemen," Melbourne said, "on behalf of King William IV, I want to welcome you. The king sincerely desires to be here, but his health will not permit, so he has asked me to appear in his stead. All of you guests were informed in your invitations that this gala event was in the honor of two very special people. Those two special people have come here unaware of this."

Melbourne set his gaze on Victoria and Albert, gestured toward them, and said, "Our lovely Victoria, Princess of Wales, and Prince Albert of Saxe-Coburg-Gotha, Germany, will you please rise?"

Mary and Louise grinned at each other as Albert stood first, then gave his hand to Victoria and helped her to her feet. They both held their gaze on the prime minister as he said, "Princess Victoria, Prince Albert, on behalf of King William IV, I proclaim this concert to be in your honor. May it be an evening you will long remember."

Tears were welling up in Victoria's eyes as the entire crowd rose to its feet, applauding. Many shouted out, calling Victoria's name.

The conductor led the orchestra in a rousing number, and everyone sat down to enjoy the evening.

It had indeed been a magical night, and when Victoria shed her beautiful dress, put on a robe, and brushed her hair, there was a light in her bright eyes that had not been there for many a year.

Pausing as she brushed the tangles from her long hair, she held the brush with both hands as her thoughts returned to the magnificent evening. Closing her eyes, she relived every moment spent with Albert, savoring especially the way he looked at her before they parted.

Opening her eyes, she looked at herself in the mirror. A tranquil smile graced her lips as she observed her dreamy countenance and whispered softly, "Is this what love feels like? If it is, I like it."

Giving herself a mental shake, she finished brushing her hair, then walked down the hall toward her mother's room. The smile never left her face, and her eyes continued to hold their happy glow.

Albert had been in London for nearly a week when time came for him to head for home. As Mary and Louise looked on, the young couple's parting words were quite touching, and their attraction for each other could plainly be seen in their eyes.

This pleased Mary, and after Albert was gone, Mary and her daughter had a private talk. She was delighted to hear her daughter say that she thought she was falling in love.

Letters were exchanged between Victoria and Albert as time passed, and they found themselves becoming more and more interested in each other.

As 1837 came, King William IV was growing weaker each day. By April, he was shaking with palsy, fighting for breath, and had to be moved from room to room in Windsor Castle in a wheelchair by the two nurses who stayed with him at all times.

During the first week of April, Victoria went to visit her uncle alone, and sitting beside his bed, she told him what Gordon Whitaker was up to and asked what she should do.

William looked at her through droopy eyes and said weakly, "Sweet girl, I had no idea that this Gordon Whitaker thing has been going on all of these years. I am shocked to hear it. I thought he was loyal to you and your mother out of respect, not greed."

Taking hold of his hand, Victoria said, "I am sorry to lay this on you, Uncle William, but I need to know how to handle Gordon when—when the time comes that I ascend the throne. Mother has promised him a great sum of money, and he is expecting to become my personal financial controller."

William wheezed, "Victoria, I cannot think clearly enough to give sound advice, but you are a brilliant young lady. When you become queen, you will have to take the matter of getting rid of him into your own hands. You will have the power as queen to do so, and I am sure you can handle it."

When Victoria left Windsor Castle with Louise at her side and four palace guards riding behind, she shared with Louise what her uncle had said.

"I agree with the king, honey," said Louise. "You are a brilliant young lady, and as queen, you will find the proper way to rid yourself of Gordon Whitaker."

◦◦◦

At Kensington Palace on the morning of May 24—her eighteenth birthday—Victoria awakened on the cot in her mother's room, stretched herself, and opened her eyes. Suddenly she was aware of the bright harmonies of a choir. At first, she was at a loss as to where the music was coming from, then as her head cleared, she realized the choir was outside the palace, below the window.

"Oh, it's my birthday!" she exclaimed happily, and bounced off the cot.

As she put on her robe, she noted that her mother's bed was already made up. She padded barefoot to the window and opened it wide. Waving to the singing group who were wishing her happy birthday, she smiled and called out her appreciation.

The choir sang for some ten minutes, then dispersed, each member waving to Victoria as they walked away. The princess waved back, smiling for all she was worth, then wheeled about and hurried down the hall to her room.

When she was groomed and dressed, Victoria went down to the kitchen where she found her mother, Louise, and Maude.

"Did you like the choir, dear?" asked Mary.

"I sure did, Mother," replied the princess, letting her eyes roam over the kitchen.

It had been gaily decorated, and topped off with a big sign that said: Happy Birthday, Princess!

"Who did this?" Victoria asked, smiling.

"All three of us," said Mary.

Running her gaze to each face, she said, "Thank you." Then she said to her mother: "Did you order the choir?"

"I wish I could take credit for it, honey, but it was your Uncle William."

"Oh, bless his heart," said Victoria. "He's such a dear man."

Mary took her daughter by the hand. "Come on, dear. You must hurry and eat your breakfast. I've arranged a special birthday reception for you. Your Uncle William lent his help."

Victoria tilted her head, gave her mother a loving look, and said, "You didn't have to do that."

"Oh, but I did," said Mary, pushing her toward her usual chair at the table. "Because I love you."

Victoria kissed Mary's cheek. "I love you, too, Mother."

In less than an hour, carriages began rolling into the Kensington Palace courtyard—some having come from over a hundred miles away—bearing visitors who were eager to attend the princess's birthday reception and sign their names in her guest book. Delegations from Manchester, Birmingham, and other large cities arrived, along with crowds of Londoners. The women were in their best bow-trimmed full-skirted dresses and poke bonnets, and the men were in tight coats and gaudily patterned waistcoats, their necks stiff in high collars and wide neckcloths.

Victoria stood at the door in the foyer, her mother and governess beside her, and showed grace and dignity as she welcomed each visitor. Her guards looked on from all over the foyer.

Victoria's eyes widened when she saw Baron Robert Quinton, King William's personal controller and financial advisor coming through the door. Stepping up to him, she said, "Welcome, Baron. It is so nice to see you."

Quinton bowed, kissed Victoria's hand, and said, "Happy birthday, Princess."

"It is much happier because you are here," she said with a lilt in her voice. She looked past him. "Is Mrs. Quinton with you?"

The baron was explaining that his wife was visiting a sister in Wales when Victoria's eyes fell on a very familiar face coming up behind him. Her eyes grew wider. "Oh, Albert! It's you!"

Prince Albert stepped up, smiling.

Victoria said to Quinton, "I'm sorry she couldn't be here, but I understand."

As the baron thanked her and moved away, Albert took Victoria's hand, bowed, clicked his heels, said, "Happy birthday, my lovely," then kissed her hand.

Mary and Louise were exchanging delighted glances.

Then Mary stepped up, greeted Albert, and said, "I guess we really surprised her this time, didn't we?"

"We sure did, ma'am," said the young prince.

"Mother!" said Victoria. "You were in on his coming?"

"She was," Albert answered for Mary. "I sent a wire, telling her I would like to be here for your birthday, and she wired back a royal invitation."

"Well, thank you both. Oh, Albert, it's so wonderful to have you here for my birthday!"

Albert wanted to say he would love to be with her on every birthday for the rest of her life, but kept it to himself. "I'm honored, sweet lady."

"Albert," said Mary, "I want you to stay close to Victoria during the entire day. Of course, Louise will always be close by."

Albert smiled, nodded at Louise, and said, "That's fine, ma'am."

Mary turned in response to a woman who spoke to her, and while she was turned away, Albert bent low and whispered to Victoria, "I don't mind Louise being near, as long as I can be in Your Majesty's presence."

Thrilled at his words, Victoria whispered back, "I love being in Prince Albert of Saxe-Coburg-Gotha's presence, too!"

Everyone was gathered in the palace's largest room while Baron Robert Quinton—who had been assigned by King William to be master of ceremonies—gave a brief speech about the princess. There was much applause at his high points. When he finished, he asked Victoria to step forward and say a few words to her admirers.

Victoria thanked them graciously for coming, then gave praise to her Lord and Saviour Jesus Christ for giving her a second birthday a few years previously when she had opened her heart to Him. There were some amens among the crowd.

Baron Quinton then took center place and announced that there would be a carriage parade as the princess took a ride through a portion of the city so the people of London could express their wishes for a happy birthday. Everyone was invited to join the parade. He then announced that at eight o'clock that evening, there would be a reception for the princess at London Music Hall, and all were invited.

The gala day passed in a round of receptions and appearances in many parts of London. While being taken from place to place in the palace carriage with her guards close by, and the Whitaker family following, she saw on every street, grocers, linen drapers, gentlemen's outfitters, women's clothing stores, and the like, displaying banners and signs in their windows, wishing her a happy birthday.

Victoria was sitting in the backseat of the carriage with Albert at her side, and as the carriage moved along slowly, she said in her heart, *Dear Lord, You know I want Uncle William to live as long as it is Thy will for him to live. But I want to thank Thee that the people of Great Britain are, for the most part, so loving toward me. I do look forward to being their queen.*

Six

At precisely eight o'clock that evening, the crowd gathered in London Music Hall, where Baron Robert Quinton once again appeared as master of ceremonies under orders from the king.

Quinton once again wished Victoria a happy birthday, and the crowd stood to its feet, applauding. From where she sat near the front, Victoria stood and waved, smiling graciously. Quinton then announced that the orchestra was going to play four of the princess's favorite songs.

When the fourth song came to a climactic close, Victoria was once again on her feet, applauding the orchestra.

As she sat down between Albert and her mother, the baron took center stage once again and said, "All of you guests here tonight are well aware that our Princess of Wales is an accomplished pianist and songstress herself."

There were cheers and applause. When they subsided, Quinton looked down at the eighteen-year-old. "Princess Victoria, could we impose on you to come to the platform and give us a number?"

Instantly, applause burst forth, mingled with cheers. As Victoria started to get up, Albert jumped to his feet, took her hand, and helped her. Mary and Louise smiled at her as she allowed Albert to guide her to the aisle, where she took his arm. He escorted her to the stairs, and they made their way up to the platform. Victoria let go of Albert's arm as they stepped up to the baron.

Quinton looked at the audience. "Ladies and gentlemen, let's have a round of applause for our princess's escort, Prince Albert of Saxe-Coburg-Gotha, Germany!"

Albert bowed to Victoria—who was applauding—turned, and bowed to the applauding crowd, then descended the stairs and returned to his seat.

"Now, Princess," said Quinton, "before you sit down at the piano, someone would like to make an announcement."

Victoria saw the popular Lord Chamberlain coming toward her from the wings, smiling broadly. She smiled in return, wondering what kind of announcement Chamberlain was going to make.

He drew up, bowed, kissed the princess's hand, then holding it, spoke loudly so the audience could hear. "Princess Victoria, I would like to wish you a very happy birthday."

She curtsied. "Thank you."

Chamberlain then said, "Princess, I am here as representative of King William, who is too ill to attend. But your uncle has sent you a birthday present, and has asked me to present it to you."

With that, Chamberlain looked toward the wings and nodded.

Victoria's mouth dropped open as she saw three men wheeling a brand-new concert piano toward her. Tears misted her eyes as the crowd stood up once again and applauded. A fourth man arrived, carrying the matching bench as the piano was rolled up in front of the princess.

"Oh, it's beautiful! Lord Chamberlain, I will express my gratitude to the king in person tomorrow."

"Of course," said Chamberlain, smiling. "The piano will be delivered to Kensington Palace also tomorrow. Now, will the princess honor us with a number on her new piano?"

Victoria nodded, stepped to the bench, then before sitting down, she ran her gaze over the audience and said, "I would like to play and sing for you my favorite hymn, 'Amazing Grace.'"

The delighted audience applauded.

"Before I do," said Victoria, "I would like to pay tribute to the composer of 'Amazing Grace,' John Newton."

She then took a few minutes to tell the story of how Newton had been a wicked, hard-drinking deckhand on a slave ship. She told of Newton's Christian mother, who came to know Christ after her son had grown up and gone to sea. On occasion, he returned home, and his mother witnessed to him of the saving grace of God, but John would not heed her message. Every time she spoke to him of Christ, and he rejected Him, his mother told him she would be praying for his conversion.

On the high seas, God had sent another deckhand and a teenage cabin boy to witness to him. On a dark night at sea, the cabin boy managed to get alone with Newton and once again give him the gospel. The Spirit of God worked in Newton's heart, and under powerful conviction, he repented of his sin and asked the Lord Jesus Christ to save his wretched soul.

"Shortly thereafter," said Victoria, "the born-again John Newton sat down with tears flowing, and composed this great hymn which has touched thousands upon thousands of lives. Later he became a preacher of the gospel."

There were cheers from some in the audience.

Victoria than gave testimony of her own salvation, saying that Jesus had saved her by His amazing grace when she opened her heart to Him a few years ago. She sat down at the piano, and many tears were shed as the Princess of Wales played the piano and sang the hymn with great feeling.

Victoria was escorted by Albert back to her seat, and the orchestra did several more pieces.

It had been a glorious day for England's Princess of Wales. Victoria entered her mother's bedroom wearing a soft cotton gown and robe. Mary was sitting up in bed, an array of pillows at her back.

Victoria sat down in a nearby brocade chair, and drew her bare feet under her. "Oh, Mother, what a wonderful birthday! I'll never forget this day. I'm so happy that Albert was here to share it with me."

A fanciful expression crossed Victoria's face.

Mary smiled to herself and nodded in a knowing way. Something good was definitely happening between her daughter and the young prince. "I think it's time for us to turn in, honey."

Rising from the chair, Victoria stretched and covered a yawn. "I agree." With that, she climbed into her small bed and told her mother good night.

Soon both women were snuggled in their beds, and a sweet, peaceful sleep claimed them from their busy day.

The next morning, Victoria and Albert had a sweet moment on the veranda of Kensington Palace as he bid her good-bye. She thanked him for coming, saying it had been the best birthday of her whole life.

Albert kissed her hand as Mary and Louise looked on, then told her he would be back to see her again as soon as possible.

Weeks passed. At nine o'clock on Tuesday morning, June 20, Mary and Victoria were in the Kensington Palace sitting room in discussion with Gordon Whitaker, who had negotiated the day before with one of Mary's creditors, and had dropped by to tell her that he had provided collateral for a new loan.

Looking at Victoria, Whitaker said, "This loan was necessary, Princess, because of the extra expense your mother went to in order to give you a nice birthday last month. I'm glad I could help."

Victoria gave him a forced smile and thanked him. She knew exactly what he was doing. He was attempting to gain more of a hold on her, which he hoped would remain when she became queen. Secretly, she was formulating plans for him. Mr. Gordon Whitaker was in for a big surprise.

At that moment, Louise Lehzen came into the room. "Please excuse me, Duchess," she said in a strained voice. "Lord Chamberlain is here, and asked to see you immediately."

"Of course," said Mary. "Show him in."

Louise stepped into the hall, said something in a low voice to Chamberlain, then escorted him into the room. One look at the man's gray features told Victoria, Mary, and Gordon what had happened. All three rose to their feet.

Victoria bit her lower lip as her heart leaped in her chest.

Chamberlain ran his gaze between the faces of mother and daughter. "It is my grievous task to inform you that King William died in his bed at four-thirty this morning."

Gordon had to cover his mouth to hide a sly grin.

Mary nodded and looked to her daughter.

Tears welled up in Victoria's eyes as she asked, "Did my uncle suffer before he died?"

"No, he didn't," said Chamberlain. "Your uncle slipped out peacefully. And though I am saddened at his parting, may I be the first to address you as Queen Victoria? My congratulations, dear. The people of Great Britain are blessed to have you as our new monarch."

The eighteen-year-old queen wiped tears from her cheeks. "Thank you, Lord Chamberlain. I appreciate your kind words. I am leaning hard on the everlasting arms of my heavenly Father to help me be the queen that my subjects deserve."

Mary moved up and touched her daughter's arm.

Victoria looked at her through a veil of tears. "I need a few minutes alone, Mother. I'm going up to my room." She wheeled and dashed into the hall.

Louise said to Mary, "Should I go to her?"

"I think not, Louise. Let's give her the few minutes she needs alone, then I'll go up."

"As you wish," said Louise. "I'll go tell Maude about King William. If you need me, I'll be in the kitchen."

Chamberlain took hold of Mary's arm. "Please sit down, Duchess."

He guided her to the overstuffed chair where she had been sitting.

Looking at Whitaker, who stood beside him, Chamberlain said, "I know you have always been a pillar of strength to the princess and her mother, Mr. Whitaker. They will need you now more than ever."

A secret elation was fluttering through Gordon Whitaker, and it was all he could do to keep from shouting for joy. The long-awaited day had finally come. Putting a somber look on his face, he said, "I will do my very best, sir."

Chamberlain talked about how the news of the king's death would strike the country with mixed emotions. They loved King William, but at the same time, they knew he had not functioned as a monarch should for quite some time. They also loved Victoria and would joyfully rally behind her as queen.

Mary rose to her feet. "If you gentlemen will excuse me, I'll go up to my daughter. Both of us will be back shortly."

When Mary entered Victoria's room, the new queen was lying face down on the bed, weeping.

Mary sat down on the edge of the bed and laid a hand on her shoulder. Victoria looked up at her and drew a shuddering breath. "Oh, Mother, I loved Uncle William so much. I'll miss him terribly."

"I understand, honey," said Mary, "but now as Queen of England, you must maintain control of your emotions in the presence of your subjects and carry yourself at all times with the dignity befitting a monarch."

With great difficulty and a prayer in her heart for God's help, Victoria brought her emotions under control. Leaving the bed she went to the washbasin, splashed water on her face, and patted it dry with a towel. Looking in the mirror she dabbed at her hair, then taking several deep breaths and straightening her shoulders, she turned to her mother. A look of determination filled her eyes.

"All right, Mother," she said softly, "with the Lord at my side, I am ready to assume my role as queen of this great nation."

Mother and daughter returned to the sitting room, and both men rose from their chairs.

Lord Chamberlain looked at the queen with compassion. "Please know that I understand your grief. I know you loved your uncle very, very much."

"And please know that I also understand your grief," said Whitaker.

Victoria thought, *You are going to have some grief, Mr. Gordon Whitaker.*

Chamberlain told Victoria and her mother that at precisely eleven o'clock, Prime Minister William Melbourne would be there to discuss the procedures necessary to inaugurate Victoria's reign.

Glancing at Whitaker, Chamberlain said, "The meeting will be a private one, sir."

"I understand. I'll be gone by then."

Gordon left a few minutes later, giving his condolences to Mary and Victoria.

When the prime minister arrived at precisely eleven o'clock, he was guided to the sitting room by Louise Lehzen. Melbourne told Victoria and Mary that if they wished, Louise could remain. Both said they wanted her there.

As the distinguished man sat down with the women, he said, "I am sure you understand, Miss Victoria, that you officially became queen the moment King William died."

"Yes," said Victoria in a serious tone. "I understand."

"Tomorrow, Queen Victoria, you will meet with Parliament and myself at Westminster Palace to discuss your governing procedure with us. It is important that you spend time right away with men who will be your political advisors. You and your mother will be moved into Buckingham Palace the day after tomorrow, and will also have Windsor Castle as a second residence."

Mother and daughter exchanged pleasant smiles.

"I have already begun planning your coronation day, Your Majesty," said the prime minister. "I will advise you and your mother of the exact date within a week."

The queen and the duchess walked William Melbourne to the door, thanked him for his fine work as prime minister, and waved as he rode away in his carriage.

When Mary closed the door, Victoria said, "Mother, I am queen, now. And when we move to Buckingham Palace, I am going to have my own private bedroom, and there is nothing Gordon can do about it."

"Of course, dear," said Mary. "With so many servants in the palace, and a healthy supply of guards to boot, I am sure you will be totally safe in your own room."

"And Maude is no longer going to have to sample my food, Mother. Neither will any of the other cooks. Gordon's rules no longer apply."

Mary made a smile. "Why, ah…of course, dear."

"This also means that starting this Sunday, I am going to attend church regularly with Louise. I will allow a minimal number of palace guards to accompany us, but I am getting back in church."

Knowing that with Victoria now being queen, there was nothing either she or Gordon could do about it, Mary said, "I know it makes you happy to go to church, dear."

Victoria took hold of Mary's hand and looked longingly into her eyes. "You know what would make me extremely happy, Mother?"

Mary's features stiffened. "I don't mean to make you less than extremely happy, Victoria, but I will not be attending church with you."

Tears misted the queen's eyes. "Mother, I want you in church with me so you will hear the preaching of the Word of God. The Lord uses preaching more than anything else to open the eyes of lost people so they will see their need to be saved and open their hearts to Jesus. I have talked to you about it over and over again since I took Jesus as my Saviour, and still you haven't turned to Him. I'm sure if you just heard my pastor preach, you would understand your need and be saved."

Mary patted her daughter's arm. "As I've told you before, Victoria, this religion business just isn't for me."

"And as I've told you before, Mother," Victoria said with a break in her voice, "what I have isn't religion. I have salvation. You need salvation, too."

"We have a lot to do to get ready for the move," said Mary. "We'd better both get busy." With that, she turned and headed down the hall.

As Victoria watched her mother walk away, there was a deep grief in her heart.

Queen Victoria met with the prime minister and Parliament on Wednesday as scheduled, and on Thursday, the big move was made to Buckingham Palace.

Wires had been sent to dignitaries across Europe on June 20, and ample time was given so those who wished to attend King William's funeral could do so. A return wire came from Edgar I, Duke of Saxe-Coburg-Gotha, stating that certain problems he was forced to handle at the present time would keep him from attending the funeral. He added that Prince Albert was also deeply involved with handling the problems and would be unable to make it for the funeral.

Victoria was thrilled to be back in church on Sunday, and was given a rousing welcome by pastor and congregation.

On Tuesday, June 27, Victoria, her mother, and Louise—who was now called Victoria's "companion"—were taken to the funeral service at Westminster Abbey in a royal carriage. As always, they were flanked by the palace guards.

As befitted a well-loved and respected monarch, King William's funeral was large and elaborate. Important dignitaries from all over the British Isles and from many other European countries were in attendance.

It was an unusually warm day, and the abbey felt close and stuffy. Every pew, as well as every inch of standing room, was filled with mourners and the curious.

The service was solemn and tedious. The great responsibility that now lay on Victoria as Queen of England weighed heavily on her small shoulders. As if to counter the weight, she sat as straight and tall as her height would allow.

As the service moved slowly along, Victoria prayed earnestly in her heart for God's mighty hand on her as she visualized what the days ahead would entail.

When the choir rose and began to sing, Victoria was brought back to the present. She let her gaze rest on the ornate black-and-gold-encrusted coffin. Tears threatened to fill her eyes, and she thought of her mother's words about maintaining her composure before her subjects. No doubt many eyes were on her. Only by her own intense will was she able to blink the tears back.

The queen's heart was sorrowful over the loss of her uncle and friend. Her mind went back to her childhood days when Uncle William was always there for her, filling the spot that was left empty by the death of her own father.

"I promise you, Uncle William," she said, barely moving her lips in a low whisper, "that with the help of Almighty God, I will love and rule these subjects in a way that would make you proud."

Lifting her chin as the choir was finishing the last line of "A Mighty Fortress Is Our God," Victoria ran her gaze over the portion of the congregation that she could see without turning completely around. A fierce determination filled her young heart, and a prayer for guidance enveloped her mind.

When the service was over at Westminster Abbey, there was a long procession to the royal cemetery where King William's coffin would be placed in a stone mausoleum. Since William had no other family, Victoria and her mother rode directly behind the funeral carriage.

The cemetery service was brief and when it was over, Victoria was in conversation with Prime Minister William Melbourne with Louise at her side. They were standing near the door of the mausoleum, where the coffin rested on a cart. While Melbourne was saying something about another meeting the queen would soon have with Parliament, Victoria noticed that a few yards away, Gordon and Alice Whitaker were talking to her mother with no one else nearby. There was a tingling along her spine. Mr. Gordon Whitaker was about to meet his Waterloo.

Picking up on what Melbourne was saying, Victoria continued her conversation with him.

Knowing they were out of earshot from Victoria, Gordon held his voice low and said, "Mary, the king's been dead for a week. I would like my promised fortune as soon as possible."

"We thought we'd have it before now," put in Alice, her features stonelike.

A bit miffed because Gordon and Alice were so greedy that they couldn't even wait to approach her about the money until after the king's body was entombed in the mausoleum, Mary wanted to lash out at them. She contained her ire. "We don't have the money yet. Mr. Melbourne told Victoria and me that the queen's money will be transferred to an account in Victoria's name at the Bank of England tomorrow. He is to let me know the exact amount this evening. He did tell me it would be at least six hundred thousand pounds. This will be the initial deposit. Others will follow periodically. I will then tell Victoria of the promise I made you so many years ago, Gordon. And I will also remind her how marvelously you have taken care of our finances."

A smile curved Gordon's lips.

"It no doubt will take a day or two for Victoria to accustom herself to having the bank account," said Mary. "But no later than Monday, I'll have her make out a check to you. It will be no less than two hundred thousand pounds. And as the queen's personal financial controller, I can assure you, there will be a generous monthly salary."

Delight showed in the eyes of the Whitakers.

Gordon chuckled. "Mary, I appreciate your willingness to follow through on your promises."

Mary smiled. "It's only right that I do. You've done us a great service all of these years, Gordon."

A look of concern captured Alice's features. "Mary, all three of us know that Victoria is not particularly fond of Gordon. Do you think she will rebel at any of this?"

"With her own mother advising her on these things, and my reminding her of how well Gordon has handled our finances since her father died, I have no doubt that she will go along with anything I say."

Alice heaved a sigh of relief. "You don't know how much this means to us, Mary. There is no way we can fully express our appreciation to you."

Mary smiled. "There is no way I can fully express my appreciation for all your husband has done for us, Alice. I can assure you, my promises will be fulfilled."

"Good," said Gordon. "Well, Alice, we need to be going."

Mary watched the Whitakers walk across the lawn to their carriage, then turned and headed for the spot where Victoria stood with her companion at her side as she talked with the prime minister.

Under her breath, she said, "Daughter of mine, please don't make a liar out of me. You've got to make good my promises. We both owe it to Gordon."

Seven

lice Whitaker was clinging to her husband's arm as he guided the carriage out of the royal cemetery onto the street and pulled into traffic. She was bending forward and giggling like a schoolgirl.

"I don't know when I've seen you so giddy," Gordon said, smiling at her.

Alice sat up, threw her head back and said, "I've never been so happy, darling!"

"Come to think of it," he said, "I haven't either."

Alice giggled and shook her head for joy.

Turning on a street that would eventually take them to their neighborhood, Gordon said, "Honey, I'll let you off at the house, then I'll go on to the bank and quit my job."

Reaching up and patting his cheek, she giggled again. "Oh, it feels so good to be filthy rich. I'm just so happy, I could shout!"

Gordon laughed. "Well, go ahead!"

"Really?"

"Sure!"

"All right!" Raising her hands overhead, she waved them and

shouted, "Yahoo-o-o! Yahoo-o-o! Yahoo-o-o!"

People on the street gawked at her, wondering why an English lady would put on such a demonstration in public.

When Alice walked into the Whitaker house, still giddy with joy, her two daughters were in the sewing room making dresses. Marianne, who was twenty-one, heard her mother giggling and looked at her twenty-year-old sister with a frown. "Lorene, what do you suppose happened at the king's funeral that would make Mom so happy?"

"I don't know," said Lorene. "We'd better go find out."

When the sisters stepped into the hall, they saw their mother coming toward them. "Hello, beautiful daughters!" she said. "Where's your brother? I've got something wonderful to tell all three of you!"

"I'm right here, Mom," said twelve-year-old Edgar from behind her. "Did Dad just become president of Barings Bank?"

"Better than that, son," Alice said. "Better than that. Let's go in the parlor so we can sit down."

Edgar sat between his sisters on the couch as their mother placed herself on a chair facing them. Their faces showed the eagerness they felt, waiting to hear the good news.

"Children," said Alice, "your father and I have known for a long time that something marvelous was going to happen to our family, but we agreed not to tell you until it actually happened. Your father is on his way to quit his job at the bank, and he told me to go ahead and tell you the whole story."

Eyes bulging, Marianne gasped, "Quit his job? Really? Something real good must have happened!"

"Tell us, Mom!" said Edgar. "I can't wait any longer!"

Barings Bank president Lester Harwood looked up from his desk when the door opened. "Yes, Miss Brickmire?"

"Mr. Whitaker is back from the king's funeral, sir," said the bespectacled secretary, "and would like to see you."

"Of course," said the silver-haired man. "Send him in."

Seconds later, Gordon Whitaker entered the president's private office, a serious look on his face.

Gesturing toward one of the chairs that stood before his desk, Harwood said, "Sit down, Gordon. Tell me how the funeral went."

Easing onto the straight-backed wooden chair, Gordon said, "Well, it went about the same as any royal funeral. Lots of tears, and hundreds of sad faces."

"How did our new queen seem to be taking it?"

"She carried her grief with dignity, I'll say that."

"I don't doubt it at all. She may be only eighteen, but she has the poise of a mature woman. She's going to make us a great queen."

"Yes, sir. I believe that."

"So are you in here to report on the funeral, or is there something else you wanted to see me about?"

Gordon adjusted his position on the chair and cleared his throat. "Well, sir, actually I'm here to tell you that I'm quitting my job."

Lester Harwood looked like he had been slapped across the face with a wet dishrag. "You what?"

"I'm quitting my job here at the bank, sir."

Eyes wide, Harwood said, "You got a better offer at one of the other banks?"

"No, sir. I'm leaving the banking profession."

Harwood shook his head in astonishment. "To do what?"

"Well, sir, at the moment I'm not at liberty to say."

"I...I never thought you'd ever leave us. Can't you at least tell me why you looked into something else? Have we not treated you right? Is the pay too low?"

"Nothing like that, Mr. Harwood. I'm quitting the bank and going into another line of work for personal reasons that I cannot discuss at this time."

"I assume you'll be giving us the usual two weeks notice."

"No, sir," said Gordon, his voice taking on a bit of a crusty tone. "There will be no notice except the one I am giving you right now. I am through as of this moment."

Harwood frowned. "You are not being fair. You owe us time to fill your position."

"No time, sir. I am quitting right now."

The bank president's frown deepened, and his face flushed. "Such conduct will go on your record, mister! You'll never be able to get another bank job anywhere in Great Britain. You'd better think this over. If whatever you're going into falls apart on you and you want to go back into banking, you'll never be hired."

Gordon waggled his head in a cocky manner. "I'll never need another bank job. In Great Britain or anywhere else. You owe me my salary up to this moment, and I want it."

In anger, Lester Harwood rose to his feet and left the office. Returning after only a couple of minutes, he said, "You'll get what we owe you. Miss Brickmire will be here with it shortly."

That evening, Prime Minister William Melbourne sat down in the library of Buckingham Palace with the young queen and her mother. After commenting on how well Victoria had conducted herself at the funeral in spite of her grief, he smiled. "I have the date set for your coronation, my dear. Thursday, July 13. Of course, to follow the long-time custom, it will be held at Westminster Abbey."

Victoria reached over and took her mother's hand. "Oh, Mother, that's little more than two weeks from now. I'm really going to be nervous. I hope I do everything right."

"You'll do fine, honey," said Mary.

"You'll get a little coaching from me, Your Majesty," Melbourne assured her. He picked up the briefcase that he had set beside his chair. "Now, let's take care of your financial business."

Melbourne opened the briefcase, took out a checkbook, and handed it to Victoria. "This is your checkbook, dear. Right under the cover is the signature card. I need you to sign it now so I can take it back to the bank when I leave here."

Victoria opened the checkbook, took out the signature card, left her chair, and went to a nearby desk. She dipped a pen into the inkwell, signed the card, blotted it, and handed it to Melbourne.

Melbourne thanked her, then as she sat down beside her mother once again, he said, "Your new account will have eight hundred thousand pounds deposited into it first thing tomorrow morning.

Baron Robert Quinton advised me that costs have risen somewhat since your Uncle William became king, and suggested that more money should be allotted to you. I took this up with Parliament, and they agreed. The ceiling amount has been six hundred thousand, but as I said, it will now be eight hundred thousand.

"On the first business day of each month, Parliament will bring your balance back up to eight hundred thousand pounds. It is from this account that you will pay your official household of four hundred and forty-five servants and guards and all palace and personal expenses."

Reaching into the briefcase again, Melbourne took out a leather-bound folder. "In here are the salary amounts for each servant and each guard. It is in your discretion whenever you feel you want to raise someone's salary. I assume you will be hiring a personal financial advisor."

"Of course," said Victoria.

Mary's heart picked up pace as Gordon Whitaker's features flashed on the screen of her mind.

"Good," said the prime minister. "It is the wise thing to do. A judicious and experienced man will be a real asset to you. His salary will come from the account also. The salary amount that your uncle paid Baron Quinton is in the folder. This will guide you as to what is fair pay for your new financial advisor, whomever he may be."

"Thank you, Mr. Melbourne," said Victoria. "You have already been such a wonderful help to me."

Melbourne closed the briefcase and rose to his feet. "Well, I must be going. Lots of work to do today. When we get closer to the time of the coronation, I will contact you, and we will set an appointment for some coaching."

Moments later, mother and daughter stood on the veranda and waved at the prime minister as his carriage pulled away.

Mary said, "Honey, you and I need to talk. Let's go back to the library."

As they sat down together, Mary's heart was pounding.

"What is it we need to talk about, Mother?" asked Victoria.

"Well, it's…it's about Gordon."

Victoria felt her stomach roll over. "Yes?"

"Mr. Melbourne just gave you sound advice when he said you need to hire a financial advisor. Now…I…ah…have something to tell you."

Victoria studied her mother's nervous eyes. "Go on."

"I…I've never told you this, but eighteen years ago when your father died and Gordon volunteered to handle our finances, I made him a promise. Well, actually, two promises."

"Oh? And what were they?"

"I promised him first of all that whenever you became queen, he would be given a substantial amount of money in a lump sum for the years he had served me as my financial controller."

The news raked up resentment within the queen and changed the slant of her lips.

Mary saw it, and felt the coolness in her daughter's sudden glance. Before Victoria could speak, she said, "I want a check made out to Gordon on Monday for two hundred thousand pounds. He deserves it for what he did for us. The second promise was that when you became queen, Gordon would be hired as your personal financial controller and paid a generous monthly salary. He has already told me he will quit his job at the bank to devote himself full-time as your personal controller. He kept the creditors away from our door all these years! You can't turn him away."

Victoria's features seemed to turn to stone. She said flatly, "Gordon is getting nothing, Mother. Nothing. And I have decided to hire Baron Robert Quinton as my personal financial advisor and controller. Since Baron Quinton did such an excellent job for Uncle William in that capacity and is now out of a job, I am going to hire him."

The duchess was shaken to the core. Panic gripped her. "Victoria, you can't do this! I made Gordon those promises, and I want them honored!"

Struggling to maintain control of her emotions, Victoria put a kind note in her voice as she said, "Mother, you had no authority to make Gordon either promise. You will just have to tell him you made a mistake."

Mary's face was pale. Her voice was strained as she said, "Victoria, you are not treating Gordon right. He deserves what I promised him. He—"

"Mother, I have known since I was very young that Gordon was an underhanded, greedy, unprincipled fraud. He kept your creditors away from the door all these years, but underneath his 'good management' of your funds was a wicked avarice that drove him to cause trouble incessantly between you and me…and to make me a prisoner in my own house. Gordon Whitaker will get no money and no job."

Furious, Mary stood up, hovering over her daughter. "You're making a fool of me, Victoria!"

Rising from her chair and meeting her mother's gaze, Victoria said softly, "No, Mother. You made a fool of yourself when you let that schemer take control of both of us. I love you, and I mean no disrespect, but you let Gordon pull the wool over your eyes. I've seen him clearly for what he is since I was six years old. Just tell him you made a mistake."

Mary glared at her daughter for a long moment, then wheeled and left the room, leaving the door wide open.

Victoria sighed. "Dear Lord, You know what Gordon is, and You know he has had control of Mother and me for eighteen long years. Please help her to see that what I am doing is for the good of both of us."

At that moment, Victoria saw a pretty face at the open door.

Emily had been personal maid to King William for the past five years, and upon the new queen's move into Buckingham Palace, the queen had kept Emily in the same position for herself.

"Is everything all right, Your Majesty?" queried Emily.

"Of course. Why do you ask?"

"I saw Duchess Mary go up the stairs a moment ago, and she looked very upset. I knew she was in here with you."

"We just had a little misunderstanding," said Victoria. "Mother will be all right. Emily, will you find Wilson and tell him I want to see him?"

"Yes, mum. I just saw him in the hall by the dining room. I'll fetch him for you."

Moments later, Victoria's favorite male servant entered the library. Wilson was a man in his early forties, and in the short time the queen and her mother had lived in Buckingham Palace, he had proven himself to be very faithful and loyal.

Doing a slight bow before her, Wilson said, "You wanted to see me, Your Majesty?"

Victoria glanced at the grandfather clock in the corner. "Yes, Wilson. The evening is still young. I need you to ride to Baron Robert Quinton's home and tell him that I would like to see him here in the library at nine o'clock tomorrow morning."

When Mary awakened the next morning and looked out the window, she was surprised to see the sun so high in the morning sky. Her glance ran to the clock on the wall, and she was surprised to see that she had overslept. It was almost nine o'clock.

While Mary dressed and brushed her hair, she thought of her conversation with Victoria the evening before, and reminded herself this was why she had not slept well. How was she ever going to tell Gordon? A sick feeling washed over her. No matter how much she dreaded it, she had to tell him.

As she headed toward the door of her bedroom, Mary stopped and took a deep breath. "I'll talk to her one more time. Maybe I can at least persuade her to give Gordon the job as her controller."

When Mary entered the palace's cozy breakfast room, she found Louise and Maude casually sipping coffee together.

Maude jumped up and went to the stove where she was keeping Mary's breakfast warm.

"Good morning, Mary," said Louise. "I looked in on you a couple of times, but you were sound asleep. Victoria told me not to wake you."

Mary nodded. "I had a hard time getting to sleep. I guess once I did, I really went under. Where's Victoria?"

"She's in the library with Baron Quinton. She sent for him last night, and he was prompt getting here this morning."

"Here's your breakfast, ma'am," said Maude, setting a tray of steaming food on the table.

"Oh. Thank you, Maude. Maybe you ought to put it back in the warmer for a little while. I need to go to the library."

"Victoria gave strict orders that she and the baron were not to be disturbed," Louise said cautiously. "She has Wilson outside the door to make sure her orders are carried out."

Sick at heart, Mary realized it was too late to change Victoria's mind about the controller job. She wanted to get the ordeal with Gordon over as soon as possible. Putting shaky fingers to her temple, she said, "I'll be right back. Keep the food warm for me."

Quickly, Mary found one of the younger male servants and sent him to the bank to tell Gordon Whitaker she needed to see him immediately.

When that was done, she returned to the breakfast room. Her appetite was gone, but she knew she had to force some food down to keep up her strength. She was going to need it.

Gordon arrived just after Mary had finished breakfast, and she took him to a sitting room where they could talk in private. Before they could sit down, Mary burst into tears and told Gordon what Victoria had said about no money, and no job.

The shock of it threw Gordon back on his heels. Pale of face, he gasped and said, "Mary, you've got to change her mind! On your word that all of this was going to be as you promised, I quit my job at the bank yesterday!"

It was Mary's turn to go pale. "Gordon, I'm...I'm sorry, but no one is going to change her mind."

"You have to! Lester Harwood will not take me back because I quit without giving him two weeks' notice. He made it clear that with this on my record, no other bank in England will hire me either. You have got to make Victoria see this, and give me the job. I need that fortune you promised, too."

Feeling weak in the knees, Mary sagged onto a chair and wiped a palm over her face. "She won't listen to me, Gordon. There's no way I can get her to give you the money, and there's no way I can get her to hire you."

"You said she'd do whatever you told her!" he hissed through his teeth.

"Well, she fooled me. Her mind is made up about you, and nothing's going to change it."

Breathing heavily from his anger, the man bent over Mary. "You go get that little brat and bring her in here so I can talk to her. She's going to give me that job."

Fear was obvious in Mary's eyes. "It's too late, Gordon. At this very moment in the library, Victoria is hiring Baron Robert Quinton as her personal controller."

Cold flame leaped into Gordon's eyes, honing to a gleam that was full of lunacy. He drew a quivering breath to speak, but was cut off when a knock came at the door.

Mary struggled to her feet, brushed past him, and opened the door.

Wilson was there. He glanced over Mary's shoulder, saw the anger on Gordon's twisted face, and looked back at her. "Queen Victoria asked me to tell you, ma'am, that she wishes to see you when Mr. Whitaker is gone."

"I need to see her before he leaves, Wilson," Mary said, glancing back at Whitaker. "Gordon, you wait here. I'll be right back."

Stepping into the hall, and pulling the door closed behind her, Mary asked, "Do you know where the queen is, Wilson?"

"She was in the main foyer when she sent me to you, ma'am. She had just walked the baron to the door."

"Thank you. I'll find her."

As Mary hurried away, Wilson scratched his head thoughtfully and looked back at the sitting room door. He hadn't liked the look he saw on Gordon Whitaker's face.

Emily was coming down the hall from the main foyer when she and Mary met up.

"Do you know where Victoria is, Emily?" Mary asked.

"Yes, mum. She went up to her room."

Mary thanked her and hurried toward the winding staircase. Her mind was in a whirl as she ran up the stairs and headed down the hall toward Victoria's room. The look she had seen in Gordon's eyes frightened her. He was liable to do something drastic in an attempt to get his money and the controller's job.

Tapping on her daughter's door, Mary called, "Victoria! It's your mother."

The door came open almost instantly. "Oh. Wilson got the message to you already. Come in, Mother. I wanted to let you know that I have hired Baron Quinton. He will begin on Monday."

Moving into the room, Mary said, "Gordon's still here. I told him what you said about no money and no job. He's very upset. He quit his job at the bank yesterday, on my word that you would make him your personal controller."

"He shouldn't have done that until he was sure he had the job. It was a foolish thing to do."

"Well, it's done now. I want you to talk to him. Since you won't give him the money or the job, it's your responsibility to talk to him and explain it."

Victoria shrugged. "All right. I'll be glad to."

"Let's go. He's waiting."

When mother and daughter drew near the sitting room, they were unaware that Wilson was watching from a recessed door a short distance down the hall. When they went into the room, Wilson hurried to the nearest intersection of the hallway, got the attention of a guard, and motioned to him.

Upon entering the sitting room, Victoria saw that Gordon's face was red with anger and there was a dangerous look in his eyes.

Moving toward her stiffly, he snapped, "So I don't get the lump sum nor the job, eh?"

Lifting her graceful chin, Victoria said, "That's right. I'll tell you what I told Mother. She did not have the authority to make such promises to you."

"But what about all these years I kept you and your mother out of the poorhouse? Doesn't that mean anything?"

"I know why you did it. You have never fooled me."

"You immature ingrate! You owe me."

The young queen didn't bat an eye as she stood before the man who towered over her. "Since I was very young, I've seen through your facade, all the way to your sordid, unprincipled core. You gained control over my mother in an underhanded way, then to protect your interests, you made me a virtual prisoner with the intent of keeping anything from happening to me so you would end up wealthy. Well it's all over, Gordon. You get nothing."

Eyes flashing with fury, Gordon spat, "You smart-mouthed brat! You're light-minded at best; mentally unbalanced at worst. If the management of your affairs is not in my hands, immediate disaster will follow. Neither you nor your mother know anything about handling money. There's nobody can take care of your financial affairs like me!"

"I just hired Baron Robert Quinton for the job. He did quite well in that capacity for King William IV, and he will do the same for me."

A devil's temper stirred behind Whitaker's fiery eyes. Suddenly his right hand lashed out and struck the queen's face a heavy blow, and Victoria hit the floor with a thud.

Eight

*I*n horror, Mary screamed at Gordon Whitaker as she hurried toward her daughter. "You beast! How dare you strike the queen!"

The door burst open, and two guards rushed in with Wilson on their heels. Having heard the blow and Mary's words, the guards quickly grabbed Whitaker, bending his arms up behind his back.

"Let go of me!" he wailed. "Let go of me!"

"You be quiet right now!" growled one of the guards. "Or we'll break both your arms."

Wilson pointed a stiff finger between Whitaker's eyes. "You'll pay for this, mister!"

As Mary dropped to her knees beside her fallen daughter, Emily burst into the room, took one look at the queen on the floor, and dashed to her, kneeling on the opposite side from Mary.

Victoria was slightly dazed as Mary lifted her upper body into her arms. Her eyes were seeing spots, and she was shaking her head trying to clear it.

Emily focused on the bright red spot on Victoria's left cheek. "Oh, Duchess Mary, he must have hit her awfully hard!"

"He did!" she hissed, looking up at Gordon. "You will indeed pay for this, you heartless beast!"

Victoria's eyes began to clear as Wilson bent over the women and said, "We'll take him to another room and send for the police."

As the guards forced Gordon toward the door, he looked over his shoulder at Victoria. "It's all your fault, you spoiled little brat! You stole my fortune from me! You—"

Both guards rammed his arms higher up his back and the sudden pain cut off his words. He let out a scream as they dragged him into the hall with Wilson following. A door somewhere down the hall slammed shut.

"Let's get her up in the chair, Emily," said Mary.

Together, they lifted the queen up and eased her into the over-stuffed chair. The angry red welt on her pale cheek was beginning to swell. She lifted a trembling hand and began to rub it. Looking up at Mary, she said, "This little demonstration ought to show you what the man really is, Mother."

"I'll fetch water and a cloth, Your Majesty," said a shaken Emily, and hurried out the door.

Mary dropped to her knees, took both of Victoria's hands in her own, and with tears spilling down her cheeks, said, "Victoria, please forgive me. I…I knew Gordon had his dark side, but I didn't realize what a truly despicable man he was. I'm so sorry for all the years I have let him control our lives. Can you find it in your heart to forgive me, child?"

Victoria gave her mother a loving look. "Of course I can, Mother." Leaning forward, she kissed Mary's soft cheek. "I forgive you."

"Thank you, sweetheart."

"You don't have to thank me. When Jesus forgave all my sins, He taught me how to forgive. He will forgive all your sins too, Mother, if you'll let Him."

Avoiding the subject, Mary looked at the welt on Victoria's cheek and said, "Does it hurt much?"

"It stings like fire right now, but it'll be all right. It'll heal in a few days."

Even as Victoria was speaking, Emily bustled into the room with a cool, wet compress and gingerly pressed it to the queen's cheek. Victoria winced at first, then took the compress in her own hands, holding it to her face.

A rustling of skirts was heard from somewhere down the hall. "That will be Miss Louise," said Emily. "I heard Wilson telling her what happened."

"She never has liked Gordon in the least," Mary said, shaking her head. "This is going to make her like him even less."

"The compress will make the swelling go down soon, Your Majesty," said Emily. "Good as new you'll be, in short order."

Victoria started to smile at her, but the pain quickly wiped it from her face.

Louise bolted into the room, paused to look at the queen, then dashed to her. "Oh-h-h-h! If I were a man, that Gordon Whitaker would get such a beating, he wouldn't get out of the hospital for a year!"

"I feel the same way," said Mary.

Louise bent down close. "Honey, let me see it."

Victoria took the compress from her cheek, meeting Louise's gaze.

Fury was in Louise's eyes as she hissed, "If he ever—! If he ever—!"

"He won't," said Victoria, placing the compress back over the bruise. "He will never have the opportunity again."

There was a tap on the wall at the open door.

"Duchess Mary," said Wilson, "the police are here. They are putting Mr. Whitaker in a paddy wagon. One of the officers told me that Police Chief Norman Halley will be here shortly."

"Thank you, Wilson," said Mary. "And thank you for being so alert. Who knows what might have happened if you hadn't had the guards just outside the door."

"It's just part of my job, ma'am," he said. "Is the queen all right?"

"I'm fine, Wilson," spoke up Victoria. "I just have a big red welt on my cheek, and it's swelling up some. Nothing worse."

"We can thank the Lord for that, Your Majesty."

"Yes. I already have."

"Wilson," said Mary.

"Yes, ma'am?"

"Since Chief Halley is on his way, it would be best if we talked to him in the reception room. Would you mind helping us get the queen down there?"

"Be my privilege, Duchess," said Wilson. "If she will allow it, I will carry her to the reception room."

"I'm still just a bit light-headed, Wilson," said Victoria. "I will very much appreciate it if you carry me."

Within an hour, Police Chief Norman Halley arrived at Buckingham Palace. He was ushered into the reception room by Wilson, where Mary and Louise sat with Victoria. She was still holding the compress to her cheek.

Halley greeted Mary and Louise as he moved directly to the queen and dropped to one knee before her. "I am so sorry for what happened, Your Majesty. May I see the bruise?"

Victoria pulled the compress away.

"Oh, my. He did strike you hard, didn't he?"

"It could have been worse, Chief," said Victoria. "At least he hit me with an open hand, rather than a fist."

"Yes. You're right about that. To what extent do you want to press charges against Gordon Whitaker, Your Majesty?"

Victoria placed the compress back against her face. "I am not acquainted with this kind of thing, Chief. Will you explain it to me?"

"It's quite simple. Because Whitaker's violent act was on the Queen of England, by law, he could get up to ten years in prison. If he had injured you seriously, it could mean twenty years or more, depending on just how serious the injury. You can call the blow to your face very serious if you wish."

"I will not press charges, Chief Halley. You can let him out of jail. However, there will be one stipulation. Gordon Whitaker is never to set foot on this property again, and he is never to come anywhere near my mother or me, no matter where we might be."

Halley looked at the queen in amazement. "No charges. You are indeed a gracious lady, Your Majesty."

"As a Christian, I try to be. But I want the stipulation made very clear to him."

"I will take care of it," he said, rising to his feet. "I will warn him that if he violates your directive in this matter, he will suffer the consequences." Halley bent his head and rubbed the back of his neck. "Your Majesty, you said for me to let him out of jail. If you will give permission, I would like to keep him behind bars for a month. The man dared to strike the queen. He really needs to learn a lesson."

"All right. A month, then. I do want him to learn his lesson."

In his cell at the jail, Gordon Whitaker sat on the bunk, his head hung low. Before leaving for Buckingham Palace, Chief Halley had told him if the queen pressed charges, he could get twenty years or more in prison. It depended on how serious she declared her injury to be. If she did not deem it serious, he could still get up to ten years for his deed.

Hatred toward Victoria burned in his heart. She had taken his entire well-designed future away from him. His plan for wealth and his scheme for prestige as the queen's personal financial controller had gone up in smoke.

Somehow, in spite of being in prison, he would find a way to get even.

At the Whitaker home, Alice opened the door and was surprised to see two uniformed police officers standing there.

"Ma'am," said the oldest of the two, "I am Officer Ben Dolford, and this is Officer Kenneth Stone. You are Mrs. Whitaker?"

"Yes."

"May we step inside, Mrs. Whitaker?" asked Dolford. "Some of your neighbors are looking at us, and we don't want to attract any more attention than necessary."

"W-well, of course," said Alice, widening the door opening. "Please come in. What's this about?"

As she closed the door behind them, Stone said, "We understand you have two daughters and a son living here, ma'am. Are they home?"

"Ah…no. They're shopping downtown."

"All right. Maybe that's best. You can break this to them in your own way."

"Break what? Please. What is this about?"

"It's your husband, ma'am," said Dolford. "We have him in jail."

Alice's jaw slacked. "In j—in jail? Why is Gordon in jail?"

"We understand he has been the Duchess of Kent's personal financial advisor for many years."

"Yes," said Alice, brow furrowed.

"He was at Buckingham Palace this morning, Mrs. Whitaker. For some reason, he lost his temper and struck Queen Victoria. He hit her hard enough to knock her down."

Alice's face blanched. Her eyes became round in the pallor of her skin. "I…I—" Her trembling hand went to her temple. "I…I don't know what to say. What's going to happen to him?"

"It all depends on the queen, ma'am. If she presses assault and battery charges against him, he could spend the next twenty years or more in prison. The government does not take it lightly when someone strikes a British monarch. The very least he could get is ten years."

Alice's knees started to give way.

Officer Ben Dolford gripped her shoulders. "Here, ma'am. Let me help you sit down."

When she was seated on a straight-backed chair, she took a deep breath, scrubbed a hand over her eyes, and said, "I need to go to my husband. They will let me visit him, won't they?"

"Oh yes, ma'am," said Officer Kenneth Stone. "We're in a buggy. We came that way because we figured you might need a ride to the jail. We'll be glad to take you and to bring you back home."

"Thank you. Let me have a moment to leave my children a note."

When Alice was taken to the cell block where Gordon was locked up, she was placed in a small visiting room where she sat at a barred window. The guard who had escorted her, stood in a corner and observed as Gordon was brought in and seated.

It bothered both of them that the guard remained, but Gordon proceeded by saying dully, "I assume you've been told why I'm here."

"Yes. Two police officers came to the house. They told me all about it. Gordon, what were you thinking? That was a foolish thing to do!"

"Well, she made me mad!"

Alice ran her eyes in the direction of the guard, who stood off to one side behind her.

Gordon knew what she was doing, but ignored the guard. "Alice, she took everything from us. She refused to give me the bonus Mary had promised, and she refused to give me the job. All our plans are destroyed. I tried to reason with her, get her to see that she needed me to take care of her finances. She coldly told me she had already hired Baron Quinton. So…I lost my temper and hit her."

"Have you been told what the consequences could be?"

"Yeah. If she presses charges, I could get more than twenty years in prison."

Alice clasped her trembling hands together. "I…I hope she'll be lenient and not press charges."

Gordon showed her a sullen face. "Don't count on it. She hates me with a passion. Do you realize that we're practically broke? If they send me to prison, what are you and the kids going to do?"

Alice's face pinched, and tears misted her eyes. "I don't know. I just don't know. If this courtship Marianne is in now works out, she'll be getting married. Lorene has that young grocer interested in her, and maybe they'll end up married. But Edgar and I will have nothing."

The guard stepped close. "Your allotted time is up, ma'am. You'll have to leave now."

Alice nodded and stood up.

"Do the kids know?" asked Gordon.

"No. They were downtown shopping when the police came. I left a note telling them I had to leave and would be home as soon as I could. I'll be back to see you soon."

With that, Alice turned and preceded the guard out the door. As she walked down the long narrow hall toward the offices, tears were coursing down her cheeks. She didn't know what to tell Marianne, Lorene, and Edgar. Should she try to cover it over and make it look less serious than it was? Or should she tell them the whole truth? Marianne and Lorene would probably handle it. They were quite stable and mature. But with Edgar it would be much different. He had the same kind of temperament as his father.

She was still wiping tears when she reached the offices. Officers Dolford and Stone were waiting for her.

Some twenty minutes after Alice had gone, Gordon was lying on his bunk in the cell, his eyes closed. The hatred he felt for Victoria was a boiling volcano in his chest.

The iron door at the end of the cell block opened and closed, and echoing footsteps were heard in the narrow corridor. The footsteps came to a halt in front of his cell. "Whitaker, you awake?"

Gordon opened his eyes and sat up. "Yeah."

"Chief Halley wants to see you in his office. Let's go."

The guard inserted a key in the lock, turned it, and slid the barred door open. Pulling handcuffs from his belt, he said, "You deaf? Get off that bunk and turn around."

Moments later, a sullen-faced Gordon Whitaker was ushered into Chief Norman Halley's office with his hands cuffed behind his back. A second guard stood next to the chief's desk as Whitaker was seated before Halley by the first guard.

"I just got back from Buckingham Palace, Whitaker," said Halley.

Gordon felt his mouth go dry and braced himself for what was coming.

"Queen Victoria is not pressing charges," Halley said. "You'd better be thankful for that."

Relief washed over Gordon like a warm ocean wave. He heaved a sigh and let a smile curve his lips.

"She's a gracious lady," said the chief. "Not too many monarchs would let you off."

Gordon couldn't bring himself to speak a word of agreement, but nodded silently.

"However," said Halley, "you are going to be kept in jail for a month for what you did. And that's my doing. Believe me, there's nothing you can do to fight it, so don't waste your time trying."

The smile vanished from Gordon's lips. He felt his temper rising and struggled to contain it.

"Now, before you go back to your cell, Whitaker," said Halley, "there is a matter of a directive laid down by the queen that I need to tell you about. She wants it understood that you are never to set foot on royal ground again, and no matter where she might go, you are never to be anywhere near her. If you ever disobey the directive, you won't like the consequences, I guarantee you. Understand?"

"Yes, sir. I understand."

"Fine. Now, you can go back to your cell."

As Gordon was being ushered back to his cell, he ground his teeth silently. *Somehow, someday, you spoiled little brat, you'll pay for what you've done to me.*

All the way home, Alice Whitaker had a mental battle. What was she going to tell her son and daughters?

Finally, when the police buggy turned the corner on the block where the Whitakers lived, she decided it was best to simply tell them the whole truth, in spite of how it would affect her hotheaded son.

Marianne, Lorene, and Edgar were watching through the window when the police buggy pulled up in front of the house. Alice thanked the officers for providing the transportation and hurried inside.

All three collected just inside the door.

"Mom, why were you in a police vehicle?" asked Lorene.

"Because your father is in jail, and I went to visit him," she said flatly.

"Jail!" gasped Edgar. "Why's Dad in jail?"

"Let's go in the parlor and sit down," Alice said. "It's a long story."

She first explained to her children that the lump sum of money promised by the duchess and the controller job their father was supposed to get had both been denied him by the queen. She told them about the incident at Buckingham Palace that morning when their father lost his temper at the disturbing news and knocked Victoria to the floor. She followed this by explaining the prison sentence their father faced if the queen pressed assault and battery charges.

Edgar jumped off the couch where he sat beside his mother and began to cry. "It isn't fair! It isn't fair! I want Dad to come home!"

Both girls wept silently as Alice stood up and wrapped her arms around their little brother, trying to calm him.

Suddenly there was a knock at the door.

Edgar stifled his crying. Dashing to the door, he opened it to see two uniformed palace guards on the porch. One was exceptionally tall and the other quite short.

"Hello, young man," said the tall one. "Is your mother home?"

Alice and her daughters were moving toward the door.

"I'm right here, sir," said Alice. "What may I do for you?"

"Mrs. Whitaker," said the tall one, "my name is Jordan and this gentleman is Rex. We have been sent by Queen Victoria to ask you to come with us to the palace."

Alice's mouth fell open. "My, oh, my!" she gasped, wringing her hands. "Whatever could the queen want with us? We haven't done anything wrong. Oh, girls, what has your father gotten us into?"

Edgar stood like a statue, gaping at the guards, and anxiety filled the faces of his sisters.

"We assure you, ma'am," said the short guard, "it isn't because you and your children have done something wrong."

"Well, what does she want?" demanded Alice.

"We don't know, ma'am. We were just told to come here and ask you to come with us to the palace so she can talk to you. I'm sure

Queen Victoria has a good purpose in wanting to see you."

Alice swallowed hard. "All right. Just give us a few minutes to freshen up and make ourselves presentable for the queen."

"Fine," said the tall guard. "We'll wait right here on the porch."

When the door closed behind the guards, Alice and her daughters prepared themselves as quickly as possible, checking their hair and using a little face powder.

When they were almost ready, Alice's hands were shaking so badly she couldn't even pin her best hat in place. Marianne took the long pin from her mother and secured the hat on her head.

Noting that her daughters both had their hats in place, Mary glanced at Edgar, who stood by looking glum. Taking a deep breath, she placed her quivering hands over her wildly beating heart. "All right, children, let's go. I've been told by many who know Queen Victoria that she is a kind young lady. So maybe she will take pity on us."

"If she's so kind, why did she do what she did to our dad?" Edgar said.

"Enough, Edgar," said Lorene. "She wants to talk to us. We've done nothing wrong. She won't mistreat us."

"Let's hope so," said Marianne. "When the British monarch says we are to come to the palace, we have to go to the palace."

When Alice and her children were brought into Queen Victoria's presence in the drawing room at Buckingham Palace by Wilson, they were amazed to find that she welcomed them warmly and was very kind. Alice and the girls cringed at the purple bruise on her cheek.

They sat down together and Victoria said, "Wilson, would you tell Emily she can bring in the tea and crumpets now, please?"

"Yes, Your Majesty," said Wilson, and hurried out the door.

"I asked you to come," said Victoria, "because I wanted to talk to you about Gordon and what happened here this morning."

"I'm so sorry, Your Majesty," Alice said with genuine sympathy in her voice.

"It was no fault of yours," Victoria said with a smile. "The police told me that you had been to the jail to see Gordon. Have they contacted you yet to tell you my decision about pressing charges?"

The girls fixed their eyes on the queen as their mother said, "No, they haven't."

Edgar sat with arms folded, staring at the floor.

"I want you to know that I am not pressing charges," said Victoria.

This brought Edgar's head up.

The girls looked at each other with relief as tears filled their eyes.

Alice blinked at her own tears as she said, "Oh, Your Majesty, I don't know how to thank you!"

"Yes," said Marianne. "Thank you."

"I thank you, too, Your Majesty," said Lorene.

Edgar only stared at the queen.

Victoria then told them what Chief Halley had said about keeping Gordon in jail for a month, and followed this by explaining the directive she had laid down.

Wiping tears, Alice said, "I can't blame you for not wanting my husband anywhere near you. Not after what he did this morning. And…and I can't blame Chief Halley for keeping him locked up for a month. It was a terrible thing that he did."

Emily came in with a tray of tea and crumpets. Alice and her daughters thanked Victoria and partook of the refreshments, but Edgar declined, saying he wasn't hungry or thirsty.

As Emily was leaving the room, Victoria said, "Alice, do you have enough money for groceries and other necessities until Gordon gets out of jail and can find a job?"

Alice was slow to answer, but finally said, "Why, ah…yes. We're fine, Your Majesty."

Victoria looked her square in the eye. "Why do I get the feeling you are not telling me the truth?"

Alice's face crimsoned. "Well-l-l—"

"Let me give you some money to help get you by," said the queen, picking up an envelope from a table next to her overstuffed chair.

Marianne, Lorene, and Edgar looked stunned.

Handing Alice the envelope, Victoria said, "Please accept this as a gift from me. Two hundred pounds. That should help, won't it?"

"Yes," Alice said, sniffing and wiping tears from her eyes. "It certainly will. Thank you so very much."

"You're quite welcome."

"Thank you, Your Majesty," said Lorene.

"Yes," said Marianne. "You've been so kind to us. Thank you."

Alice set level eyes on her son. "Edgar, what do you say to Queen Victoria?"

"Thank you," he said in a low tone.

When Alice and her children left the royal carriage and entered their house, the girls were singing the praises of the queen.

With a pout on his face, Edgar started toward his room.

"Wait just a minute, Edgar," said Alice.

The boy stopped, pivoted, and gave her a sour look.

"Listen to me, young man. You get that pout off your face. You embarrassed me in front of the queen. She did a wonderful thing letting your father off without pressing charges. And she did a very generous thing in giving us this money."

"I'm glad Dad won't have to go to prison," Edgar said. "But that kid queen could have kept him from having to spend a month in jail. Worse than that, though, she cheated Dad out of that big lump of money her mother promised him, and she cheated him out of the job he was supposed to get. I wish I could get my hands on her. I'd choke the life out of her!"

Alice's mouth dropped open. Moving up to look him in the eye, she snapped, "Edgar Whitaker! That is no way to talk! You should learn from your father's mistake that it doesn't pay to lose your temper—especially when it comes to the queen."

"That's right, Edgar," said Marianne. "Look where it got Dad. He could've gone to prison for over twenty years."

"Can I go to my room now?" Edgar said.

"You may," Alice said stiffly, "but you'd better have an attitude change by morning. I'm not putting up with your insolence."

Edgar shoved his hands in his pockets, wheeled, and went to his room. When he closed the door behind him, he walked to the mirror, looked at his reflection, and said, "Someday, Edgar Whitaker, you're going to find a way to punish that kid queen for what she did to your dad."

Nine

At nine o'clock the next morning, Queen Victoria stood before the body of over four hundred palace servants and guards in a room at Buckingham Palace which had been provided for such gatherings when the palace was built. She was glad for the small platform, which raised her some ten inches from the floor.

Running her gaze over their curious faces, she said, "With all that is in the offing in the next several days, you are probably wondering what this meeting is about. I know you all have your jobs to do, so I will be brief."

Her lips quivered a bit. She put a hand to her mouth and cleared her throat gently. "I know you all understand that a great responsibility has been placed upon my shoulders. I am going to need God's hand on me as I rule the people of Great Britain. I need the wisdom that only He can give me. Also, I want His blessings on the palace and its staff. Therefore, starting tomorrow morning at eight o'clock, we will meet for prayer and Bible reading. This will be a regular thing from now on. I realize that there are duties on some of you that will make it so you will have to alternate with each other, so you will only be able to attend every other day.

"Except for those I just mentioned, everyone else will attend the meeting every day, which will last for some twenty minutes to half an hour." She looked over their faces again. "Any questions?"

When there were none, Wilson raised a hand.

"Yes, Wilson?"

"Your Majesty, may I say how very much I appreciate this. We indeed want the Lord's hand on you as you lead this great country, and I know He is going to bless your reign because you are putting Him first. God bless you!"

There were voices of agreement all across the crowd, which pleased the queen. And she was pleased even more when they all stood and applauded her.

She thanked them for the encouragement, asked them to pray for her, and dismissed the meeting. While most of the crowd scurried off to get to their places, the others made a circle around Victoria as Wilson was helping her down the two steps at the side of the small platform. These servants—male and female—and the guards, assured her they were born again, and told her they were looking forward to the meetings.

Victoria was very much encouraged, and as she headed back toward the main part of the palace she thanked the Lord in her heart for the attitude all the staff had just shown her.

For some ten days prior to Victoria's coronation, the people of London were in a festive mood. The warm July nights found people on the streets carrying signs and banners lauding their new queen.

On Monday morning, July 10, Prime Minister William Melbourne came to the palace to meet with the queen by arrangement. Mary and Louise were with her when she led Melbourne into the library and they sat down together. The women were on an overstuffed couch, facing the prime minister, who sat on an overstuffed chair.

Smiling happily, Melbourne said, "Your Majesty, your subjects are very much excited about the upcoming coronation. Old-timers are spreading the word, saying never has London been so crowded; never the streets so choked with carts, carriages, wagons, and omnibuses. Thousands have come from all over the British Isles to watch the coronation parade and to join in the festivities that are going to precede the great day.

"Every day since last Friday, people are arriving by coach and private carriage, and by railroad lines coming into London from Greenwich, Southampton, and Birmingham. Lodging houses are already packed, and every vacant house along the coronation parade route has been rented far in advance, with the landlords making shamefully high profits."

Shaking her head in wonderment, Victoria said, "Mr. Melbourne, I'm overwhelmed. All I can say is praise the Lord for His mighty hand on me."

"Well, that mighty hand is on you, Your Majesty. Without a doubt."

The queen's eyes misted. Her lips quivered. "I have prayed earnestly that the Lord would put it in the people's hearts to love me and follow my leadership. Already I am seeing my prayers answered."

Melbourne smiled. "Your Majesty, with your faith in God, I know you will be given the wisdom you need to successfully lead the people of Great Britain."

"Yes," put in Louise. "I have no doubt of that, sir."

Melbourne looked at Mary. Knowing that he was expecting a comment from her, she made a smile and said rather weakly, "That's for sure."

Victoria's heart was heavy for her mother, who was such a skeptic about God and the Bible. It grieved her that her mother would not open her heart to Jesus, nor give Him the glory for His mighty work in her daughter's life.

Taking two sheets of paper from his briefcase, Melbourne said, "Your Majesty, I need to tell you of the events planned for the next three days and nights. I had a copy made for you so you will have it."

As he spoke, he handed Victoria her copy, which she quickly began scanning.

"As you see, Your Majesty," said Melbourne, "concerts are planned for tonight, Tuesday, and Wednesday at various London music halls."

"Yes."

"And there will be a grand military review Wednesday afternoon at three o'clock at Hyde Park."

Victoria's eyebrows arched. She smiled. "Lots of pomp."

"Yes. Great Britain only has one monarch on the throne at a time, so we do it up big when a new one ascends the throne."

Victoria turned and said to her mother, "I'm getting nervous."

"Don't be nervous, sweetheart. You'll do fine."

"Especially after you and I have the session Wednesday morning so I can coach you on procedure, Your Majesty," said Melbourne. "I'm waiting until the day before the coronation so it will be fresh in your mind."

"Thank you. I appreciate that."

"You will please note that Niccolò Paganini will be playing his violin tonight, Tuesday, and Wednesday nights at the London Opera House."

"Oh, my!" said Victoria. "How am I going to attend those concerts and the other ones?"

"You will have to pick and choose, Your Majesty. When I know which ones you will attend, I will see that it's done right, so that it is held in your honor."

"So I have to decide before you leave here, don't I?"

"Yes."

"All right," she said.

"You simply won't be able to attend all the things that are going on," said Melbourne. "During these next three days, the late-rising wealthy set will attend elaborate 'breakfasts' at noon. Night after night, the same people will crowd into the salons and dining rooms of London mansions, eager to see and be seen. Underneath it all, of course, they are celebrating your ascension to the throne and will be on hand for the coronation, even though most of them will not be able to get seats inside Westminster Abbey."

Victoria smiled at Louise and shrugged.

"You will see there, Your Majesty, that I have set the coronation at one o'clock in the afternoon on Friday. This has been custom for decades."

Victoria nodded. "The British people are very traditional, Mr. Melbourne. You are wise to hold to custom."

"Yes," agreed Mary. "Well, Victoria, you'd better pick and choose when and where you're going to appear these next three nights. I'm sure Mr. Melbourne needs to get back to his office."

The next morning Queen Victoria finished reading Scripture to her guards and servants, then had Wilson lead in prayer.

When the meeting was over, Victoria had been escorted to the library by Louise so she could join her mother to talk about the events of the day. Just as they were sitting down with Mary, a servant named Walford stood at the open door and knocked on the wall. "Your Majesty," he said, "there is someone here to see you."

Mary and Louise exchanged smiles and turned their attention to the servant.

"Who is it, Walford?" asked Victoria.

"He prefers to come in and let you see for yourself. The guards have approved him."

Victoria's flawless brow furrowed. "Well, show him in."

Walford pivoted and stepped back into the hall. "Queen Victoria says you may go in, sir."

Again, Mary and Louise smiled at each other.

When Prince Albert came through the door, Victoria gasped. "Albert!" She jumped from her chair and hurried toward him.

Having been caught up in the plans and festivities leading to coronation day, Victoria had been very busy. However, each night when she lay in her featherbed, there had been a strange uneasiness deep within her. She had done her best to analyze the nagging feeling, but it remained a mystery.

Until now.

When Albert appeared, she immediately knew what the feeling had been. Albert had told her in his latest letter, which had come some ten days earlier, that his father was sending him on a diplomatic assignment to Paris, France, and that he would be gone until sometime in the third week of July.

This told Victoria that the one person she wanted at the coronation more than anyone else would be absent on her big day. She realized now that knowing Albert wouldn't be coming to the coronation had spawned the strange uneasiness.

Albert opened his arms as Victoria drew up, and folded her close to him. Victoria felt his masculine strength, and loved it. When he released her, gently gripping her upper arms, she looked up at him with a bright smile. "Albert, I'm so happy to see you! What happened to your assignment in Paris?"

"Nothing," he said, a sly look in his eyes. "I took care of it in two days."

"But you said you would be gone until sometime in the third week of July."

"Exactly. I just sort of forgot to tell you that after Paris I would be coming to London for the coronation. By the time I get home again, it will be sometime in the third week of July."

The queen said, "Prince Albert of Saxe-Coburg-Gotha, you are a sneak!"

He laughed. "Does this mean I'm in trouble?"

"Oh no!" she said. "I'm just so happy you're here! Thank you for coming to share this momentous occasion with me."

Albert embraced her again, then held her at arm's length with a twinkle in his eyes. "Sweet Victoria, I wouldn't miss this time with you for anything in the world."

Then taking her right hand in his left, he bowed, clicked his heels, and placed a kiss on it.

"Hello, Prince Albert," Mary said softly.

"Nice to see you again, Prince Albert," said Louise.

"You too, Duchess, Miss Lehzen."

"Well, it worked," Mary said. "She was surprised."

Victoria turned around. "Mother! You knew Albert was going to surprise me like this?"

"She sure did," Louise answered for her. "And she shared it with me."

Victoria laughed. "Well, it seems I'm surrounded with sneaky people!" She looked back at Albert. "But what a wonderful surprise!"

Albert winked at Mary, then said to Victoria, "We have another surprise for you."

Victoria shook her head in wonderment. "I have no idea what to expect now."

Practically unnoticed, Walford was waiting at the door. When Albert nodded to him, he stepped into the hall and quickly returned with a slender, distinguished-looking man in his early thirties.

Victoria's mouth flew open and her eyes widened. She recognized Johann Strauss, the Austrian musician, composer, and orchestra leader. She had attended one of his concerts some two years ago, and had long been an admirer, which everyone close to her knew.

"Oh! Mr. Strauss!" she said. "What an honor to have you here."

Strauss stepped up, took the queen's hand, bowed, and kissed it. "Thank you, Your Majesty, but the honor is all mine."

Victoria ran her gaze first to Albert, then to her mother. "You two are responsible for this wonderful man's presence here?"

"Yes, dear," said Mary. "Albert and I have been working together through the mail."

Victoria laughed, shaking her head. "Talk about sneaky people! Tell me about it."

"Well, dear," said Mary, "Albert wrote me in March and said he had been to Vienna in February. He had met Mr. Strauss while there, and told him he had been getting well acquainted with Princess Victoria of England. Mr. Strauss showed interest, asking about King William's health."

"You see, Your Majesty," spoke up Strauss, "I have close friends who live here in London, and they keep me up to date on what is going on in Great Britain. I was aware of your uncle's poor health and that you were next in line for the throne. I also knew that you were an accomplished musician. Prince Albert told me you had often spoken of your admiration for me."

"Yes, sir," said Victoria. "I love your music. I had the privilege of attending the concert you did at London Music Hall two years ago. At the time, I was keeping a low profile for reasons I won't go into, so you weren't informed of my presence. Anyway, I have admired you for a long time."

"May I say, Your Majesty, that I am indeed flattered."

"And when I saw how flattered he was when I told him how you admire him," interjected Albert, "I asked him about the possibility of bringing his orchestra to London for the coronation celebration when the time came. He was immediately interested, and said if at all possible, he would do it. When I received your letter after your Uncle William died, telling me the date of the coronation, I contacted Mr. Strauss. He rearranged his concert schedule. His full orchestra is in London with him."

Smiling from ear to ear, Victoria said, "Mr. Strauss, this is marvelous. Thank you for coming."

Mary laid a hand on her daughter's arm. "Sweetheart, Mr. Strauss's concert is set for this evening in the great room right here in Buckingham Palace. I couldn't let on this morning when you were telling Mr. Melbourne which places you would appear in his schedule, but I got word to him later about Mr. Strauss's concert. I knew you would want to be here tonight."

"You're right about that, Mother!" Victoria said. "Thank you for your part in all of this."

"It was my pleasure, dear."

Victoria turned to Albert. Raising up on her tiptoes, she kissed his cheek. "And thank you, Albert, for what you did to bring this about."

Albert touched fingertips to the spot she had kissed and looked deep into her eyes. He wanted to say something, but refrained. It showed on his face, however, and did not escape Victoria's notice.

It was a gala occasion that evening as hundreds of guests—previously invited by Mary—attended the concert by Johann Strauss and his orchestra.

The great room in Buckingham Palace was ablaze with literally hundreds of flickering candles in glittering crystal chandeliers. Men dressed in satin breeches and multicolored brocaded vests and waistcoats escorted ladies arrayed in splendid gowns representing every color of the rainbow and more. Diamonds, rubies, emeralds, and sapphires sparkled with every movement the elegantly dressed women made. Huge urns were spilling over with white and coral roses; the wondrous aroma filled the air.

Lord Chamberlain was there as master of ceremonies to introduce the queen, and to present Maestro Johann Strauss and his orchestra. Both received standing ovations.

Victoria sat mesmerized by the music as the orchestra played piece after piece, including waltzes composed by Strauss. She sat between Albert and her mother, with Louise at Mary's other side.

From time to time, Victoria caught Albert and her mother smiling smugly at each other because of the surprise they had successfully pulled off. When the orchestra had played for almost an hour and a half, Strauss climaxed a Viennese waltz with a heart-stopping crescendo, snapping his baton in his own inimitable way. While the audience applauded vigorously, he turned and walked to center stage.

When the applause finally died out, Strauss said, "Ladies and gentlemen, I have known for some time that the young lady who is now your queen is an accomplished pianist. I would love to hear her do a number for us."

There was instant applause, punctuated with cheering voices.

A bit intimidated because of Strauss's stature in the music field, Victoria was a bit nervous.

Looking down at her, he said, "Your Majesty, I have been told that you have a captivating rendition of 'The Battle of Prague.' Would you do all of us the honor of coming to the stage and playing it for us? My orchestra would be delighted to accompany you."

Again there was applause, along with cheers.

Victoria sat absolutely stunned for a long moment, then was aware of Albert standing over her, extending his hand. She placed her hand in his. He helped her to her feet, then escorted her up the carpeted stairs to the stage. The applause and cheering became louder as she moved toward the grand piano, where Maestro Strauss waited for her. He bowed, kissed her hand, then allowed Albert to seat her.

Albert took a few steps back, positioning himself to wait until it was time to escort her back to her seat.

While the applause and cheering diminished, Victoria sat quietly with her hands in her lap, head bowed, collecting her thoughts. Then all went still. Raising her head, she noted Strauss standing in front of the orchestra, baton in hand. She smiled, nodded at the maestro, and struck the first chord.

As the orchestra beautifully blended in to accompany her, Victoria became absorbed in her music. For the duration of the number, even the upcoming coronation faded from her mind. She played like never before, thrilled beyond measure to actually be playing with the famous maestro and his orchestra.

When "The Battle of Prague" came to its climax, the crowd was immediately on its feet, and while the queen stood at the piano with a smiling Albert at her side, they gave her an ovation that lasted nearly three minutes.

After the concert, Albert walked Victoria to the parlor, where they had a few minutes together with Louise looking on from the hall but out of earshot.

Holding both her hands in his, Albert looked into her eyes longingly. There was a positive magnetism between them. Both hearts were throbbing as he said softly, "Victoria, you are so wonderful. I—"

"Yes, Albert?"

He swallowed hard, glanced toward Louise, who was looking on from the hall. Once again gazing into Victoria's eyes, he said, "I…I really enjoyed your number tonight. You did a marvelous job."

She blushed. "Why, thank you."

"I really mean it."

"I know you do." She gave him a warm smile.

Albert lifted both hands to his lips and kissed them. "My carriage is waiting. I guess nobody told you that I'm staying with some friends here in London."

"No. I thought maybe Mother had offered you a room here in the palace."

"Oh, she did. But my friends are from Germany, and I sort of owe them a little time."

"Of course. I understand."

"Did your mother tell you that she has invited me to ride in the royal carriage with you for the coronation day parade?"

"No, but she has hardly had a moment to talk to me alone since you and Mr. Strauss arrived today. That's great! If she hadn't invited you to ride with us, I would have done so."

"Really?"

"Of course. After all, you are very, very important to—to me."

His eyes lit up. "I am? Two 'very's'?"

Holding his gaze, she smiled. "Maybe even more than two."

Albert said, "You don't know what that means to me."

She lowered her eyelids slightly. "Maybe I do."

Albert wanted desperately to take her into his arms and kiss her, but Louise was watching. "I must go now. I'll see you tomorrow."

"Yes. Tomorrow."

The next two days were busy ones with Victoria attending more concerts, the grand military review, and various other festivities, accompanied by her mother, Louise, and Prince Albert.

Early in the morning on the day of the coronation, Victoria was in a robe and slippers, kneeling beside her bed in prayer. Tears were on her cheeks as she said, "Dear Lord, I know I've reminded You of James 1:5 a lot lately. I'm sure You won't care if I bring it up today of all days…the day of my coronation. 'If any of you lack wisdom, let him ask of God, that giveth to all men liberally, and upbraideth not; and it shall be given him.'

"Thank You that You will not scold me for asking again. As queen of this great nation, I need the wisdom that only You can give me. I want to lead my people correctly at all times. I know my advisors from Parliament will be a great help, but I still need wisdom beyond theirs…wisdom that comes from You. Please quiet my nerves and help me as I go through the coronation ceremonies. Mr. Melbourne has gone over it all with me, and will be at my side to coach me, but I still need Your divine help. Thank You for promising wisdom to me."

Victoria went on to pray concerning Prince Albert, asking the Lord to lead and guide them, and to have His will and way in their lives. Just as she said her amen, there was a knock at the door.

She went across the room and opened the door to find her mother standing there. Mary had a folded newspaper in her hand as she stepped into the room. "Honey," she said, unfolding the paper, "I want you to see the headlines of the *London Times* this morning and read this fantastic article on the front page about you. It was written by England's most prominent journalist: Charles Greville."

"Oh, my!" said Victoria as her eyes took in the bold headlines which told of Queen Victoria's coronation that would take place that day at Westminster Abbey. Smaller headlines told of the colorful parade that would move through the city prior to the ceremonies.

Victoria's eyes ran down to the article at the bottom of the page.

"I have always liked Mr. Greville, Mother. Ever since he started doing a write-up in the *Times* every time I had a birthday, I enjoyed him interviewing me. He is a such a pleasant man."

Extending the paper to her, Mary said, "Here. Read it."

Putting her hands to her mouth, Victoria said, "You read it to me, please."

Mary smiled. "All right."

The mother read the early paragraphs which paid tribute to her daughter and praised her for being such a fine young lady. Greville told about his interviews with Princess Victoria over the years, commenting on how very warm and personable she had always been.

When she reached the last paragraph, Mary paused and wiped tears. "Now, honey, listen to this. 'Though the lovely lady has known much tragedy in her young life, she has turned a strong and pleasant face toward the world, impressing guests at Buckingham Palace with her distinctive blend of dignity and unaffected charm. She never ceases to be a queen, but is always the most charming, cheerful, obliging queen in the world.'"

Victoria burst into tears. "Oh, Mother, I don't deserve those nice words."

Folding her daughter's small frame in her arms, Mary said, "Oh, yes, you do. Mr. Greville is known for his accurate assessment of people. He has it exactly right. The people of Great Britain who don't know you will read this article, and it will make them feel that they do know you. I have no doubt you're going to be a great leader, sweetheart."

"By God's help I will be, Mother."

Mary smiled without comment. "Honey, I want to talk to you about Albert."

"Mm-hmm?"

"These past days as I've observed you and the handsome prince together, I couldn't help but notice the way you and he look at each other. Are you falling in love with him?"

Victoria blushed. "Yes, I am. Head over heels."

"I can read it quite clearly in your eyes when you look at him. Just wanted to hear you confirm it. And it isn't hard to tell that Albert feels the same way about you. Has he come out and told you he is in love with you?"

Victoria's crimson features went darker. "Well-l-l-l…"

"Did he?"

"Well, almost. On Monday night. I'm pretty sure he started to say it, but Louise was close by, and maybe he felt she would read his lips."

Mary chuckled. "Well, take it from me, honey. It's written all over his face."

Victoria drew a sharp breath. "Really?"

"Really. A person would have to be blind not to see it."

A wide smile spread over the young queen's features.

Ten

As the day progressed, Buckingham Palace was a virtual beehive. The servants pitched in to do their part to help Queen Victoria prepare for her coronation.

Head dresser to the queen was Marianne Skerrett, whose job it was to oversee the practical work of ordering all the queen's clothing, shoes, and hats. Marianne had ordered a special dress made for Victoria's coronation day. She would be seen in the dress during the parade prior to the coronation ceremonies at Westminster Abbey and afterward. It was customary for all British monarchs to wear a Parliament robe for the coronation ceremony, itself.

Marianne and Louise worked together that morning to get Victoria ready. When Louise had finished fixing her hair, Marianne helped her get into the lavish dress. A group of older women surrounded the queen to tend to other important matters. The group was made up of eight bedchamber ladies and eight maids of honor, who formed an inner circle to serve as the queen's official attendants. On this day of days, they were all busy, making sure everything was just right for her majesty.

Prince Albert arrived an hour before the royal carriage was to leave the palace and head for the spot in London where the parade was to begin. When he was ushered by Wilson into the drawing room where Victoria was surrounded by her maids, he stopped short.

Victoria smiled and hurried to him. "Good morning, Albert!" she said cheerfully. "Did you get a good night's rest?"

Albert stared at Victoria as if he was in a trance, running his gaze from head to foot. Drawing a quick breath as he looked into her shining eyes, he said, "Oh, Victoria! You look so beautiful. Absolutely stunning."

The little queen's face flushed. "Why, thank you, Albert."

He rubbed his temple. "I'm sorry. You asked me something. What was it?"

"I asked if you got a good night's rest."

"Oh. Yes, I did, thank you."

One of the maids stepped up. "Excuse me, Your Majesty. Is there anything else we can do for you?"

"I don't think so, Cora. You've all done a marvelous job. You go get yourselves ready."

Wilson excused himself and followed the maids out of the room.

"I assume your mother and Louise are getting ready," said Albert.

"You assume correctly. Please, come sit down."

When they were seated, facing each other, Victoria said, "Can you believe it? We're actually alone."

Albert's eyes were fixed on her, trancelike again. "Yes. And how fortunate I am to be alone with the most beautiful, most charming, most stunning woman in all the world."

Victoria was without words. She was pleased to hear the heartfelt compliments coming from the man she loved.

Rapid footsteps were heard, and they turned to see Louise coming through the door.

Albert sighed and said in a whisper, "Well, it was good while it lasted."

Soon the royal carriage that was to carry the queen rolled up in front of the palace. It was decorated with brightly colored flowers and flanked by eight mounted armed guards.

Wilson stood on the wide veranda and spoke to the driver. "Charles, I will bring the queen and her escorts out in just a moment." His attention then went to the front seat where Prime Minister William Melbourne sat with Lord Chamberlain and his wife. Melbourne was a widower.

"Good morning, Lady Chamberlain," said Wilson, then greeted the men. "Queen Victoria has asked that her companion, Louise Lehzen, sit in the second seat with you beside her, Mr. Melbourne."

"That will be an honor for me," said the prime minister, rising and stepping out of the carriage.

Smiling, Wilson nodded. "She will be here in a moment."

With that, Wilson turned and entered the palace. Less than a minute later, he stepped out the door and held it open while Louise moved past him. The prime minister hurried up the steps, gave Louise his hand, and said, "Allow me, Miss Lehzen."

She nodded and gave him a warm smile.

When Melbourne had helped Louise into the carriage onto the second seat he climbed in and sat beside her.

Wilson moved to the duchess, escorted her down the steps, and helped her onto the rear seat. As Mary was thanking him, the queen appeared with Prince Albert at her side, her hand locked in the crook of his arm. Albert helped Victoria aboard the carriage, seated her beside her mother, then sat down next to her. Wilson mounted the steps, smiled at the queen, and thought how small she looked sitting between the duchess and the prince.

He watched the carriage and its mounted escorts as it pulled away from the palace and headed down the tree-lined lane toward the street. When it turned onto the street, he pivoted to see the string of other carriages coming from behind the castle, which would carry all of the palace servants to the coronation site by a different route than the queen's carriage was taking.

The royal carriage moved through the streets of London toward the south side, where the procession would begin. Few people were visible along the way, for they were already lining the streets where they knew the queen would appear on her way to Westminster Abbey.

It took almost an hour to reach the place where the parade would begin. The men of Parliament were waiting in carriages that would follow the queen's carriage through the streets.

Charles guided the horses to a spot just ahead of the first parliament vehicle and pulled rein. Just ahead of the royal carriage was a military band, dressed in bright colored uniforms.

As the bandleader stepped in front of his men, Victoria squeezed the prince's arm. "Oh, Albert, I'm so nervous."

Patting the hand that gripped his arm, Albert said, "You will do fine, Victoria. The Lord planned for you to be queen of England before you were ever born. He has given you what it takes to fulfill His plan for your life."

Mary looked at her daughter and said softly, "You have royal blood in your veins, sweetheart. You will make us all proud today."

Victoria swallowed hard and looked straight ahead as the bandleader signaled for the band to begin playing, then led them in a precision march as they led the procession forward.

Trumpets blared and drums beat as horses clopped down freshly swept streets. Bright banners and countless British flags waved in the breeze, while thousands of people lined the streets to cheer Queen Victoria and to catch a glimpse of her as she smiled and waved.

After a while, Albert turned to Victoria as she waved, smiling at her elated subjects. "Look how they love you. I have to say that you are a magnificent queen already. You have captured their hearts in such a short time."

Victoria gave him an affectionate glance as the crowds cheered, calling out her name. "Albert, you are the most wonderful man I know."

Mary smiled to herself, happy to see that something serious was definitely happening between her daughter and the handsome prince.

At the same time, Gordon Whitaker sat in his cell at the London jail, listening to the other prisoners in the cell block talking about the coronation. Hatred toward Victoria boiled inside him as they spoke of her in approving and admiring terms.

Soon the sound of the marching band could be heard as the procession passed the jail, and the roar of the crowd met their ears.

Gordon stood up and began pacing his cell, mumbling something the others could not understand. A man two cells down looked at him. "What are you angry about, Whitaker?"

All the others were now looking at him.

Gordon scowled at him. "What makes you think I'm angry?"

"It's written all over your beet red face."

"Mind your own business," Whitaker snarled, and kept pacing and mumbling. In his mind, he told himself that someday he would get even with Victoria for what she did to him. The fact that she did not press charges against him didn't alter a thing as far as he was concerned. She did him wrong, and she was going to pay.

The vast crowds that packed Westminster Abbey for the coronation were moved by the sight of the queen's figure, garbed in the parliament robes of crimson velvet trimmed with ermine and gold lace, walking slowly down the aisle toward the platform where she would be crowned.

Beside her was Prime Minister William Melbourne. On their heels was the Duchess of Kent, magnificently dressed in regal purple, with Louise Lehzen at her side. Prince Albert had taken his place in the audience near the platform.

Victoria's immensely long train was held by Lord Chamberlain and eight young female attendants, their white and silver gowns sprinkled with roses.

When the queen ascended the platform, which was flanked by a large choir and the London Symphony Orchestra, everyone in the audience rose to their feet. The orchestra began to play while the queen, her mother, her companion, and Prime Minister William Melbourne were being properly seated. Once they were on their chairs, the crowd sat down.

The orchestra continued to play to set the mood for the coronation.

While the music went on, Victoria let her eyes roam over the faces in the crowd, seeing many people she recognized. When her eyes fell on Alice Whitaker and her children, she smiled at them, nodding her head. Alice smiled back, as did Marianne and Lorene. Edgar met the queen's gaze, but kept his lips pressed tight. He would not give the queen the satisfaction of seeing a smile on his face. Victoria then ran her line of sight to Albert, who flashed her a loving smile. She returned the smile in the same manner.

Soon the orchestra was finished with their number, and the coronation ceremony began with Prime Minister William Melbourne at the podium, asking the queen's pastor to step up and lead them in prayer.

When this was done, Melbourne introduced six members of Parliament, who filed to the podium from the side of the platform. Leaving the six men to carry on the ceremony, Melbourne sat down beside the queen. As the formalities proceeded, Victoria found the steadying presence of Melbourne with his fatherly glances very heartening.

With the prime minister at her side to coach her through the long ceremony, Victoria managed to perform each one of the twenty-one separate sections of the coronation ritual without a mistake. Throughout the five-hour ceremony, with its thunderous orchestral interludes and the deafening choral anthems, its moments of high drama and rich pageantry, the queen remained the center of all attention.

There was loud applause when the gleaming crown, its diamonds, rubies, and sapphires flashing, was lowered carefully onto her neatly coiffed head by Prime Minister William Melbourne.

As planned before the ceremony, Victoria then left the chair where she had been crowned and knelt beside it in reverence, bowed her head, and prayed silently. The sight brought forth whispers of prayer from even the most hardened in the audience.

When the queen had finished praying, Lord Chamberlain helped her to her feet, then placed the golden royal scepter in her hand. The audience leaped to its feet, cheering and applauding. William Melbourne led the queen down the steps from the platform and escorted her up the aisle with her mother and companion on the arms of men of Parliament behind them. Prince Albert followed on their heels. Soon they were at the royal carriage outside with thousands of people cheering while Victoria's mounted guards kept an eye on the crowd. When everyone was seated in the carriage as they had been before, the procession began with the marching band out front.

As the carriage rolled along the crowd-lined street, Victoria sighed and looked at Albert as she gripped the golden scepter. Though the ceremony had been long, she felt surprisingly buoyant and energetic, for which she silently thanked the Lord.

"You did marvelously, lovely lady," said Albert.

"You most certainly did," said Mary. "You made us all proud."

Along the return route to Buckingham Palace was a section known as Birdcage Walk. Standing in the crowd that lined the street in that section was a tall, hollow-cheeked, stoop-shouldered man who wore an overcoat. People eyed him, elbowing each other and pointing at him. He had a strange look in his eyes, and held his mouth in a weird, turned-down manner. His right hand stayed out of sight inside the long, bulky sleeve while he continually rubbed his three-day growth of beard with the left hand.

Two teenage boys were laughing as they looked at him. One of the boys snickered and said, "Hey, mister, don't you know it's July? Why are you wearing that overcoat?"

The man widened his peculiar eyes and fixed them on the boy. "Are you blind? This is no overcoat. It's my royal robe."

"Royal robe?" The other boy laughed. "Man, are you crazy?"

The man's eyes bulged wildly. "Don't you call me crazy!"

People turned to look at him then put their attention back up the street where the queen would soon appear in her royal carriage.

"What's your name, mister?" asked one of the teenage boys.

The man squared his shoulders, holding his head high. "My name is William."

"William what?"

"William V, King of England."

One boy poked an elbow in the rib of his friend and laughed. "You couldn't be William V unless William IV was your father, and he didn't have any children."

"Oh yes, he did!" insisted the wild-eyed man. "I'm his son, and I should be the one who got crowned today, not that—that pygmy girl, Victoria!"

The boys looked at each other, then one laughed again. "You really are crazy, mister. C'mon, Gerald, let's get away from him."

The man gave them an angry look as they filtered into the crowd and moved up the street.

At the same moment, the sound of the military band was heard, and someone shouted, "Get ready, everybody! The queen's coming!"

As the entourage slowly turned onto Birdcage Walk with the blaring band out front, Victoria was smiling and waving at her admiring subjects. Mary leaned past her daughter. "Albert, I'm so glad you could be with us for Victoria's coronation. It just wouldn't have been right without you here."

"Thank you, Duchess," said Albert. "I appreciate you feeling that way about me."

"I do, too," said Victoria as she waved at the cheering crowd. "It wouldn't be the same without you here, Albert."

"There isn't anywhere else in the world I'd rather be, sweet Victoria," Albert said.

"God bless you, Queen Victoria!" shouted a large woman who stood at the edge of the curb.

"And God bless you, too!" Victoria said.

A few feet further down the street, the wild-eyed man was also at the forefront of the crowd. His whole body trembled. He eyed Albert, who was sitting at Victoria's side, knowing he would have to make his move fast and sudden to get between the horses of two of the guards and leap up onto the carriage past Albert.

As the carriage drew near, he steeled himself like a spring coiling, ready to strike. Victoria was waving and smiling at the crowd. Albert was leaning past Victoria, saying something to her mother. The man's jaw was clenched tight. The veins were bulging in his forehead and neck.

The man waited until one mounted guard passed, then timing his move with a sudden ferocious anger, he sprang up to the carriage, a knife flashing in the sunlight. Two women in the crowd screamed, and before Victoria could let out a cry, Albert whipped around in time to see the man leaping toward the queen, raising the knife.

Reacting in a split second, Albert sprang from the seat, grasped the wrist of the hand that held the knife, and threw his weight against the man. Both men landed in the street, wrestling for supremacy. By this time Charles had pulled rein, and the guards were sliding from their saddles, pulling their revolvers.

Albert quickly rolled on top of the man and sent a solid punch to his jaw, stunning him. He viciously slammed the hand that held the knife against the street repeatedly until it fell from the man's grasp.

One of the guards picked up the knife, and at the same time, the man was trying to clear his head and was flinging his fists at Albert. The young prince chopped him twice more, once with the left, and then with the right. He sagged, closed his eyes, and went totally limp.

By this time the guards were gathered around, some kneeling next to Albert. "We'll take it from here, Prince Albert," said one of the guards.

Two others took hold of the unconscious would-be assassin while Albert stood up, breathing hard, and turned to look at Victoria. William Melbourne was out of the carriage, standing next to the seat where the queen and her mother sat, talking to them in low tones. Mary had an arm around her daughter, and Victoria was holding a handkerchief to her mouth with shaky fingers. The police had arrived and were pushing the curious crowd back from the spot.

Albert rushed up beside Melbourne, eyes fixed on the queen. "Victoria, darling, are you all right?"

Victoria was not alone in picking up on the endearing word that Albert had just used. The queen nodded, her features pallid. "Y-yes. I'm all right."

Albert nodded, gave her a quick smile, then wheeled and went back to the guards who were just lifting the man to his feet. His eyes were dull, but he set them on the queen. "You have no right to the throne, Victoria! I am King William IV's son, and should have been crowned today, not you!"

"The man's insane!" shouted a man in the crowd.

"That he is," replied a policeman who was standing in front of the would-be killer. "He'll be locked up in Bedlam and examined by the doctors."

Two other police officers joined him, handcuffed the man, and took him away in a paddy wagon.

One of the guards looked at Albert and said, "You're to be commended for your quick thinking and courageous action, Prince Albert."

The others spoke their agreement.

Albert's features tinted slightly. "I only did what any man sitting in my position would have done." Looking back at Victoria, he said, "Excuse me, gentlemen."

Most of the eyes in the crowd were on the prince as he climbed back into the carriage and settled on the seat beside the queen. Lord Chamberlain and his wife looked on with smiles.

Victoria's eyes, huge in her pale face, turned to rest lovingly on Albert. He could tell that she was deeply shaken. Blinking to dispel any trace of tears, Victoria gave Albert a tremulous smile, searching in her heart for the proper words to thank him for risking his life to save her own. "Albert, how can I thank you? That—that man could have killed you instead of me. You are the bravest man I know."

"That's right, honey, he is," said Mary, smiling at the young prince.

Pulling herself together, Victoria said to the others around her, "We had best get on with the parade. People are waiting."

Moments later, the band, mounted guards, and royal carriage were once again moving slowly down the street with the crowds cheering their queen. The guards rode alongside the carriage, their eyes continuously looking from side to side, their cautious eyes inspecting the crowd.

Albert was also watching the crowd with a newfound alertness. Victoria watched him while waving at the crowds, a deep emotion filling her still fluttering heart. The words *Victoria, darling* kept resounding through her head.

When they were nearing Buckingham Palace and the end of the ride, Prime Minister William Melbourne turned around on his seat and set admiring eyes on the prince. "You should be given a medal for what you did."

Embarrassed, Albert shook his head. "I don't deserve a medal, sir. Besides, I already have my reward. The queen is unharmed."

Victoria took hold of Albert's arm and gave him an appreciative smile.

Albert asked Victoria for time alone with her. Now that she had been crowned, she felt it was time for her to be able to meet with Albert in private. She first talked to her mother and Louise, explaining her position on it, and they found it necessary to agree.

When Albert and Victoria were alone in the library, she thanked him again for saving her life, saying the British press would make a big thing of it.

Albert's face reddened a bit. "I wish they wouldn't. I would risk my life to save yours a thousand times and more, if necessary, but it would be because of how I feel about you, not for people to brag on me."

Victoria and her mother had discussed Albert's use of the word *darling* at breakfast that morning. Her mind went to it again. "Well, Albert, just how do you feel about me?"

A shy grin curved his lips. "I think you're the most beautiful, most wonderful lady in the whole world. That's how I feel."

Victoria was hoping the word *love* would come from him, but when it didn't, she smiled anyway. "And I think you're the handsomest, most wonderful man in the whole world."

"I guess that makes us even, doesn't it?"

"Looks like it." Victoria's heart was pounding.

She didn't know it, but so was Albert's, though he was hesitant to go any further at that time.

Taking a deep breath, he smiled at her and said, "Could we pray together before I go?"

Thrilled that he would ask to pray with her, Victoria said, "Oh yes. I would love that."

In his prayer, Albert asked the Lord to guide the two of them in their lives, saying they both needed His hand on them and their future. After the prayer, Albert embraced Victoria in a proper manner. "I must be going. I will be back again as soon as possible."

"I…I wish it could be tomorrow," she said softly.

Albert smiled and kissed the tip of her nose.

Victoria walked Albert to one of the sitting rooms where her mother and Louise were in light conversation. Both women thanked Albert once more for what he did to save Victoria's life, and walked to the door with the couple.

When Albert climbed into the carriage, Victoria had a lump in her throat. She was in love with the handsome young prince, and her love was growing stronger by the minute.

Eleven

At the same time as Queen Victoria was watching Prince Albert's carriage drive away from Buckingham Palace, Alice Whitaker was ushered into the cell block at London's jail by a guard and seated in the visitor's room at one of the barred windows. She held a folded newspaper in her hand.

A moment later, Gordon was brought in by another guard, and sat down at the barred window, facing Alice. The guard who stood beside Alice took a few steps backward and leaned against the wall.

Pressing a smile on her lips, Alice asked, "How are you doing, honey?"

"As well as can be expected in this place," replied Gordon levelly, glancing at the guard who stood behind her.

"Have you heard about the incident on Birdcage Walk yesterday?"

"Yeah. It's the talk of the jail." His eyes went to the newspaper in her hand. "I suppose the newspapers are full of it."

Alice unfolded the early edition of the *London Times* and held it up so he could see the front page. The bold headlines read: INSANE MAN ATTEMPTS TO ASSASSINATE QUEEN VICTORIA!

"So he's definitely been declared insane, eh?"

"Yes," said Alice, folding the paper and laying it in her lap. "His name is William Bender. They have him locked up in a padded cell at Bedlam Asylum."

"So his name really is William. We heard that he screamed at Victoria that he was William V and should have been crowned king because William IV was his father."

"Yes. Poor man. He's totally out of his mind."

"Is it true that he almost got to Victoria with his knife and was stopped in the nick of time by her boyfriend from Germany?"

"Yes. If Prince Albert hadn't acted as quickly as he did, Bender would have buried the knife in her heart."

Gordon started to comment, then checked himself when he remembered that the guard was standing within hearing distance. Alice noted it, and was sure her husband was about to say he wished the would-be assassin hadn't failed.

Silently, Gordon told himself that maybe fate was going to give him the chance to get even with Victoria.

For the next month, which was dubbed Coronation Month by Parliament, Buckingham Palace was host to several concerts and grand dinners, while every night there were parties and receptions for the elite guests.

Queen Victoria was required by her station to attend the concerts and dinners as well as to entertain the many attending dignitaries and be hostess at the gala parties.

One hot summer morning, Victoria sat at a small lace-covered table in her private sitting room adjacent to her bedroom. On the table was a stack of important papers which she had been perusing since returning to the room after breakfast. She was studying one of the papers with great interest when she heard a knock at the door, followed by the muffled voice of Louise Lehzen. "Your Majesty. It's Louise."

"Please come in, Louise."

Louise entered, carrying a tray with a pot of aromatic hot tea and a plate of scones, fresh from the oven. Victoria sniffed the sweet scents, flashed Louise a grateful smile, and pushed the stack of papers to the side. "How did you know that tea and scones were exactly what I needed?"

Louise smiled as she placed the tray on the table. "Sweet girl, I've been with you since you were just a wee thing. I pretty much know all of your likes and needs by now."

"Of course you do, and I'm so thankful to have you with me. Your quiet wisdom and unselfish support are always such a comfort to me."

Pouring the tea into the cup, Louise said, "You give me far too much credit, Your Highness."

"Oh no. If anything, I don't praise you enough. You mean more to me than I could ever tell you."

Louise set the teapot on the table, and blinked at warm tears that were trying to fill her eyes as she sat on a chair opposite the queen.

With a small sigh, Victoria picked up the cup, took a sip, and leaned back in her chair. "This is wonderful, Louise. I needed a break. I am enjoying all of the frivolity and festivities of Coronation Month, but to be quite honest, I'm getting rather tired. I'm looking forward to settling into a routine that is not so rigorous and demanding. Being involved every night in one activity or another is rather wearying. I know I'm young, but I want to be at my best when decisions are required of me."

"I know what you mean," said Louise. "But only a few more days, and everything will settle down."

After another bite of scone, and another sip, Victoria said, "I still have so much to learn, Louise, and sometimes I do feel totally overwhelmed by it all. I can only take it one day at a time. I couldn't do it at all without the guidance of my heavenly Father."

"That's true of every Christian, but especially of you. Most of us will never be in the demanding position you are in."

Victoria set loving eyes on her companion. "Louise, dear, I owe you so much. You are the one who witnessed to me of salvation in Jesus Christ and took me to church where I could hear the gospel preached. And after I opened my heart to the Saviour, you are the one who saw to my spiritual growth all of my growing-up years. I really do owe you so much."

As she spoke, Victoria pushed her chair back, stood to her feet, leaned over Louise and embraced her. "Thank you. My life as queen of England wouldn't matter at all if my soul was not secure in God's hands. Thank you for caring about my eternal destiny. Thank you for leading me to give my heart and life to Jesus." Victoria planted a kiss on Louise's cheek.

A bit embarrassed by Victoria's accolades, Louise dipped her head. Then with the tears spilling unbidden down her cheeks, she looked up at Victoria and said, "It has been my pleasure and joy to have a part in your coming to the Lord and growing in Him, Your Majesty. As long as God leaves me in this world, I will always be here for you and will daily hold you up in prayer."

Victoria kissed her cheek again. "Thank you, my sweet Louise. I love you."

Louise laid a palm on Victoria's cheek. "I love you, too. More than you will ever know."

Moments later, Louise carried the tray from the room and the queen sat down at the table, slid the sheaf of papers in front of her, and began reading once again.

A few days later, Alice Whitaker and her three children sat in the family carriage in front of the London jail.

"How should we conduct ourselves, Mama?" asked Marianne. "Should we just act like none of it has happened?"

"Yes, as best you can," replied Alice. "Your father is still carrying a heavy grudge against Queen Victoria. It's eating like a canker in his soul, and the less we talk about her, the better. Let's just put on happy faces and make the best of our situation."

"Have you told Papa about Queen Victoria giving us the money, Mama?" asked Lorene.

"No, honey. He might get angry because I accepted it from her. It's best he not know about it."

"Even if he did know about it," said Edgar, "it wouldn't make any difference—not after what she did to him. As far as I'm concerned, she's still a bad woman."

Alice frowned at her son. "Try to remember, Edgar, that it was the queen's mother who made your father those promises, not the queen. Victoria really owes your father nothing."

"Not the way I look at it," Edgar said stubbornly.

"Well, you just keep it to yourself," said Alice. "We've got to go on with life, and the quicker you and your father get over your grudge, the better off we'll all be. Don't you tell him about her giving us the money, either. I don't need him angry with me."

Edgar stuck out his lower lip.

"I mean it," Alice said sternly.

"I won't tell him," said the boy.

"Promise?"

"Promise."

"Thank you."

"Here he comes, Mama," said Lorene.

All eyes went to Gordon, who was accompanied by a uniformed policeman as he came out of the jail. The officer smiled and spoke to Gordon's family while Gordon climbed into the front seat of the carriage. Then to Gordon, he said, "I hope we don't see you in here anymore, Mr. Whitaker."

Ignoring him, Gordon took the reins from Alice's hands and put the carriage in motion.

"We're glad to see you, Papa," said Marianne.

"We sure are," said Lorene.

"That goes for me, too, Papa," said Edgar. "It'll be nice to have you home again."

Gordon turned on the seat, managed a smile, and said, "Thank you, children. It will be good to be home again." They rode through London's busy streets in silence for several minutes, then Gordon turned to Alice. "Anybody else try to kill the queen?"

Alice gave him a calm glance. "No."

"Too bad. Maybe the next guy who attempts it will get the job done."

Alice sighed. "Gordon, I know you want revenge on Queen Victoria, but I wish you would forget it. You need to go on with your life, get a job, and support your family. Anything you would try to do to the queen would only make things worse for you, not to mention the rest of us."

The three in the back seat remained silent, but Edgar was building up stronger resentment in his heart toward the queen for what she had done to his father.

As time passed, the young queen surprised the people of Great Britain at how well she handled the responsibilities that went with wearing the crown. She worked well with her advisers in Parliament and surprised even them with her wisdom. When they commented on it one day while meeting with her, she gave God the glory, saying He was the one who gave her the wisdom. The born-again men in the group were especially thankful that the Lord had given the country such a godly monarch.

Unknown to Gordon and Edgar, Victoria kept contact with Alice through written notes delivered to the Whitaker home by a palace messenger. Money was included with the notes, for Gordon was having a hard time holding a job for very long. Alice kept the money a secret, fearing what Gordon's reaction would be if he learned that she had accepted it from the one person in the world he hated with a passion. Marianne and Lorene were deeply appreciative of the queen's generosity, but shared their feelings only with their mother.

When Alice spent the money on groceries and other necessities, she told Gordon it came from different neighbors who knew they were having a hard time. Gordon never asked which neighbors were their benefactors, which was a relief to Alice. She knew that her husband's mind was filled with hatred for Victoria. It was consuming him. She feared that his loathing for the queen would drive him to do something desperate and foolish.

For the next two years, Prince Albert came to England every few months to see Victoria. Their hearts were knitting tighter all the time, but neither tried to hurry things between them.

In October of 1839, Albert came to see Victoria again. She and her mother, along with Louise, were now living at Windsor Castle. They went to Buckingham Palace from time to time to take part in events that took place there, but thoroughly enjoyed living in the quietness and country atmosphere Windsor Castle provided. The larger portion of the servants remained at Buckingham Palace, and the rest served at Windsor Castle.

It had been three months since Albert's last visit, and Victoria welcomed him warmly. After Mary and Louise had welcomed Albert, they left the couple alone, and in private, Albert and Victoria admitted they had missed each other terribly.

Albert was given the room next to Wilson's on the first floor of the castle, and over the next few days, the queen and the prince took walks together between her meetings with men of Parliament. They also went horseback riding, played games, and went to church together on Sunday. In the evenings, they spent hours together in the library of the castle.

On Monday evening, October 14, Albert and Victoria went together to the library to talk after dinner.

When Albert closed the library door behind them, he moved up to Victoria, took both her hands in his, and looked into her eyes. "Victoria, may I speak frankly?"

"Of course," she replied, meeting his soft, loving gaze.

"Thank you," he said, trying to catch his breath. "I…I have to tell you. I can't hold it in any longer. Victoria, darling, I am deeply in love with you. I have been for a long time."

"Albert, I am deeply in love with you, too. And I am sure I have been for just as long. I know with both of us being royalty, we are expected to move slowly when it comes to love and courtship, but love affects us the same way it does other people. We've waited long enough to let our love show."

"Yes," he said breathlessly.

Their eyes locked and held for a long moment, then a bit hesitantly, Albert lowered his face toward hers. Victoria tilted her face toward his, and their lips came together in a sweet kiss.

When their lips parted, the prince gazed into her eyes again. The moment was precious between them, and they kissed once more.

Still holding her close, Albert said in a whisper, "Victoria, my love, I…I have never proposed to a queen before. But…will you…marry me?"

Tears filled her eyes, and a smile broke over her face. "Oh, Albert! Yes! Yes, I will marry you!"

They kissed again, then Victoria said, "Darling, I am not worthy of you. It is a great sacrifice for you to give up your independence as prince of Saxe-Coburg-Gotha to become husband of the queen of England. In order to marry me, you will also have to give up your citizenship in Germany and become a British citizen."

Albert nodded. "Yes. But it is no sacrifice if I give up those things so I can be married to the most wonderful and most beautiful woman in all the world. I know it will be different than most marriages. Even though you will be my wife, you will also be my queen—the highest authority in Great Britain. Please don't think of what I am giving up as a sacrifice. I will be happy and content to spend the rest of my life as your husband."

"Oh, I love you so much!" Victoria breathed softly, and they kissed again. Looking deeply into his eyes, she said, "Even though I will be over you as queen of England, I still insist on the words 'to love, honor, and obey' in my vow to you in the wedding ceremony. God used the word *obey* when speaking of submissive wives in 1 Peter 3:6, and I want to be the wife to you that He wants me to be."

Albert smiled and tweaked her nose playfully. "What more could I ask for? I am going to be the husband of the queen of England, and I get to boss her around!"

They laughed together, then sat down and talked about all the things they had in common.

First and foremost, they both had the Lord Jesus in their hearts. They both loved being in church, hearing the Word of God preached, and listening to heart-stirring hymns and gospel songs sung by individuals, groups, and choirs. They both were romantics. They both loved music—Albert played the piano, as well as the organ, and he had written several songs.

"Oh, darling," said Victoria, "we will have such a happy life together! I love you so very much."

Albert kissed her again, then said jubilantly, "I want to tell the whole world. I am engaged to marry the most beautiful and wonderful woman!"

During the next two days, Albert and Victoria spent hours together, praying about their upcoming marriage, gazing into each other's eyes, and making promises of undying love and plans for their lives together.

Both mornings, Victoria was up before daylight, attending to her many duties and obligations so she could spend as much time with the man who had captured her heart—in between her important meetings with men of Parliament.

On the evening of Wednesday, October 16, the happy couple went to the library again after dinner, and sat down on a sofa, holding hands. Albert said, "I borrowed a calendar from Wilson. We are expected to have a proper waiting period between the official announcement of our engagement and the wedding. This is October 16, 1839. How about setting the wedding for Monday, February 10, 1840?"

Victoria smiled. "That's almost four months. As queen of England, I declare it a sufficient amount of time!"

They sealed it with a kiss, then went to the duchess and Louise Lehzen and told them of the engagement. Mary and Louise were overjoyed at the announcement and congratulated the happy couple.

Mary then told them that the proper thing for her to do was to find herself a place to live just before the wedding took place, since they needed to have privacy from relatives in their home, whether it be Windsor Castle or Buckingham Palace. Louise spoke up and said since Victoria would not need her services as companion once she was married to Albert, she would also find another place to live. Mary immediately said Louise could live with her. This pleased Louise, and she readily accepted the invitation.

Victoria then told her mother and her companion that she

would pay for their living quarters, and both would be given money to live on for the rest of their lives.

There were tears and hugs.

That evening in the library, Albert and Victoria spent half an hour in prayer as they both brought their petitions to the Lord, seeking His hand on their engagement and upcoming marriage.

When they had finished praying and rose from their knees at the sofa, Victoria set endearing eyes on the man she loved. "Oh, darling, just a few short years ago, I never could have imagined in my fondest dreams that I would ever be this happy. My position as queen is an awesome responsibility and a great honor. But my position as your wife will be an even higher calling.

"And then there's the greatest honor that could ever be bestowed on this sinner saved by grace. I'm a child of the King of kings. Being the queen of England is indeed a great blessing, but being a child of the King is an even greater blessing."

"That's for sure," said Albert.

Victoria's eyes sparkled as she said, "Being queen is a temporal thing, but being a child of the King is an eternal thing."

Albert enfolded her in his strong arms. "Yes, my love, you and I are royalty by fleshly birth, but we are heirs of the King of kings by being born spiritually into His family. And, darling, we will always put Him first in our lives and in our home. He will guide and bless us as we serve this great country that you love and I am learning to love as well."

Victoria laid a palm on Albert's cheek. "Your dedication to the Lord makes me love you even more. What a joy to know that Jesus will be the very center of our home."

The next Sunday the banns were announced by the pastor at church, and after the services, the young couple were congratulated by people as they passed by on the way out. Louise stood with Albert and Victoria, beaming.

On Monday, the British newspapers came out with large headlines, announcing the royal engagement.

By the last week in January 1840, Victoria had purchased a house for her mother and Louise in Belgrave Square, an upper-class neighborhood of London.

On Saturday, February 8, Albert's widowed father, Ernest I, Duke of Saxe-Coburg-Gotha, Germany, and Albert's twenty-year-old brother, Milan, arrived in London.

Victoria was thrilled to meet her future father-in-law and her future brother-in-law and welcomed them warmly. They were given quarters in Buckingham Palace for their stay, where Victoria had returned to make her main home as Albert's wife.

When Mary and Louise met them, there was much to talk about, and the six of them spent that evening in vibrant conversation.

Ernest and Milan, who were also dedicated Christians, attended church services with Albert, Victoria, and Louise on Sunday.

On Monday morning, February 10, Victoria was awakened early by the sound of falling rain beating against her bedroom windows. Having lain awake into the wee hours because of the excitement, she yawned, stretched her arms, and sat up. Rising from her warm bed, she padded barefoot to the window, pulled back the velvet drapes, and peered outside. A gray dawn was just breaking in the east, and there was no indication that the storm would be abating anytime soon.

Disappointment gripped her, but only for a moment. Hugging herself, she shrugged her shoulders and looked through the rain-speckled glass at the heavy sky. "Oh, well, this is what I get for planning a wedding in rainy England in February."

Twirling in a circle, she looked heavenward and said, "Dear Lord, I'm not going to let the rain dampen my spirits. 'This is the day which the LORD hath made; we will rejoice and be glad in it.' As far as I'm concerned, the sun is shining all over the world! Thank You, heavenly Father, for this beautiful day!"

Going to the wall she pulled a cord, summoning whatever personal maid was on duty at the moment.

~⊗~

At midafternoon, rain was falling in torrents as the royal carriage carried the queen, her mother, and Louise to St. James's Chapel.

Thousands of people made their way toward the huge chapel in the wind and rain.

Prince Albert was waiting inside the chapel with his father and brother. It was dark and gloomy outside, but St. James's was aglow with candlelight and bright, happy faces anticipating this joyful occasion.

Soon a blare of trumpets and a blaze of heralds in bright-colored uniforms proclaimed the arrival of the bride. Victoria, Mary, and Louise were quickly ushered inside beneath umbrellas to a room next to the foyer. Victoria was helped into her wedding gown by her mother and Louise, who also touched up her hair.

Just before Mary and Louise were to leave the room and take their places in the chapel, Victoria stopped her mother with a gloved hand on her arm. Mary turned toward her daughter.

Victoria leaned close and placed a tender kiss on Mary's cheek. "I love you, Mother," she said softly.

Mary returned the kiss as a sheen of tears filled her happy eyes. "I love you, too. Always be happy, sweetheart."

"I will," Victoria assured her.

Victoria then hugged Louise, who said, "God bless you, sweet girl. I love you."

"I love you, too," said the beautiful bride, and watched them pass through the door.

Victoria followed a moment later and found Prime Minister William Melbourne waiting for her as she stepped into the vestibule, where the rest of her attendants were gathered.

Inside the chapel proper, Prince Albert and the pastor took their places as the organ gave signal. Albert let his gaze run over the crowd, and noted that all of the queen's servants were seated in the balcony. There were royal guards positioned strategically throughout the building.

In the vestibule, the bride took a deep breath and standing as tall as possible, took hold of William Melbourne's free arm. In his other hand, he held the Sword of State, which was customary in royal British weddings.

The organ began the wedding march, and as they moved inside and started down the flower-strewn aisle, the crowd was on its feet. Victoria held her crown-bedecked head erect and set her eyes on her beloved, who waited for her at the foot of the platform.

Every eye was on the queen, who appeared small but stately in a dazzlingly beautiful white satin wedding gown with high neck and long sleeves, her round face framed with orange blossoms. Her hair was coiffed the way Albert liked it best.

Twelve lovely young attendants, all in white with white roses, bore the long train of Victoria's gown, and she sparkled with diamonds as she moved down the aisle to meet her groom.

The music reached a resounding crescendo as Victoria neared the altar, and Prime Minister William Melbourne halted as she let go of his arm.

As Albert stepped forth, smiling, and offered his arm, a verse of Scripture pushed its way into Victoria's crowded mind: "O give thanks unto the LORD; for he is good—"

Yes, her heart repeated, *He is good!*

When the ceremony was over, Albert and Victoria went in a special wedding carriage to the reception hall at Buckingham Palace where they greeted their guests around a 300-pound wedding cake adorned with cupids and satin love knots.

Later, Victoria went to a dressing room where her servants helped her put on a white silk dress trimmed with swansdown for the ride to Windsor Castle, where the bride and groom would spend their brief honeymoon.

Among the rain-soaked crowd—which had not been able to attend the wedding nor the reception—outside the Buckingham Palace grounds, Gordon Whitaker watched the wedding carriage as it came through the gate, accompanied by royal mounted guards. Hatred toward the queen burned in Whitaker's heart.

All along the route to the castle, the crowds ignored the rain and called out their good wishes to the bride and groom. Albert and Victoria held hands, smiled and waved; they were so much in love.

Twelve

ordon Whitaker's eyes were like pinpoints as he watched the royal carriage bearing Queen Victoria and her husband roll down the street. His rain-spattered face was a mask of animosity.

He thought of how he had continued to go from one job to another ever since he had spent the month in London's jail. His life was miserable for lack of the wealth he had thought for so long would be his. At this point he was between jobs once more.

He felt the muscles of his jaw hardening until they ached. There was a knot twisting in his stomach. His lips were tight in suppressed anger. "And it's all because of you, Victoria," he hissed in a low voice so those standing near would not hear him. "You're filthy rich, so what do you care about me and my family?"

The need for revenge on Victoria still ate at him, but he could think of no way to enact it without endangering himself. Giving the diminishing royal carriage one last scowl, Gordon wheeled and headed for home.

Alice Whitaker was dusting the parlor when she heard the front door of the house open and close. Laying the feather duster on a small table, she went to the door and saw Gordon removing his rain-soaked hat and coat in front of the closet in the hall.

Catching sight of her in his peripheral vision, he glanced her way, then tossed his hat on the closet shelf and hung the coat on a hook just inside the closet door.

Alice said, "Honey, where have you been? You left when Edgar and I were upstairs without saying a word."

When he turned to look at her, she could see he was in a foul mood; which was his main state of mind anymore. The frown line, which was now the most noticeable feature of his face, traversed the entire length of his forehead. Alice thought if it cut any deeper, it might expose the skull itself.

"I went to catch a glimpse of Victoria and the fool who married her when they came out of Buckingham after the reception," Gordon said evenly. "They're honeymooning at Windsor Castle, you know."

"I read it in the paper, yes."

"You should've seen the look on the little runt's face. She was the epitome of happiness." He took a short breath and scowled even more. "It gripes me to see her so happy."

"Gordon," Alice said, laying a hand on his arm, "brides are supposed to be happy."

"Not her!" he spat. "I wish her all the misery in the world! She robbed us of the happiness we could have had. But what does she care? She's got more money than she can count, and now she's got herself a prince for a husband. I'd like to—"

"To what?" asked Alice, knowing her husband wanted revenge on the queen more than anything in his life. She feared that he would end up doing something foolish to vent his hatred for Victoria, but she knew better than to interfere.

Gordon mumbled something Alice couldn't understand, cleared his throat and headed down the hall. "Never mind."

Alice went back into the parlor, picked up the feather duster, and returned to her work. While dusting the mantel over the fireplace, she thought about how kind Queen Victoria had been to her. Even though both Marianne and Lorene were now married and living in other parts of England, Victoria was still secretly making sure Alice had enough money to keep food on the table for the rest of the family.

Though it went against her basic principles, Alice had lied to Gordon repeatedly, saying kindly neighbors were giving her money because they knew the Whitakers were having a hard time financially. It was not in Gordon to express his appreciation to the generous neighbors, thus he had never learned the truth about the money's actual source.

In early March, Victoria began experiencing some strange sensations in her normally healthy body. She kept a very busy schedule most days, starting immediately after breakfast and not ending till late at night. She was in meetings with Parliament, Prime Minister William Melbourne, government officials, and Baron Robert Quinton. Often upon returning to Buckingham Palace, she had paperwork to keep her occupied until late at night.

Albert understood the necessity of such a schedule, and though he continually moved about the palace and the grounds, making sure guards and servants had everything they needed to carry on their duties, he kept himself available for whenever she needed him.

One cold, cloudy morning, Victoria awakened at her normal early hour, rolled over in bed, and found that Albert was already up and gone. He had talked the night before about wanting to oversee the changing of the guard at dawn.

Wishing she could stay in her warm cocoon of blankets but knowing she had an early meeting that morning with a parliament committee, she threw back the covers, sat up, and dropped her feet over the side of the bed. She stood up and suddenly the room seemed to be whirling around in circles.

She plopped back down on the side of the bed, putting fingertips to her temples. She closed her eyes and sat with her head bowed for several minutes. Her stomach was a bit queasy. *Guess I just have been overdoing it a little,* she thought. *Maybe something I ate last night didn't agree with me.*

Soon the dizziness subsided. Raising her head, she slowly opened her eyes. Everything seemed to be all right again. The queasiness had left her stomach.

Gingerly rising to her feet, she stood still for a moment. Though she didn't feel totally normal, she wasn't actually ill, either. Moving to her small desk, she sat down, read a chapter of Proverbs in her Bible, had her prayer time, then rang for her maid. Emily came quickly to help the queen prepare for another busy day.

Two days later, when attempting to get out of bed, Victoria found the same sensations assailing her. Albert was already up and gone.

Once again sitting on the edge of the bed, she said aloud, "Whatever is going on here?"

Suddenly, her hand flew to her mouth and she darted for the water closet. After losing what little food was still in her stomach, she washed her face in cold water, then returned to the bed and lay down, sinking back onto her pillows.

After a few minutes, she felt fine and sat up. "Oh, well," she muttered, "it's another day and I have much to do."

During the next two weeks, Victoria experienced the same thing almost daily, but each time, Albert had already departed the bedroom, and was unaware of it. Sometimes she had to excuse herself to whomever she was with and make a hasty departure. And most afternoons, after a light lunch, she felt the need for a nap. Usually she was too busy to give in to her body's desire, but occasionally she would lie down for a few minutes.

When questioned by her personal maid, Emily, Victoria attributed her weariness to the busy schedule she was keeping. Though Emily was aware of the queen's sudden departures to a water closet on some days, she said nothing. But when Victoria referred to her schedule for the fifth or sixth time as the source of her weariness, Emily secretly smiled to herself. Other than the fact that these incidents were annoying, Queen Victoria had not yet realized the real cause of her discomfort. Being in such demand, Emily thought, the queen didn't seem to have a moment to ponder her symptoms.

One evening when Albert and Victoria were dining together alone, Albert noticed her listlessly picking at her food as she had been doing so often lately. On closer scrutiny, he saw that she was quite pale. Reaching across the table, he took Victoria's hand in his. "Darling, are you all right? You've barely touched your food, and you look rather fragile."

"Oh, I'm all right, love," Victoria replied with a wan smile. "I've been a bit tired lately. My stomach has been queasy sometimes."

"How long has this been going on?"

"Mmm, better than two weeks, I'd say."

"This queasy stomach…has it been that way at any particular part of the day?"

"Mostly in the mornings."

Albert's brow creased. "Do you have any idea what's causing this?"

"Just my heavy schedule, darling. It seems that once the crown was placed on my head, everything fell on me at once. And there's been little letup."

Surprised that his wife hadn't guessed what was causing these symptoms, Albert said, "Let's go up to our room."

Victoria leaned heavily on Albert's arm as they climbed the stairs, moved down the long hall, and entered their bedroom. Albert paused and tugged on the bellpull by the door, then guided his wife to a chair.

As she eased onto the chair with his help, Albert said, "I want you to take the opportunity of no engagements this evening and go to bed early. I'm going to have Dr. Rice examine you tomorrow."

Victoria looked up at him, eyes wide. "Now, Albert, there's no need for that. I'll just see if I can't manage to get more rest."

Albert shook his head. "No, darling. You are my wife, and I'm concerned. I want Dr. Rice to look at you."

Victoria smiled at him. "You wonderful man. I love you so much."

"I love you so much, too," Albert said as a light tap came at the door. "Emily's here. She'll help you get ready for bed. I have some paperwork to do. I'll look in on you shortly."

Calling for the maid to come in, Albert bent over, kissed his wife's cheek, then turned to Emily. "Her Majesty is going to bed early. Will you help her, please?"

"Of course, sir," said Emily, moving quickly to the queen.

Albert passed into the hall, a knowing grin on his face.

An hour later, he moved down the hall and quietly opened the bedroom door. Peeking in, he saw by the light of the single lantern that Victoria was fast asleep, curled up in the large bed like a kitten.

Tears filmed Albert's eyes. "Dear Lord," he whispered ever so softly, "please protect her and our baby."

At midmorning the next day, Albert, Mary, and Louise sat together on a bright-colored sofa in the hall, outside of the palace's main bedroom.

"From everything you've told us, Albert," said Mary, "it sounds like I'm going to become a grandmother. Thank you for sending the carriage for us."

"Yes, thank you," said Louise. "We wouldn't miss this moment for anything in the world."

Even as Louise was speaking, the door opened, and Dr. Cecil Rice, the palace physician, appeared with a broad smile on his face.

His nurse, Jean Miller, appeared at the door behind him, also smiling.

"I was right!" said Albert, jumping off the sofa. "I was right, wasn't I, doctor?"

"You sure were, Prince Albert," said the silver-haired physician.

"Her Majesty wants to see you."

"And I want to see her!" he said excitedly. He started toward the door, then stopped and looked back at Mary and Louise.

Before he could speak, Mary said, "We'll come in pretty soon. You two need this moment alone. Go on."

Albert grinned, hurried through the door past Jean, and rushed up to the bed as Jean closed the door to give them privacy.

"Oh, sweetheart!" Albert said. "We're going to have a little prince or princess running around this place."

Still lying on the bed, Victoria held her arms up to him. "Yes, we are, darling!"

They embraced, kissed twice, then embraced again. Breathing into her ear, Albert said, "Oh! I forgot to ask Dr. Rice when the baby will be born."

"Sometime the latter part of November," she said, squeezing him tight. "Oh, Albert, I'm so happy!"

"Me too," he said, and kissed her cheek.

After a few minutes of rejoicing together and praising the Lord for His goodness, Albert said, "Sweetheart, I…uh…took the liberty of sending a carriage for your mother and Louise so they could be here to share this wonderful moment with us."

The queen grinned. "Oh, you did, eh? Pretty sure, weren't you?"

"Mm-hmm. I was."

Mary and Louise were called in, and they both hugged Victoria with the joy they felt at the good news.

Within the next two days, every British newspaper carried the story, announcing that the queen would be giving birth to a child sometime in late November.

One warm evening in June, Albert took Victoria for a drive in one of the smaller royal carriages to relax after a long, tedious day in parliament meetings. The ever-present mounted armed guards rode in front and behind the carriage.

"Where would you like to go, sweetheart?" Albert guided the horses down the lane toward the gate.

"How about Green Park?"

"Sounds good to me."

Some thirty minutes later, the carriage wheeled into the large park, catching the attention of people scattered across the green lawns and among the flower gardens. Many called out the queen's name, waving, and Victoria waved back.

They were approaching a thick, wooded area where a large group of young people were gathered. All of them waved to their queen, some of them calling out that they loved her. Victoria smiled, returned the wave, and said to Albert, "It means so much that the younger people show their love for me."

"I think it's great." Just then, Albert caught sight of a man swiftly coming around a tree, pointing a revolver at Victoria. He quickly pulled Victoria down across his lap as he shouted to the guards, "Assassin!"

Before the guards could react, the man fired his gun and the slug hissed past Albert's ear.

There was a rapid staccato of gunshots as the guards opened fire on the would-be assassin. There were screams and shouts from the group of young people as the man fell under the barrage of bullets. Albert had to pull hard on the reins to keep the team from bolting.

The gunman got off another shot before he collapsed, and the slug almost hit Albert.

People from all over the park were running toward the scene.

The chief guard knelt beside the fallen gunman, felt for a pulse on the side of his neck, and said, "It's all right now, Prince Albert. He's dead." He stood up, called for one of the guards to bring the police, then hurried to the carriage where other guards had formed a circle around it, guns still in their hands.

Drawing up to the side of the carriage, the chief guard looked at the queen. "Your Majesty, I'm sorry we didn't see him sooner."

Victoria wiped a hand across her sweat-beaded brow. "It's all right, Weldon. God knew he was there and let Albert see him in time."

"Yes, Your Majesty. And we are thankful to Him for that."

"I'm going to take her home, Weldon," said Albert as the crowd was growing.

"Yes, sir," said Weldon. "I'll leave one of my men here to stay with the body until the police can be summoned. The rest of us will go with you."

The chief guard explained the situation to his men, ordered one to stay, then the rest of them mounted up.

"Albert," said Victoria, "because of the way news travels in London, I would like to go by Mother's house and let her know I'm all right."

"Certainly," said Albert, and put the carriage into motion. He took hold of her trembling hand. "I can't understand why anyone would want to kill you, darling. They've tried it twice now."

"It goes with the territory," she said, snuggling up close to him. "No matter who or what a monarch or national leader of any kind may be, there is always someone who dislikes them."

"Well, praise the Lord for keeping His mighty hand on you."

"Yes," she said. "Praise His precious name."

Upon reaching the home of Mary and Louise, Albert and Victoria told them of the assassination attempt. Mary took her daughter into her arms, saying how glad she was that the man's bullets missed her. Louise praised the Lord for His hand of protection on both Victoria and Albert. Mary made a feeble comment.

The next morning, when the London newspapers hit the streets, Gordon Whitaker was on his way to the construction job he had just landed and heard a newsboy calling out the headlines about the assassination attempt in Green Park.

He stopped, bought a paper, and took time to read the front-page article. When he had read the story, he shook his head in wonder. "I don't know about you, Victoria. You must have a host of guardian angels watching over you."

Tossing the paper into a trash can, Gordon headed down the street, telling himself that though he wanted to have his revenge on Victoria, it would have to be something other than just trying to kill her. He didn't want to end up like yesterday's would-be assassin. He must find a way to make her suffer without attempting to take her life.

In late October, Wilson escorted a lovely young woman into one of Buckingham Palace's sitting rooms, where the queen sat with her husband.

Albert left his chair as Wilson said, "Miss Lucy Granville, Your Majesty."

Victoria stood up, her maternity dress showing fully that she was eight months along. "Welcome, Lucy. Please come sit down."

"Thank you, Your Majesty."

"And I am Prince Albert," said the handsome man, gesturing toward the proper chair.

"Yes, sir. I know. And thank you."

When all three were seated, Lucy said, "Your Majesty, I am deeply honored that you would give me the opportunity to be governess to your new baby."

Victoria smiled. "You come highly recommended to us, Lucy. Martin Owens, director of London Orphanage, says you are the very best."

Lucy's features crimsoned. "I don't know about that, Your Majesty, but I promise if you give me the job, I will do my utmost to please you and Prince Albert."

"We have no doubt of that," said Albert. "We understand that you have worked with infants and little children for four years."

"Yes, sir."

"You are twenty-three years of age."

"Yes, sir."

"You may wonder why we are hiring a governess this far ahead of the baby's birth," said Victoria. "We want her to be accustomed to the palace routine before the baby is born, and we want her to have time to be taught how the baby's parents will want him or her to be taken care of."

"I can understand that, Your Majesty. I think you are wise to do it this way." Lucy paused. "Do you have other questions?"

"Only one or two," said Albert. "Are you planning on getting married anytime soon?"

A sad look captured Lucy's eyes. "No, sir. My…my fiancé left me for another woman. It will be some time before I'm ready to trust another man."

"Of course," said Victoria. Then to Albert: "You had another question?"

"Yes," he replied, then looked Lucy in the eye. "Do you understand that this is a Christian home, and that you will be expected to attend church services with us?"

"Yes, sir. I would say there are very few people in Great Britain who do not know of your walk with the Lord. I am a born-again child of God, and a member of the church where you are. It's just so large that you have never noticed me."

Albert and Victoria looked at each other and smiled. Then the prince said, "You were told by Mr. Owens what the starting salary is?"

"Yes, sir, and I feel it is very generous."

Albert smiled again. "And after all these questions, do you want the job?"

"Oh yes, sir!"

"Then, Miss Lucy Granville, you are now the official governess of our unborn prince or princess."

A pale, wintry sun made its way into the eastern sky on Saturday, November 21, 1840, just as a lusty cry reverberated through the upper halls of Buckingham Palace. Dr. Cecil Rice, with the aid of nurse Jean Miller, brought Princess Victoria Adelaide Mary Louise into the world.

A jubilant husband entered the bedroom when called by Jean, and looked at his beautiful baby daughter with tears in his eyes. The parents had agreed that since the baby's first name was Victoria, they would call her Vicky.

Albert and Victoria were thrilled with their new daughter, and Mary was thrilled with her new granddaughter. Louise announced that she would be "Aunt Louise" to little Vicky, and after Mary had held the baby for a lengthy time, she took the infant into her arms, kissed her chubby cheek, and said, "Hello, sweetheart. I'm your Aunt Louise, and I love you."

Lucy Granville had her moment of joy when she was allowed to hold the baby and announce to her that she was her governess, and that she also loved her.

As the days passed, Albert and Victoria often sat for long periods of time, just watching little Vicky sleep.

When the baby was a month old, the family's pastor was invited to Buckingham Palace, and before all the guards and servants, she was dedicated back to the Lord as the pastor held her in his arms. He prayed that the Lord would bring Vicky to Himself when she was old enough to understand her need of the Saviour, thanked Him that she was safe until then, and prayed that He would guide her life and use her for His glory.

The little princess was barely three months old when the young queen of England began to experience a familiar pattern to her mornings.

Their second child, Albert Edward, Prince of Wales, was born November 9, 1841. He was called Bertie.

Albert and Victoria were very happy with the way Lucy Granville had taken care of Vicky and were satisfied that she would do as well with Bertie.

The 1840s in Great Britain were proving to be a time of intense self-scrutiny. Newspapers and journals were calling their era "Victorian," and the term was becoming associated with proper morals and decency, a humane spirit, and a deep reverence for God and the Bible. All of this, according to the press, was due to the leadership being given by Queen Victoria and her husband, who faithfully stood beside her.

The press reported that by survey, atheism and agnosticism was lower per capita than it had been since King James I was on the throne in the early seventeenth century. Though some atheists and agnostics spoke their adverse feelings toward the queen and her Christianity, even the majority of them had something good to say about her and her reign.

One day in late 1842, Gordon Whitaker bought a copy of the *London Times,* and during his lunch hour as a janitor in a large office building, he read an article written by a newsman who greatly admired the queen and her husband. The article lauded the queen for her stand against immorality and the example she showed the world as to what a moral and upright woman should be.

When Gordon finished reading the article, he angrily wadded up the newspaper and tossed it into a wastebasket. "If she's so good, why did she cheat me out of the wealth I had coming, and the job that should have been mine?"

Thirteen

*I*n March 1843, the royal family moved their main home to Windsor Castle. In April, Albert and Victoria's third child, Alice Maud Mary, was born.

On a beautiful sunlit morning in London, hundreds of people were milling about Hyde Park, enjoying the colorful flower gardens, the sparkling fountains, the sun-kissed ponds, and the deep shade of the trees. Children laughed and played on the lawns.

At one of the ponds near the winding path that traversed the park, an elderly couple stood together in the shade of the trees, holding hands. They were watching the fish swim near the surface of the water. Soon they were aware of a young couple in their midtwenties standing close by, also holding hands.

The young pair studied the fish for a few minutes, then the woman glanced at the elderly couple. "Look, John. I hope when we are their age, we'll still have the romance in our marriage."

Her husband set appreciative eyes on the silver-haired pair. "Me, too."

The elderly man smiled. "The secret of keeping the romance in your marriage is to work at it. Too many married people reach middle age and get so wrapped up in all of life's trials that they forget to cultivate their love for each other. Just make up your minds to never let the fire go out even when the wrinkles and gray hair come along."

The young couple moved up close.

"That's sage advice, sir," said the man, extending his hand. "I'm John Barlow, and this is my wife, Amanda."

As they shook hands, the old gentleman said, "I'm Alister White, and this is my wife of fifty-nine years, Lorraine."

The usual greetings were exchanged, then John asked, "Do you folks live here in London?"

"Yes," replied Alister. "Our home is only a few blocks from here. We come to the park two or three times a week, except in the dead of winter."

"Are you Londoners, too?" asked Lorraine.

"No, ma'am," said John. "We're from Wales. My father and I operate a riding stable just outside of Cardiff."

"Oh. Alister and I have been to Cardiff a few times over the years. Beautiful place."

"We love it," said Amanda.

"How long have you been married?" asked Alister.

"Almost three years," said John. Chuckling, he added, "That leaves us about fifty-six years behind you."

The Whites laughed, and Lorraine said, "Any children, yet?"

"Yes," John said proudly. "We have a son who just turned a year old. His name is Stephen."

Alister smiled. "Well, we have four children, fifteen grandchildren, and three great-grandchildren. Most of our family lives in—"

Someone shouted, "It's the queen! Queen Victoria is coming!"

Word was spreading all over the area that the queen's carriage was coming along the path, and people were collecting quickly.

John and Amanda looked the direction people were pointing, and saw the royal carriage coming along the path under the huge shade trees, accompanied by the mounted guards.

"Have you two ever seen the queen before?" asked Lorraine.

"John has," said Amanda. "Eight years ago. But I've never had the privilege."

"We get to see her quite often," said Alister. "She and Prince Albert come into Hyde Park a lot."

"Where did you see her, John?" asked Lorraine.

"She came to our stable in Wales, and I had the joy of taking her horseback riding."

"Oh! That must have been a thrill."

"It sure was, ma'am," said John, craning his neck to see past the crowd that was gathering along the edge of the path. "Come on, Amanda, let's get up close. Nice to meet you folks."

The Whites smiled and watched as the Barlows hurried toward the path where the royal carriage would soon pass.

As John and Amanda drew up to a spot yet unoccupied, others were crowding up behind them.

"Look, Amanda!" said John, fixing his gaze on the approaching carriage. "It's her, all right. She still looks the same. She's holding one of her children. And that must be the prince and the governess behind her with their other children."

Victoria and Albert were smiling and waving to their admirers.

The guards that preceded the carriage were passing the spot where John and Amanda stood, and just as the carriage came near, a man bumped John's shoulder from behind as he darted toward the carriage, raising a revolver and pointing it at two-year-old Vicky, who was on her mother's lap.

Reacting by impulse, John sprang after him as the man shouted angrily, "I'll make you suffer by killing your daughter!"

Screams and shouts rose from the stunned crowd.

At the same instant, Albert threw himself in front of Victoria and Vicky.

John Barlow was on the gunman's heels and reached him in time to seize his gun hand and thrust the muzzle skyward just as the weapon fired. The sharp report echoed across the huge park, drawing the attention of people who were unaware of the queen's presence.

Lucy Granville was holding Bertie on the rear seat with Alice Maud Mary lying on the seat beside her, wrapped in a blanket. Eyes wide, she clutched the children close to her.

A frightened Victoria held Vicky tightly with trembling hands as the guards and John Barlow wrestled the gunman to the ground and disarmed him. While the guards were shackling the man as he ejected a stream of curses, John stood up to see Prince Albert coming toward him.

Amanda was pushing her way through the crowd that now encircled the carriage when Albert offered his hand to the man who had kept the bullet from finding its mark. "Sir, I don't know how to thank you. What you did was a wonderful display of quick thinking and courage. I'm Prince Albert, Queen Victoria's husband. I know the queen will want to speak to you. Please come with me."

Amanda drew up, took hold of her husband's arm, and said, "Darling, that was marvelous!"

"Honey," said John, "this is Prince Albert, Queen Victoria's husband. Sir, this is my wife, Amanda."

"Honored to meet you, ma'am," said Albert. "I was about to take your husband to meet the queen. I know she will want to thank your husband for what he did."

Albert hurried them toward the carriage.

Suddenly Victoria's eyes fell on the face of the man who accompanied her husband. "John!" she cried. "John Barlow!"

"You know him, sweetheart?" said Albert, as they drew up to the side of the carriage.

"Oh yes! John, what can I say? You just saved my little Vicky's life, and maybe mine, too."

"You don't have to say anything, Your Majesty," said John. "I am one of your proud subjects. I only did what any other man would have done."

Holding little Vicky close to her heart with her left arm, Victoria reached out her right hand. "It's been a long time, but I knew you the instant I saw your face. It's so nice to see you again."

"You, too, Your Majesty," he said, bowing and kissing her hand. Then taking hold of his wife's trembling hand, he drew her up. "Your Majesty, this is my wife, Amanda."

Victoria offered her hand to Amanda. "Your Majesty, I am honored to meet you. John often talks about the time Princess Victoria came to the stable in Wales and he had the privilege of escorting her on a horseback ride."

"So that's how you know my wife," said Albert.

The chief guard stepped up. "Excuse me, Your Majesty. Are you all right?"

"Yes, Weldon," said the queen, "thanks to this man's fast thinking and brave move."

Weldon smiled at John. "Thank you, sir. England will be forever grateful to you."

John's cheeks blushed as Weldon turned back to the queen and said, "Your Majesty, two of my men are taking the gunman to police headquarters. While we were shackling him, he was cursing and saying he is an atheist and he hates your Christianity. He wanted to take Vicky's life because this would make you suffer. He'll be in prison for the rest of his life."

"As he should be," said Albert. "Thank you, Weldon. I'll let you know when we're ready to move on."

"Yes, sir," said Weldon, and moved back among his men.

Tears were in Victoria's eyes as she said, "John, I often think about that day you took me riding. You were so kind and gentle. I…I want to honor you in a special way for saving Vicky's life; and as I said, maybe mine, too."

"I agree, sweetheart," said Albert. "He deserves to be honored."

"You are still living in Wales, John?" asked Victoria.

"Yes. My father and I still run the stable together. My parents are here in London with us, also. Little vacation. Right now, they're at the Holborn Hotel, taking care of our little one-year-old son, Stephen."

"Well, I would like to see your father again," said Victoria, "and if you recall, your mother was in Birmingham at the time and I didn't get to meet her. I want to meet her, and your little Stephen, too. Prince Albert and I would like to have all of you for dinner this evening at Windsor Castle."

Amanda's face lost color, and a tiny, unbidden gasp escaped her lips.

Victoria asked, "Is there anything wrong, Amanda?"

"Oh no, Your Majesty," replied Amanda, swallowing hard. "It's just—just that I…I never dreamed that I would ever have dinner with the queen of England and her family. I'm overwhelmed."

Victoria smiled. "The honor is going to be ours. Having you in our home for dinner will be a blessing to us."

That evening, Hugh and Kathleen Barlow sat down at the dining room table at Windsor Castle with their son and daughter-in-law after Queen Victoria and Prince Albert had made over little Stephen, then turned him over to Lucy Granville to take care of during the evening.

Albert led in prayer, thanking the Lord for the food before them and for putting John Barlow in Hyde Park that morning.

As the food was being passed around the table while three servants looked on, Hugh Barlow ran his gaze between the queen and her husband. "I want to thank you both for giving us rooms here in the castle for the rest of our stay. It is very kind of you."

Albert smiled. "That's the least we could do."

"John and I had a little discussion at the hotel before the carriage came to pick us up. We were trying to decide which one of us should tell you something that is on our hearts. Finally, John decided the prerogative should go to his dear old dad. Kathleen and Amanda were in full agreement."

There was light laughter around the table.

"What it is, Your Majesty, Prince Albert, is that just recently the four of us came to know the Lord Jesus Christ as our personal Saviour."

"Wonderful!" exclaimed Victoria.

"Yes!" agreed Albert. "Tell us how it happened."

While they ate, the four Barlows gave their testimonies, telling how a visitor at the stable gave them a printed copy of the sermon "Sinners in the Hands of an Angry God" by the famous American preacher Jonathan Edwards, and by reading it, they had all repented and turned to the Lord for salvation. They were all members of a Bible-believing church in Cardiff.

Victoria and Albert wiped tears and praised the Lord.

"What we want you to know, Your Majesty," said Hugh, "is how much we appreciate the powerful influence you and Prince Albert are having in Great Britain for the gospel, and for the strong testimony you both have of your faith in Christ."

Victoria blinked at the tears that were filling her eyes and took Albert's hand. "We just thank God for using us. It is such a privilege to serve Him."

"Yes," said Albert. "A privilege we don't deserve. But we praise Him every day for allowing us to proclaim the wonderful name of Jesus."

As the meal continued, and the Barlows were enjoying their meal with the queen and her husband, Victoria noticed that Amanda seemed ill at ease. Twice, her shaking hands almost dropped her teacup.

When the third time came, Victoria set soft eyes on her and said, "Amanda, dear, you seem nervous. Are you all right?"

Amanda placed the cup in its saucer, touched a cloth napkin to her lips, and said, "Your Majesty, I am totally in awe. I can hardly believe I have met the queen of England in person. That's enough to put butterflies in my stomach. But here I am, sitting at your table in Windsor Castle. I feel like I'm dreaming. It just doesn't seem possible that I am in this castle, in your presence."

Victoria smiled, pushed her chair back, and stood up. She moved to Amanda, leaned down, put an arm around her neck, and said, "Amanda, dear, I appreciate the way you feel about me, but please understand that I'm just human like you. I eat, sleep, inhale, exhale, weep when I'm sad, laugh when I'm glad, and am a sinner saved by the grace of God through the precious blood of the Lamb just like you. Please relax. Albert and I are so honored to have you here."

With that, Victoria kissed Amanda's cheek and moved back around the table toward her chair.

Albert was smiling as he stood up, and helped his wife to be seated.

Amanda wiped a tear from her cheek. "Thank you, Your Majesty. I love you."

Victoria smiled warmly. "I love you, too, Amanda."

～∞～

Later that night, when the palace was quiet and the guests were in their appointed rooms, Albert and Victoria were in overstuffed chairs in the sitting room which was part of their bedroom suite, enjoying hot tea and a few moments of privacy.

Setting loving eyes on her husband, Victoria said, "Darling, we've hardly had opportunity to be alone since the incident this morning. I have to say that you have been my hero for a long time, but when you threw yourself in line with the bullet you thought was coming at Vicky and me, you endeared yourself to me more than ever."

Albert smiled. "I love you and my children more than life itself, sweetheart."

"You proved that this morning. I'm so proud that you are my husband."

"Thank you. And speaking of being proud, you made me more proud of you than ever tonight when you put Amanda at ease. You have such a special way with people. You always know just what to say and to do to make them comfortable."

Victoria smiled shyly. "After being raised in almost total solitude, thanks to Gordon Whitaker, I enjoy being with people. I love having guests, and I pray daily that God will bestow on me the gift of hospitality. And even though we live in a castle, I want our guests from every walk of life to feel welcome here."

"Amen to that," said Albert.

Suddenly, Victoria put a shaky hand to her forehead as tears filled her eyes. Albert left his chair and knelt in front of her. "Honey, what is it?"

Victoria pulled a hankie from her sleeve, dabbed at her eyes, and said in a tear-clogged voice, "Albert, I'm so thankful John Barlow was in the park today. That atheist could have killed both Vicky and me with the same bullet."

"That he could have." Albert took hold of her hand. "Let's just stop and thank the Lord right now for the way He protected both of you."

"Yes. And while we're thanking Him, let's pray for that atheist. He needs to learn the truth."

When Albert finished praying and rose to his feet, Victoria left the chair and said, "You go ahead and get ready for bed, darling. I must go and look in on each of our children before I can rest."

"All right, darling. Your heart is a mother's heart before it is a queen's heart, and that's the way it should be."

Albert walked her to the door, and stood there watching her move down the hall, loving her with his eyes.

The next day, a special ceremony was held on the castle grounds with most of Parliament in attendance, honoring John Barlow for his heroic deed.

The day following, there was a tearful good-bye as the Barlows headed back for Wales.

Because of the near-successful attempt on Vicky's life, more guards were added to Windsor Castle to better protect the royal family whether at home or on the streets of London.

When Gordon Whitaker read in the *London Times* about the attempt on Princess Vicky's life, and what the gunman had shouted before he was disarmed, he pondered it.

Certainly, he told himself, for someone to even threaten one of the queen's children would bring her great sorrow and worry.

But what could Gordon do?

It wouldn't be worth it if he were to be caught and sent to prison like that atheist would be. Still, Gordon told himself, the day would come when he would get back at Victoria for what she did to him.

On May 24, 1845, Gordon Whitaker, Alice, and twenty-year-old Edgar joined the throng that lined the streets of London for the big parade honoring Queen Victoria's twenty-sixth birthday.

Gordon had finally gotten a good job in the construction business, and was bringing home a decent paycheck every week. The secret money was still coming from Queen Victoria, and Alice was socking it away just in case Gordon lost his present job.

The crowds waved British flags and banners that wished the queen a happy birthday.

Gordon had positioned himself and his family across the street from Westminster Abbey, where the royal carriage would appear after special services had been held by Parliament to celebrate the queen's birthday.

He had observed a group of palace guards standing outside the gate, but had not noticed the three children they were hovering around until he heard a tall, slender man close by explaining the customary procedure that had been established the year before to a friend who was obviously from elsewhere.

The man told his friend that the three children were the queen's three oldest: Vicky, who was four years old; Bertie, who was three; and Alice, who was two. The young woman with them was their governess, Lucy Granville.

The tall man went on to explain that Queen Victoria had established the procedure last year. She had the governess stand in the same place with Vicky and Bertie. She felt that her children should be among the people for her birthday parade, rather than riding in the royal carriage. She knew it sat well with the citizens of London to see this, and did not fear for them because of the guards who were watching over them.

Soon the gates were opened, and a marching military band appeared first, followed by members of Parliament in carriages. Behind them, the queen and her husband rode in the royal carriage with Victoria holding little one-year-old Alfred in her arms.

While the enthusiastic crowd cheered, Gordon was deep in thought. Rubbing his chin, he told himself he just might have the solution he had been looking for. If it worked out, he would have his revenge on Victoria, plus line his pockets with the fortune she owed him at the same time.

As the months passed, a master plan was forming in Gordon's vicious mind. By wire, he contacted Olaf Kalmar, who had worked under him at Barings Bank for several years then had gone home to his native Norway, and now was a chief executive in Oslo's largest bank. Gordon's plan, when fully developed, would provide him a way to cause a diversion at the queen's birthday parade in front of Westminster Abbey next year, so he could grab one of the queen's children. He knew it wouldn't be easy, but convinced himself that with careful planning, it could be done. He would hide the child somewhere in London and demand a ransom of 400,000 pounds. He would mastermind the perfect plan and have his revenge on Victoria. He would like to have the revenge sooner, but told himself he must be patient.

With this plan ever in mind as the months went by, Gordon went about his daily routine on his construction job.

One day in April 1846, he was working with two men—Chester Mackey and Donald Chaffin—on the fifth floor of a new office building in downtown London. Positioned some distance from them, he overheard Mackey use the queen's name in a derogatory manner, and Chaffin came right back in agreement and said something even worse about her. As the conversation went on, the two men agreed that with her influence and the country's wealth, Victoria should do something for hard-working men like themselves so they could live better. She lived in all that luxury and they practically lived in poverty.

All the time, Gordon's mind was working, but he didn't say anything to them until the fourth day in a row they had spoken their hatred for the queen.

At the close of the work day, Gordon approached Mackey and Chaffin. "Hey, guys, could I talk to you in private before you head for home?"

"Sure," said Mackey. "We can find a spot in the alley."

When they had located a private place, the two men looked at him, waiting for him to speak.

"I've got real good ears, guys," said Gordon. "Since we've been working up there on the fifth floor the past few days, I've picked up some of your conversations. Sounds to me like our pint-sized queen isn't one of your favorite people."

Mackey and Chaffin exchanged fearful glances.

"Now look, Gordie," said Chester Mackey, "we didn't mean no harm. We just—"

"Hey," said Gordon. "I'm in total agreement with you."

"Oh," said Donald Chaffin, "that makes me feel better."

"Let me tell you about Her Little Majesty," said Gordon, and proceeded to relay the story of what she had done to him.

Both men were sympathetic with Gordon's loss of the promised fortune and the job as the queen's personal controller and financial advisor.

Chaffin shook his head in disgust. "No wonder you feel toward her like you do."

"Yeah," said Mackey. "She really did you dirty."

Gordon chuckled. "Well, I've got a little plan worked out in my head so I can get back at her for it, and pick up some money at the same time. But I need help. If you guys will help me, I'll see that you get some money, too."

The two men grinned at each other, then Mackey said, "We're listening."

Gordon then told them about his plan to kidnap one of the royal children at the queen's birthday parade next month, and hold the child for a ransom of four hundred thousand pounds.

"As you can see, I will do the actual abducting," said Gordon, "so the greater risk will be mine. But if you will help me, I'll give you both a generous portion."

"I'm in," said Chaffin.

"Me, too," chimed in Mackey.

A grin spread over Gordon's face. "Good. How about we meet right here tomorrow after work and I'll explain the plan to you."

Both men agreed.

At the close of the next work day, the three men met at the same spot in the alley and Gordon explained his plan in detail. As he laid it before them, Mackey and Chaffin liked what they heard and were especially impressed with the crafty way Gordon would make the pickup of the ransom money with no danger of getting caught.

On the morning of Queen Victoria's twenty-seventh birthday—May 24, 1846—the Whitakers were eating breakfast.

Edgar said, "Dad, I'm glad you're not making Mom and me go to the parade this year. I felt like a hypocrite last year, standing there acting like I was wishing that low-down queen happy birthday."

In her heart, Alice wanted to go, but remained silent.

Gordon had not revealed any of his plan to Alice or Edgar, but it was time to tell them about his deal with Olaf Kalmar.

Taking a sip of coffee, he said, "I have something to tell both of you, and it's really good."

Wife and son smiled.

"It's time we had something good happen around here," Alice commented. "Let's hear it."

"Well, we're moving to Oslo, Norway."

"What?" gasped Alice.

"Oslo?" said Edgar. "Why, Dad?"

"Because I just landed a job with Oslo's largest bank."

Wife and son sat in silence, eyes wide.

"Alice, you remember Olaf Kalmar, don't you?"

"Of course. You were his immediate supervisor at Barings Bank. And come to think of it, he was from Norway."

"Right. Well, he went back to Norway a short time before I quit my job, expecting to come into the money the duchess had promised me. I remembered that Olaf had landed a good job with First Bank of Oslo, so I contacted him by wire. We exchanged a few wires, and it wasn't long till he offered me a very good, well-paying job. Half again the salary that I had at Barings."

"Oh, honey, this is wonderful!" exclaimed Alice. "When will we be going?"

"Well, I have us booked on a train in three days." In his plan, this would give him time to get his hands on the ransom money and leave for Norway without raising suspicion. The move would be simple, since they were now renting and would not have a house to sell. The furniture would be left behind. He would tell Alice and Edgar the whole story later, when he felt it was time for them to know.

Edgar took a sharp breath. "Three days?"

"Yes. I've got things all worked out. How does this sound?"

"It will take some doing," said Alice, "but I like it."

"Me, too, Dad," said Edgar.

"Great!" Gordon said, reaching across the table and gripping Alice's hand. "We'll get a brand new start in life."

Alice laughed happily. "Yes! And in Norway, you can forget all about Queen Victoria and your grudge against her."

Gordon forced a smile. "Right. I'll just do that."

An hour later, Gordon drew near Westminster Abbey and stepped into an alley. He had purchased a fake mustache and beard at a costume shop the day before, and had found a worn-out old cap in the trash disposal behind a hotel. Donning the disguise, he left the alley and hurried to his chosen spot in front of Westminster Abbey near where Lucy Granville and the queen's older children would stand in about three hours.

At Windsor Castle, the royal family was making preparation for going to the parade. Baby Helena, their fifth child, was almost a year old, and once more Victoria was great with child. Her baby was due in two to three weeks.

As Victoria and Lucy were making last-minute touches on the children, Albert came into the room and said to Victoria, "Sweetheart, I'm really concerned about you being able to handle all the excitement of the parade. I don't want anything to happen to you or the baby. It isn't too late to cancel it."

Victoria waddled to him, smiled, and said, "Darling, the baby and I will be fine. Besides, I owe it to my subjects to put in the appearance they expect. I can't disappoint them."

Albert sighed, a worried look on his handsome face. "How about just appearing at the abbey for the service with Parliament, then coming home?"

Victoria frowned at him.

Albert looked deep into her eyes. "I could ride alone in the royal carriage for the parade and stop every few minutes to tell the people you just weren't up to the parade because of the coming baby."

Victoria reached up and patted his cheek. "You're a worrywart, darling. I told you, the baby and I will be fine. Now let's get going, or we'll be late."

Moments later, Albert and Victoria rode away in the royal carriage, heading for Westminster Abbey with the mounted guards flanking them. Helena would remain at the castle with one of the maids to watch over her.

An hour later, Lucy Granville took Vicky, Bertie, Alice, and Alfred in a special carriage provided for them. They headed for London with orders from Victoria to stand in the same spot near the gate outside of Westminster Abbey.

Fourteen

ordon Whitaker's breathing grew ragged with excitement when he looked past the crowds that lined the street in front of Westminster Abbey and saw the carriage roll up with Lucy Granville and the queen's four children aboard. He congratulated himself for getting there plenty early so he could secure the desired spot.

The guards dismounted and some of them helped Lucy and the children out of the carriage. When that was done, the carriage pulled away and parked several yards down the street. The guards formed a semicircle around the governess, Vicky, Bertie, Alice, and Alfred, as they stood close to the curb near the abbey's gate.

Only a few minutes passed, then the crowd began to applaud, cheer, and wave their flags and banners as the military band drew up on the back side of the gate. When the gates were opened, the cheering grew louder as the band started playing a rousing tune while marching to the street. Next came members of Parliament in carriages, followed by the royal carriage.

Queen Victoria came into view, waving and smiling with Albert at her side as the carriage and its uniformed escorts moved out. The roar of the crowd grew louder.

Lucy had the four children waving at their parents. Albert and Victoria waved back.

As the royal carriage slowly pulled into the street, making its right turn, Gordon glanced furtively to the roof of the six-story building directly across the street. He could barely see the tops of Mackey and Chaffin's heads above the solid four-foot wall that bordered the roof of the building, but he knew they were ready with the firecrackers. Gordon had purposely purchased large firecrackers while wearing his disguise the day before, knowing when they went off, they would sound like guns firing.

Suddenly, several strings of hissing, smoking firecrackers sailed over the four-foot wall. Some began to pop immediately, while others exploded after the firecrackers had landed on the street. Gordon knew his partners were already making their getaway.

By this time, the carriage horses and those ridden by the guards were rearing in fright. Carriage drivers struggled to keep their teams under control. The startled horses ridden by the guards were fighting their bits and dancing about, eyes wild.

The team hitched to the royal carriage panicked and bolted. The driver was helpless to stop them. Albert put an arm around Victoria as the carriage veered around the other carriages and zigzagged down the street with terrorized people trying to get out of the way. In front of Westminster Abbey, people were screaming and crying out and running in every direction.

The guards around the royal children thought they were hearing gunshots as well as firecrackers and had their revolvers in hand, looking around in the attempt to find where the gunmen were located.

Lucy huddled over the terrified, weeping children, trying to hurry them to safety behind the gates of Westminster Abbey. Children and adults were dashing every direction. Most of the children were screaming and crying.

Finding his plan working beautifully, Gordon Whitaker rushed up to Lucy in his disguise. "May I help you, ma'am?"

"Oh yes, sir," said the governess. "They're so frightened. I want to get them inside the gate."

Instantly, a silver-haired man was there, and said, "I'll help you, too, ma'am."

"Thank you," said Lucy.

A pair of guards, guns ready, saw the two men offering to help the governess and assumed the children were in good hands.

Lucy picked Alfred up and put an arm around Vicky, fighting her way through the panicky crowd toward the gate. The older man picked up Alice and followed Lucy. Gordon was glad to take Bertie into his arms. Seconds later, when the firecrackers had stopped going off, and four of the guards were charging through the gate, Lucy was clutching Alfred and Vicky, trying to calm them. The silver-haired man had Alice in his arms, talking to her in a soothing tone.

"Miss Lucy," said one of the guards, "is everybody all right?"

"Yes," she replied, trying to catch her breath. "We're doing fine. These two gentlemen helped me get the children through the gate to safety."

The guard looked around. "Two gentlemen, ma'am?"

"Yes," said Lucy, running her gaze toward three-year-old Alice and the older man, expecting also to see Bertie and the bearded man. Her eyes darted about. Finding no sign of them, she gasped, and her face lost color.

"What's the matter, ma'am?" asked the guard.

"I—I don't see Bertie and the man who had him. Oh no! The man has Bertie!"

The guards wheeled, dashed to the street, and looked both ways. They saw the royal carriage heading toward them, the horses now calm.

Hurrying back to Lucy, one of them said, "The queen and Prince Albert are back, ma'am. We couldn't see Bertie anywhere."

Lucy could hardly breathe. Normally a very self-controlled person, she was in a complete panic when the royal carriage pulled through the gate and the guards were telling Albert and Victoria what had happened.

Victoria started to get out of the carriage. Albert jumped out, helped her down, and they rushed to a weeping Lucy, the silver-haired man, and the children.

"Lucy!" said Victoria, laying hands on Vicky and Alfred. "How did this happen?"

Lucy tried to speak, but her tear-clogged throat prevented it. The older man, who still held Alice, said, "Your Majesty, I am Walter Riggins. When the firecrackers were going off, a man moved up and offered to help the governess get the children behind the gate. I offered, too, and picked up little Alice. He had Bertie in his arms. In all the confusion, I didn't see the man leave with him."

"What did he look like?" asked Albert.

"He was about my height. Slender. Probably late forties. Had a mustache and a beard. He was wearing a worn old cap, but from what I could see of his hair, it was sort of blond, like the beard and mustache."

One of the guards had found a police officer, having told him of Bertie's abduction. The officer came up to Victoria and told her that he needed a description of the man.

Victoria's voice shook as she said, "Our governess and this gentleman got a good look at him."

The officer was given the abductor's description by Walter Riggins, which was confirmed by Lucy Granville. He wrote it down, told the queen she would be contacted at Windsor Castle by the chief of police, and hurried away.

Lucy said, "Your Majesty…Prince Albert…I—I'm so sorry. It's my fault for allowing a stranger to help me as I was trying to take the children through the gate to safety. I'm sorry-y-y! So sorry-y-y!"

Albert gripped Lucy just above her elbows and gave her a gentle shake. "Lucy, calm down. We're not blaming you. This gentleman over here is a stranger, too, but he did help you. And Alice is in good hands."

"Please, dear," said Victoria, "you were doing your best to care for our children. It is quite evident that with the firecrackers, this whole thing was carefully planned and executed. You did the best you could under the circumstances."

Catching her breath on a sob, Lucy said shakily, "But I can't help but blame myself, Your Majesty. You trusted me with these precious children, and I failed you."

Victoria put an arm around Lucy's waist and squeezed her tight. "Please, dear, get a grip on yourself. I need you to care for Vicky, Alice, and Alfred."

Lucy looked at her with wide eyes. "Y-you mean after this, you still trust me with your children?"

"Yes," said Victoria, giving her another squeeze.

"We certainly do," put in Albert. "We're trying to tell you this wasn't your fault."

"Oh, thank you, sir. And thank you, mum. Thank you. The guards and I will see them safely back to the castle."

The queen and her husband thanked Walter Riggins for what he did to help Lucy, and surrounded by guards, Lucy and the children boarded the carriage.

When it pulled away, Albert put an arm around Victoria. "Let's get you home, sweetheart. I'll go to the police station and—"

Suddenly Victoria doubled over, made a loud grunting sound, and put a hand to her swollen midsection.

Albert grabbed her, brow furrowed, and said, "Honey, is it the baby?"

Gritting her teeth, Victoria nodded. "I…I think so."

Less than a minute later, the royal carriage was racing toward King George Hospital with Albert hanging onto Victoria and the guards galloping ahead and behind. One guard had been sent to Windsor Castle by Albert to inform Lucy Granville and the rest of the castle personnel that the queen had been taken to King George Hospital, experiencing labor pains.

Making his way through the back streets and alleys of London with a crying Bertie in his arms, Gordon Whitaker went to the east side of the city. Entering a dense forest as planned, Gordon carried Bertie inside an old abandoned, isolated house. It was constructed of stone and the shutters were closed over the windows, though some were broken and allowed some light to seep inside.

The kidnapper was unaware of two twelve-year-old boys who were walking through the woods and saw him carry the weeping child into the house.

Daniel Reynolds and Wilbert Myers lived a short distance away in a small community on the edge of the forest, and knew the old stone house had been abandoned for years. They looked at each other questioningly, and Daniel said, "Why would that man take his little boy in there?"

Wilbert shrugged. "I don't know, but I guess it's none of our business. We'd better get on home."

Inside the house, four-and-a-half-year-old Bertie looked around when Gordon stood him on the floor, eyes bulging as tears washed his cheeks. "I want my mummy! Where's my mummy? Where's Lucy?"

Gordon reached down to grasp the boy's hand, but Bertie eluded him and ran to a far corner of the shadowed room, putting his face against the wall and sobbing.

Gordon moved up behind him, saying, "Come on, Bertie, I'm not going to hurt you." He reached in his pocket and pulled out a licorice twist. "Look what I have here."

Bertie turned around, spied the candy, and sniffed. Swiping his sleeve across his runny nose, he said, "I'm not s'posed to have candy unless Mummy or Daddy says."

"Come on now. One little piece isn't going to hurt you. You like licorice, don't you?"

"Uh-huh."

The little prince was just like any other boy, and even as he made his reply, he was reaching for the licorice.

When he stuck one end into his mouth, Gordon said, "Good, isn't it?"

"Uh-huh."

Gordon had previously brought snack food and water into the old house. After Bertie had devoured the licorice twist, he fed the child a snack and gave him all the water he wanted.

As Bertie was downing his last cup of water, Gordon said, "Now, Bertie, I have to go away for a little while. You'll be safe here."

Bertie's features twisted and fear showed in his eyes. His chin began to tremble. "Where ya goin', mister?"

Ignoring the question, Gordon said, "You be a good boy, and I'll be back soon." With that, he hurried to the door, stepped out, closed it, and locked it.

Bertie let out a high-pitched howl, ran to the door, pounded on it with his palms, and wailed. When there was no response, he turned around, wiped tears from his eyes, and probed the large room by the small bit of sunlight that was streaming in through the broken places in the shutters. There was very little in the way of furniture; just a table and three wooden chairs, and a broken-down old chair with the stuffing falling out.

Desperate to get out of the house, the boy went from window to window, pounding on the frames and calling out for help. But only the silence of the forest met his ears.

After several minutes of trying to be heard, Bertie went to the door where he had last seen his bearded abductor, turned his back to the wall beside it, and slid down to a sitting position on the floor. He drew his knees up and rested his head on them. Fresh tears began to trickle down his cheeks and splash on his hands.

The house was stuffy and hot, being sealed up with no way for fresh air or a breeze to enter. The trauma of his abduction by the man, along with the weariness brought on by crying soon sapped Bertie's energy. With his head against his knees and his eyes still leaking tears, he finally succumbed to sleep.

The news of Bertie's kidnapping spread through London like wildfire while Victoria was still in labor at the hospital.

When Gordon Whitaker was back in the city, moving toward downtown, he let his eyes take in those who moved along the street on bicycles. Soon he saw a boy who looked to be in his late teens and hailed him.

Bringing his bicycle to a stop, the youth said, "May I help you, sir?"

"Maybe so," said Gordon, stroking the false beard. "Do you know how to get to Windsor Castle?"

"Yes, sir. I've been past it many times. Once in a while I've gotten a glimpse of Queen Victoria, Prince Albert, and their children."

By the lack of any mention of Bertie's kidnapping, Gordon knew the boy had not yet heard. Pulling a sealed envelope from his shirt pocket, he said, "I need this letter delivered to the guards at the gate of Windsor Castle as soon as possible. You can get it there much faster than I can. I'll pay you fifty pounds to deliver it for me."

The boy's eyes widened. "Fifty pounds! Yes, sir! I will be most happy to deliver it for you."

Gordon placed folded bills in the boy's hand, then handed him the envelope. When he saw Queen Victoria's name on it, he raised his eyebrows. "A message for the queen, herself, eh?"

"That's right. Like I said, I need it delivered as soon as possible."

Stuffing the money in his pocket, the boy said, "I'm on my way, sir. You can depend on me. And thanks!"

Gordon smiled, nodded, and waved. Watching the boy weave his way through traffic, he sighed and said, "All right, Victoria. You'll soon have the ransom note. You and your husband will follow my instructions to the letter, I have no doubt. I'll appreciate it, and so will Bertie."

Daniel Reynolds and Wilbert Myers had stopped in the forest to study a family of squirrels who were busy carrying various objects into the hollow of a fallen tree. Moving on, after spending better than an hour there, they then met up with a neighbor who wanted to show them his new dog.

At the same time Gordon Whitaker was watching his hired messenger riding away on the bicycle, Daniel and Wilbert drew near the Reynolds house at the edge of the woods. Suddenly Wilbert looked up and said, "Look, Daniel! It's your dad. He's got that buggy moving really fast!"

Daniel focused on the buggy that was barreling along the road, throwing up a cloud of dust behind it. "Dad's really in a hurry. Something must be wrong. He isn't supposed to be home till late this afternoon."

Seconds later, Harold Reynolds skidded the buggy to a halt and jumped out, looking at the boys.

"Dad, what's wrong?" queried Daniel.

"Come on in the house," said Harold moving toward the porch.

"I'll tell you and your mother at the same time. You can come in too, Wilbert, if you wish. It's something you need to know, anyway."

Della Reynolds was sitting in her wheelchair in the parlor, sewing on a dress, when Harold and the boys entered.

"Honey, what are you doing home at this hour?" Della said.

"There's been a kidnapping, honey. Somebody grabbed Prince Bertie at the queen's birthday parade."

"Oh, how awful! Poor Queen Victoria. And her expecting another baby. Have the police anything to go on?"

"Only that the man is probably in his late forties, is wearing an old gray cap, and has a mustache and a beard. The last I heard, the police are combing the city."

Both parents saw the boys look at each other, eyes wide.

"Daniel, what is it?" asked Della.

Daniel swallowed hard. "Mom, Dad, Wilbert and I were coming through the woods a couple of hours ago. We saw a man exactly as you just described carrying a little boy who was crying. He took him in the old Welch house."

"That's right," said Wilbert. "Exactly as you just described the kidnapper. We didn't get a good look at the little boy, but he would be just about Prince Bertie's age."

"I'll take you boys to the police precinct on the east side right now!" Harold said, heading for the door. "We've got to tell the police about this."

When Harold and the boys entered the precinct office and Harold told the officer on the desk what Daniel and Wilbert had seen, he was told that Scotland Yard was now on the case. Two police officers immediately rushed them to Scotland Yard headquarters.

Chester Mackey and Donald Chaffin were waiting at the same place in the alley where they had met before with Gordon Whitaker. They smiled at each other when they saw Gordon come around the corner of the alley and head toward them.

Grinning with a happy light in his eyes as he drew up, Gordon said, "Gentlemen, you did a great job. The ransom note is on its way to Windsor Castle, and I'll soon have the money! I've decided to give you sixty pounds each."

Both men laughed, patting each other on the back, rejoicing in the money that would soon line their pockets.

Mackey laughed fiendishly. "I'll bet Victoria's crying her eyes out about now!"

"Yeah!" Chaffin chuckled. "And who cares? Not me!"

"Me, either," said Gordon. "I hope she's really miserable. She's dealt out enough misery to me. Well, guys, I'd better get back to the place where I've got the kid stashed. Meet me back here at four o'clock tomorrow afternoon. I'll have the money by then."

"It's a date!" chirped Chester Mackey.

The sun was slanting low in the western sky when Gordon made his way through the trees and moved up to the front door of the old house. Flipping the latch, he pulled the door open and stepped into the gloom of the interior.

As he ran his gaze around the room, he expected to see Bertie's small form somewhere on the floor or on one of the chairs. Frowning, he called out, "Bertie! Where are you?"

Dead silence.

"Bertie! I know you're in this house, somewhere! There's no way you could have gotten out! Now, you show yourself, because if I have to hunt you down, you'll get a beating you won't forget!"

Suddenly a door creaked, and a cold voice from the shadows said, "You're not beating on anybody, mister."

Pacing the floor of the small private waiting room at King George Hospital as expectant fathers are wont to do, Prince Albert waited for news from the doctors. He prayed with each step for Victoria's successful delivery of the baby and for Bertie's safe return to his family.

Suddenly Albert was aware of male voices just outside the door. Hurrying across the room, he threw the door open and was met with a wonderful sight.

There stood Chief Inspector Brent Cunningham of Scotland Yard holding a wide-eyed Bertie in his arms! Next to them was London Chief of Police Silas Altman. Both men were beaming.

When the boy saw his father, he cried, "Daddy!" and reached for him.

Cunningham handed the child to the prince and Albert folded him to his chest, kissed the top of his head, then examined him with eyes and hands. "Son, are you all right?"

"Yes, Daddy. I'm okay now, but I was scared that bad man was gonna hurt me."

Albert looked at the two men with misty eyes and said, "How— where—"

"Let's go in the waiting room and sit down, sir," said Cunningham.

As they moved through the door, Chief Altman explained that they had asked the head nurse on the floor about the queen, and she told them the doctors were with her but were not sure how soon she would deliver.

"Right," said Albert as they sat down. "I have our palace physician here, also. He told me after examining her that he thinks she will have a normal delivery."

"Wonderful!" said Cunningham. "Well, I know you're anxious to hear how we found and freed Bertie."

"I am," said Albert, squeezing the boy he held in his arms.

Police Chief Silas Altman began by telling Albert that as soon as he was informed about the kidnapping, he took two officers with him and went to Windsor Castle to talk to the parents. Upon arriving at the castle, they learned from the guards at the gate that a young man on a bicycle had arrived there only minutes earlier, bearing a sealed envelope addressed to the queen.

The guards told Altman and his men that a police officer had come to the castle earlier and informed them that Queen Victoria was on the way to King George Hospital, having labor pains. The guards went on to explain that as the cyclist rode away, they decided that one of them should ride to the hospital with the envelope and give it to Prince Albert.

It was at that moment that Chief Altman and his two officers had ridden up.

The guards gave the envelope to Chief Altman, who felt sure it was a ransom note, so he opened it. It was indeed a ransom note, demanding four hundred thousand pounds for Bertie's safe return. Explicit instructions were given as to how, when, and where the money should be left for the kidnapper, promising if it was followed to the letter, Bertie would be set free unharmed. If it was not, Bertie would be killed.

Inspector Cunningham then told Albert that when he returned to his office at Scotland Yard, he found a man and two twelve-year-old boys who had just arrived and had a story to tell.

Cunningham went on to explain the story the boys had told him and how the police and Scotland Yard officers had rushed to the old house in the forest and found Bertie alone and unharmed. Shortly thereafter, the kidnapper returned, was arrested, and now was in jail.

"Praise God for letting those boys see that bearded man!" said Albert. "And just who is he?"

"Well, for one thing," said Altman, "the beard was false, as was his mustache. Simply a disguise. The man used to be Duchess Mary's personal financial controller."

Albert's eyes widened. "Gordon Whitaker!"

"That's him, sir."

"Well, I'm not surprised. It's a long story, and I'll tell it to both of you later."

The door opened and Dr. Cecil Rice came in. "I was told a few minutes ago that you had the law in here with you, Prince Albert," said the physician, "and that little Bertie had been rescued."

"Yes, praise the Lord," said the prince.

"Please excuse my intrusion, sir, but since Her Majesty hasn't delivered yet, I thought you should bring Bertie in so she can see him. We haven't told her he's been found. We thought you would like to surprise her."

Rising to his feet with the boy in his arms, Albert said, "If she's up to it, Doctor, I'd love to! I had thought about asking if I could bring him in."

Rice grinned. "Let's go."

~~⌒~~

While concentrating on giving birth to the wee one who was about to come into the world, the queen lay in her hospital bed with doctors and nurses around her, praying for the child who was missing.

Still gasping for breath after one long, arduous contraction, Victoria opened her eyes and thought she was hallucinating, for at her bedside stood Albert holding Bertie in his arms.

Blinking rapidly, she tried to focus on the supposed illusion.

"Mummy!" a small voice penetrated into her numb mind.

Suddenly, Victoria knew it was not an illusion. "Oh, I'm not dreaming!" she cried. "Bertie! It really is you!"

"Yes, sweetheart," said Albert. "I wanted you to see for yourself that our son is safe and well. Dr. Rice said it would be all right."

Bertie's full attention was on his mother and she could tell that he wanted to go to her. Seeing it too, Albert said, "Dr. Rice told him he couldn't touch you."

Victoria managed a wan smile. "Don't you worry, son," she said. "When Mummy gets out of the hospital we can hug each other lots and lots."

"Okay," said Bertie, satisfied with the promise.

"Oh, thank You, Lord," said Victoria. "Thank You for bringing little Bertie back to us!"

Albert then told Victoria the story, and she, too, was not surprised to learn who had abducted Bertie and demanded the large sum of money. She told Albert that her heart went out to Alice and Edgar.

"Edgar is twenty-one now," she said, "and will take it hard when his father goes to prison. This will bring shame and suffering to him, and no doubt have a devastating effect on his life."

Suddenly another pain began its journey through Victoria's body. Albert gently caressed her cheek, told Victoria he and Bertie would be in the waiting room, and hurried away.

At four o'clock the next morning, Victoria gave birth to their sixth child, Louise Caroline Alberta. Leaving Bertie in the care of a nurse, Albert was at his wife's side.

When the nurses had prepared the baby for her parents to see her, Victoria took her in her arms as Albert looked on and said, "Praise the Lord, Albert! He has given us six healthy children. And when it appeared we might lose Bertie, God brought him back to us."

"Yes, sweetheart, He did," said Albert. "And I'm going to see to it that those two boys who led the police to the house in the woods are both generously rewarded."

"Oh yes, by all means," said the queen. "Very generously."

Albert bent down, kissed his new little daughter, then took Victoria's hand and said, "Let's pray and thank the Lord for His goodness."

When Albert said his amen, Victoria wiped tears and said, "Darling, would you do something for me, please?"

"Of course. What is it?"

"I want you to go see Alice Whitaker and tell her she will still get financial help from us. Gordon is going to prison. She'll need the money."

"Of course," said Albert. "I'll go as soon as I take care of some other things that are pressing right now."

"Thank you," said Victoria. "Tell Alice and Edgar how sorry I am that their lives have been so blighted."

Fifteen

At ten o'clock that morning, Edgar Whitaker was moving a heavy chair in the parlor with his mother telling how she wanted it positioned when there was a knock on the front door of the house.

Leaving the chair, Edgar headed that direction. "I'll get it, Mom."

Alice, her face drawn and dark circles under eyes, moved slowly toward the parlor door in case whoever was knocking wanted to see her.

When Edgar opened the door, he was surprised to see Prince Albert on the porch, flanked by two palace guards.

"Hello," said Albert. "You must be Edgar."

Edgar gave him a dull look, eyelids partially drooped. "Yeah. That's me. And you are?"

Feeling quite unwelcome, Albert said, "I'm Prince Albert, husband of Queen Victoria. I thought you might recognize me."

"What do you want?"

"Edgar!" came his mother's voice as she hurried to him. "You knew he was Prince Albert. What's the matter with you?" Then she said to

Albert, "I'm sorry for my son's ill manners, sir. Please come in."

The guards remained on the porch as Albert stepped in with Edgar giving him the cold eye.

"Mrs. Whitaker," Albert said, removing his hat, "let me say that I am sorry for what you are going through."

Alice tried to smile. "Thank you, sir. It indeed was a horrible shock when the police came to my door and told me that my husband had been arrested as little Bertie's kidnapper. They said his trial is set for June 4. Kidnapping is a capital offense in Great Britain."

"Yes, ma'am," Albert said.

Edgar's features looked as if they were set in stone.

Alice took a deep breath. "Prince Albert, I am so sorry for what Gordon did. It must have been horrible for you and Queen Victoria to have little Bertie kidnapped and not know whether you would ever see him alive again."

"It was very difficult, yes. But my heart also goes out to you and your son, ma'am. This has to be a terrible thing for you. Let me explain my reason for being here. Victoria gave birth to our sixth child at King George Hospital in the wee hours this morning, so of course she couldn't come with me. However, she asked me to come and tell you how sorry she is that this horrible thing has happened to you and Edgar, and she wants me to tell you that you will continue to receive the financial help she has been sending the past few years."

Edgar's mouth sagged and his eyes bulged. "You've been getting money from the queen, Mom?"

"Yes. Ever since your father left his job at the bank. The queen has been so kind to look after us, Edgar."

"I thought the money came from neighbors."

"Well, I told your father that because I knew he wouldn't accept money that came from the queen."

Edgar's teeth were clenched and his jaw muscles were rippling under the skin.

Tears surfaced in Alice's eyes. "Prince Albert, please express my deepest gratitude to Queen Victoria for her kindness. I will write her a letter, but in the meantime, I want her to know how much this means to me."

"I most certainly will, ma'am. Well, I must be going."

Edgar's eyes blazed with anger. "All of this is still Victoria's fault!" The words whipped from his mouth. "If she hadn't cheated Dad out of the fortune he had been promised, and the job he had been promised, none of this would have happened, and he wouldn't be facing execution! It's her fault!"

Alice moved a step closer to him. "You're wrong, son. As much as I hate to say it, this whole thing is your father's fault. He brought this on himself." She turned to Albert. "I apologize for my son's attitude, sir."

Edgar stared at his mother silently, his eyes still blazing.

Albert laid a hand on Edgar's shoulder. "You need to get this anger out of your system, Edgar, and try to be a help to your mother. She's going to need all the support you can give her in the harrowing days to come."

Edgar jerked his shoulder free from Albert's hand, set his jaw, and hissed, "I don't need any advice from you."

On Thursday morning, June 4, 1846, the courtroom was jam-packed. Newspaper reporters stood around the room, their backs against the walls.

Prince Albert was there, seated between two palace guards. His heart went out to Alice Whitaker, who sat with her son nearby.

Edgar kept his eyes on his father, who was seated at a table near the judge's bench. A state attorney sat beside Gordon, and two police officers stood close by.

The courtroom was silent when the Scotland Yard officers testified, saying they had caught the defendant red-handed in the kidnapping of Bertie. It took the jury only a few minutes of deliberation to return to the courtroom with the guilty verdict.

Judge Randall Nelson looked at Gordon Whitaker and said, "Will the defendant please rise?"

The court-appointed attorney rose also.

Nelson set steady eyes on the defendant and said in a level voice, "Gordon Whitaker, you have been duly tried in this court of law, and have been found guilty of kidnapping the son of Queen Victoria and Prince Albert. In this country, kidnapping is a felony punishable by execution."

Alice Whitaker broke down and sobbed. Edgar made no move to comfort her, keeping his attention on his father.

The judge waited a few seconds for Alice to gain control of herself, then looking once again at Gordon, said, "Mr. Whitaker, you are hereby sentenced to death by hanging at sunrise one week from today—June 11. And may God have mercy on your soul."

The court session was then dismissed by Judge Nelson with the bang of his gavel on the desk.

Gordon remained stiff as the two police officers led him from the courtroom. Before passing through the door, Gordon glanced over his shoulder at his weeping wife and stone-faced son.

The newspaper reporters quickly gathered around Alice and Edgar, wanting a statement from the wife of the condemned man. Alice was weeping uncontrollably and could not speak.

Prince Albert stepped up and said, "Gentlemen, as you can see, Mrs. Whitaker is in no condition to talk to you. Please stand back and let her son take her home."

"How about a statement from you, Edgar?" asked one of the reporters.

Edgar's hatred toward Queen Victoria was a fiery ball in his chest.

Through barely parted lips, he said with trembling voice, "You couldn't print what I would say. Let's go, Mom."

Alice clung to Edgar's arm as they walked together out of the courthouse and headed for the parking lot. Twice, Alice's knees buckled, and Edgar kept her from falling.

When they were in the family buggy and moving through the city toward home, Edgar was fuming with wrath. While his mother sat with her head bowed, words were burning through his mind: *Victoria, you ruined my father's life, and now, you are responsible for his execution. I will have my vengeance on you!*

⤎⤏

When Prince Albert arrived back at Windsor Castle, he found Lucy Granville carrying baby Louise from the master bedroom. Lucy paused, saying, "She just had feeding time."

Albert nodded, leaned down, and kissed the baby. "How is Her Majesty feeling?"

"She's still quite weak. Dr. Rice just examined her and said she is doing fine for having given birth under such trying circumstances. She just asked if you were back yet."

"I'll go in and see her."

Lucy moved on down the hall, baby in arms.

When Victoria saw Albert come into the room, she smiled. "There's my darling husband."

Albert bent over and kissed her, then sat down on the edge of the bed. "Lucy told me Dr. Rice says you're doing all right."

"Yes, praise the Lord. So how did the trial go?"

"Exactly as we expected. The jury was out maybe five or six minutes and came back with the guilty verdict. Judge Nelson set the execution at sunrise next Thursday."

"I…I just feel so sorry for Alice. It's going to hit Marianne and Lorene awfully hard when they learn of it. And…Edgar. I know he despises me, and from what he said to you and his mother, he blames me for causing his father to do what he did. But my heart still goes out to him."

"Yes," said Albert.

There was a brief silence, then Victoria said, "Darling, I want you to take me to Judge Nelson. I want to talk to him."

"But you're too weak to do that. What do you want to talk to him about?"

"I…I just feel that I should keep Gordon from hanging. Have his sentence commuted to life in prison. This would make it easier on Alice and her children."

Albert squeezed her hand. "Why doesn't this surprise me? You are such a compassionate person. All right, but instead of my taking you to see the judge, I'll send a messenger to him, saying the queen would like to talk to him tomorrow. How's that?"

Victoria smiled and sighed. "Fine. Thank you."

Albert cleared his throat. "That is, if Dr. Rice says it's all right for you to do this. You'll have to leave this bed, dress for the occasion, and walk to the drawing room downstairs."

"I can do that."

"Let me talk to Dr. Rice first."

Some ten minutes later, Dr. Cecil Rice stood next to Prince Albert beside Victoria's bed, with Emily beside Albert.

The queen spent several minutes attempting to convince her husband, her physician, and her personal maid that by the next morning she would be perfectly capable of leaving her bed to meet with the judge. "I promise not to overdo," she said, smiling sweetly at the trio. "It will be wonderful to leave this room and see something different. Now, Albert, dear, you need to get the appointment set for tomorrow, and if you gentlemen will excuse me, it's time for Emily to give me my spit bath."

Knowing they had been rather summarily dismissed, the men looked at each other, smiled, and walked out the door.

At precisely ten o'clock the next morning, Judge Randall Nelson was ushered into the drawing room at Windsor Castle and welcomed by Queen Victoria from her chair. Albert stood next to her.

When Nelson had bowed and kissed the queen's hand, she said, "I was so glad when Albert told me you could come this morning, Judge Nelson."

"Well, it just happened that I had no court date this morning, Your Majesty. But let me hasten to say that even if I had, I would have postponed it in deference to my queen's wishes."

Albert shook hands with Nelson, and they sat down.

Nelson smiled at Victoria. "I have to confess, Your Majesty, not knowing what you wanted to see me about, I had a rather restless night."

"Oh, I'm sorry," said Victoria.

Nelson chuckled. "Please don't be. It's just that this is the first time I have been summoned into the presence of England's monarch. Now what did you want to talk to me about?"

"Gordon Whitaker's execution," she said flatly.

With his hands cuffed behind his back, Gordon Whitaker was ushered into the office of the police chief by two guards.

When he was seated in front of the chief's desk and the guards stood flanking him, Altman leaned forward, putting his elbows on the desktop. "Mr. Whitaker, I have some very good news for you."

"Good news? What possible good news could you have for me?"

"How about a commuting of your death sentence to life in prison?"

Gordon's head bobbed and his eyes widened in shock. He was speechless.

"Well, it's true," said Altman. "Queen Victoria had Judge Randall Nelson brought to Windsor Castle and told him she wanted the sentence changed to life in prison. What do you think of that?"

Gordon's jaw worked as he tried to find his voice. Finally, he croaked, "I…I just can't believe it."

"Take my word for it. You will miss the noose. You will spend the rest of your life in London's Newgate Prison."

"Has someone…has someone let my wife and son know?"

"Yes. You will be transferred to Newgate in about an hour. You won't be able to have visitors until sometime tomorrow."

Gordon licked his lips. "I—I just can't believe it. Why would Vic—Queen Victoria do this for me?"

"I can't say, but it shows me one thing."

"What's that?"

"She has a heart as big as the Milky Way."

The next morning, Victoria was seated in the drawing room and smiled up at Alice Whitaker when Wilson escorted her into the room.

"Thank you, Wilson," said Victoria as Wilson seated Alice.

"Yes, Your Majesty," said Wilson. "Please let me know if there is anything else I can do."

As Wilson left the room, Alice said, "Your Majesty, thank you for granting me this audience."

"My pleasure. Now what can I do for you?"

"Your Majesty has already done a wonderful thing. I wanted to see you so I could thank you for sparing my husband's life. Words are poor vessels of communication at a time like this, but please look in my heart if you can, and know how very much it means to me."

Victoria smiled. "I can see it in your eyes, Alice, as well as in your heart."

Alice's brow furrowed. "Your Majesty, may I ask you a question?"

"Of course."

"How can you be so kind to Gordon after what he did to you and Prince Albert? He kidnapped your son. It had to have been a terrible thing for both of you."

Victoria nodded. "It was a terrible ordeal, indeed. But let me explain. I can be kind to Gordon because the Lord Jesus Christ was kind to me. He saved my wretched soul, Alice. I was a guilty sinner before Him who deserved to spend eternity in hell. But when I came to Him in repentance of my sin and received Him into my heart as my Saviour, He washed my sins away in His precious blood and saved me. He has promised me a place in heaven when I leave this world."

Alice batted her eyes and shook her head. "I...I've never heard it quite like that before, Your Majesty. Y-you actually know you are going to heaven?"

"Absolutely. Through His blood and by His grace. Not by my works or any religious rites. Jesus said in John 3:3, 'Except a man be born again, he cannot see the kingdom of God.' According to John 1:12, I was born again...born into the family of God when I received the Lord Jesus into my heart. You can have the same salvation and assurance, Alice, if you want it. Jesus died on Calvary's cross for you, too."

Alice rubbed her temples. "Your Majesty, I have often thought about dying, and wondered where I would go when I die. I would like to know more about this."

"Wonderful," said Victoria, picking up a Bible from the table next to her chair. "Let me show you right from the pages of God's Word."

It was just after one o'clock in the afternoon when Alice was taken into the visiting room of Newgate Prison and seated in front of a barred window.

Other visitors were there, talking to prisoners.

When Gordon came in with a guard at his side and sat down, Alice put her face close to the bars and said, "Oh, Gordon, I was so happy when they told me what Queen Victoria had done for you! Isn't it great?"

Gordon let a tiny smile curve his mouth. "It was good news when Chief Altman told me, yes. The thought of spending the rest of my life in here isn't pleasant, but it's better than dying."

"Honey," she said, eyes sparkling, "something wonderful just happened to me."

"Oh? What?"

Alice proceeded to tell her husband how she had gone to the castle to thank Queen Victoria for sparing his life, and how the queen had shown her in the Bible how to be saved and know she was going to heaven.

"Gordon," she said excitedly, "I opened my heart to the Lord Jesus Christ like Queen Victoria showed me, and now I'm saved! I'm a Christian and a child of God! Oh, Gordon, I want you to be saved, too. Queen Victoria gave me a small Bible and marked the verses for me so I could read them again. It's in my purse. I can show you—"

"I don't want anything to do with it, Alice," Gordon interrupted.

"But—"

"No! If that makes you happy, so be it, but I don't want any part of it. Let's talk about something else."

That evening when Edgar came home from his job at one of London's department stores, Alice said, "Honey, I went to see your father today after I went to Windsor Castle to thank Queen Victoria for sparing his life."

"Mm-hmm. Did you tell Dad I'd be there to see him as soon as I can?"

"Yes. Just before I left him. But let me tell you what happened to me at the castle today."

Edgar listened as his mother told him about becoming a born-again, heaven-bound child of God. When she started to ask if he would let her show him in the Bible how to be saved, he threw up his hands. "Mom, I'm not interested in that religious stuff."

"But this isn't religion. It's salvation, forgiveness of sins, and the sweet peace of knowing you're going to heaven and not to hell when you die."

Jutting his jaw, Edgar said, "Mom, I said I'm not interested, and I know if you talked to Dad about it, he said the same thing."

Alice's face paled.

"So you did, didn't you? I'm right, aren't I?"

"Yes."

"You asked me a few weeks ago what it was that caused me to break up with Darlene. I didn't tell you the whole thing, Mom. I told you she got upset every time I said something derogatory about the queen, and after a while, I got sick of it. Well, there's more to the story. She went to some church and did the same thing you're talk-ing about. She got this born-again thing and all that. It was hard enough hearing a lecture every time I had my say about the little runt queen. I put up with it anyhow because I was really in love with the girl. But when she took on that fanatical religious stuff, that was it. That's the real reason I broke up with her. So please…I don't want to hear it from you, either."

Alice nodded silently, telling herself she would pray for both the men in her life.

"And another thing, Mom," said Edgar, "why don't you just tell Victoria you don't need her money? I'm making decent wages now. I can provide for both of us."

"How about when you finally do get married, son? Will your wife want you shelling out money to your mother?"

Edgar rubbed the back of his neck. "Well-l-l…"

"So I'll let the queen do what she wants to help me. She's such a kind and generous person."

Edgar's features hardened. "If she's so kind and generous, why didn't she give Dad the fortune and the job he had been promised?" He walked away without waiting for an answer.

Two years later.

On a cold day in November 1848, Alice and Edgar entered Newgate Prison to visit Gordon as usual. Approaching the counter where they always signed in, Edgar said to the guard, "Hello, Mr. Ames. My mother and I are here to see my father."

Ames wiped a hand over his mouth. "Sorry, you can't see him today. He's in the infirmary."

"The infirmary!" said Alice. "What's wrong with him?"

"He has pneumonia, ma'am."

Alice's face twisted. "He was all right four days ago. Is it serious?"

"I don't know, ma'am. You would have to talk to Dr. Faulkner."

"Why hasn't my mother been notified of his illness?" asked Edgar.

"It isn't prison policy to keep in touch with inmates' families."

"Well, can't we see him, even if he is in the infirmary?" asked Alice.

"No, ma'am. It is against prison rules."

"Well, somebody needs to change the rules!" gusted Edgar. "Why are there such rules?"

The guard looked at him askance. "This isn't a vacation resort, Mr. Whitaker. This is a prison."

Edgar's face turned crimson. He banged his fist on the counter. "I want to see my father, and I want to see him right now!"

"Edgar," said Alice, "calm down."

"Calm down, nothing! I want to see Dad!"

Instantly, two guards rushed up and seized Edgar by both arms, bending them up behind his back. "You are leaving," said one of them. "This kind of behavior is not tolerated here."

As her son was being forced out the door, Alice said, "I'm sorry, Mr. Ames. Would it be possible for me to see Dr. Faulkner?"

Moments later, Alice was seated in the doctor's small office, asking his opinion of Gordon's condition.

Faulkner said, "Mrs. Whitaker, I must be honest with you. Your husband is going to die."

"But…but last Wednesday he didn't have pneumonia!"

"He did, ma'am. But apparently he didn't let on to you. It was that very night that he was put in the infirmary. The pneumonia has progressed quite rapidly, which it is known to do in this cold, damp place."

Hot tears filled Alice's eyes and began streaming down her cheeks. "Please, Doctor, may I see him?"

"All right. Under the circumstances, I will let you."

Moments later they approached the door of the room where Gordon was being kept. The doctor whispered, "He may be asleep."

Alice followed Faulkner into the small, single-bed room. Gordon seemed to be sleeping, but when the doctor looked down at him, he gave Alice a fearful glance and pressed fingers to the side of his neck.

"Doctor, is he—"

"I'm afraid so, ma'am," Faulkner said solemnly. "Had to have happened only moments ago. He's still warm. I'm sorry."

Lips trembling, Alice said, "May I…may I have a moment with him?"

"Of course. I'll be just outside the door."

When the doctor was gone, Alice sat down on a chair next to the bed and took her husband's lifeless hand into her own. Gazing at his face through her tears, she saw that even in death, there was no peace on his pallid countenance.

"Gordon," she whispered while wiping tears with her free hand, "I'm sorry that you lived the last years of your life with such bitterness and hatred. It has been so empty and wasted. If only I could have convinced you to repent and make Jesus your Saviour, at least now you would be in heaven. As it is, you will spend eternity in hell with only regret as your companion."

The love Alice had once felt for her husband had waned over the

years as the bitterness and hatred he felt for Queen Victoria con-
sumed him. Yet there was a void in her heart that he had filled, and a
great sadness gripped her as she rose to her feet and walked slowly to
the door, not looking back.

Edgar was pacing outside the prison gate when his mother came out,
weeping.

Rushing to her, he said, "Mom, what happened?"

Alice looked up at her son through a veil of tears. "Your father is
dead, Edgar. He died only minutes before the doctor took me in to
see him."

Edgar was both grieved and furious. He wept for his father and
at the same time upset Alice further by swearing vehemently and
cursing the name of Queen Victoria.

The next day, when Victoria had been advised that Gordon
Whitaker had died from pneumonia, she sent a carriage for Alice.
When the two of them were alone in a sitting room, Victoria
handed her an envelope containing a special amount of money and
assured her again that she would see that she had sufficient funds to
live on.

Alice embraced the queen with tears streaming down her face.
When she rode away in the royal carriage toward home, she was
heavy in heart because she knew her son was more bitter than ever.

By 1850, Queen Victoria's leadership of Great Britain was strong and
very influential. The Bible preaching churches were flourishing and
missionaries were being sent from England all around the globe to
spread the gospel of Jesus Christ. A new wave of prosperity was spreading over the land, and God was getting the glory. Victoria's subjects
moved with assurance and optimism. Morals were at an all-time high.
Alcohol consumption and blood sports were on the decline.

The queen was on her throne, God was blessing from heaven,
her heirs were thriving, and for Great Britain, all seemed right with
the world.

In the fall of 1850, Prince Albert talked to Victoria about the blessings that God had showered on England since she became queen and how the rest of the world looked to Great Britain as a leader for peace. He explained that he would like to plan a "Peace Festival" for the next spring, and invite nations all over the world to send their leaders.

When Victoria showed her enthusiastic favor of the idea, Albert told her that as a gesture of peace to all nations, he would like to have what he would call a "Great Exhibition" during the festival, and arrange for a vast array of exhibits from as many nations as would send their goods to be displayed.

Victoria agreed and asked where he would have the festival and the exhibition. He told her he would need a building erected for it. She agreed to this, also, saying England was thriving financially and could well afford it.

Albert immediately picked out a choice piece of vacant ground in Hyde Park, and construction was begun on a huge glass building that would be used as a cathedral to the glory of God when the festival and exhibition were over.

When the newspapers announced Prince Albert's plan, the people of Great Britain—for the most part—were excited about it.

Sixteen

The morning of May 1, 1851, was fine and clear, with only an occasional passing cloud, and the great glass cathedral shimmered in the sunlight. Multicolored flags flapped in the breeze on the rooftop of the cathedral, whose airy brightness cheered and dazzled the multitude of spectators from far and wide who crowded into Hyde Park.

It was nearly noon when nine state carriages arrived, and the queen and Prince Albert alighted from the royal carriage with their two oldest children and entered the sparkling glass building with an escort of uniformed guards.

Inside, they were greeted instantly by a blast of trumpets, and the thousands of people seated in the galleries burst into cheers and applause. The queen, holding Bertie by the hand, was great with child, but handled herself well.

Victoria and Albert, with Vicky and Bertie, took their place under the huge nave, a crystal fountain to their backs. Behind the fountain was a large leafy tree, its topmost branches reaching almost to the domed ceiling. As soon as the royal family was seated, a 600-voice choir broke into the "Hallelujah Chorus" with a full orchestra and pipe organ.

Victoria smiled at Albert, who had not told her of this part of the program, and he smiled back as she rose to her feet, which she had done for years every time "Messiah" had been sung when she was in attendance. The audience, all knowing what the queen would do, also stood up. Albert put an arm around his wife's shoulders as the choir sang, and she dabbed at the tears that streamed from her eyes.

When the choir was finished, Prince Albert left the queen's side and made his way to the huge platform. The acoustics in the building were perfect, and everyone could easily hear Albert as he stood at the podium and welcomed all the foreign dignitaries in attendance, the men of Parliament, and all guests.

Albert then pointed out that only three years earlier, the states of the European continent had been convulsed in revolution, but now, with the rebel governments overturned through advice that came from Parliament under Queen Victoria's leadership, peace and order had been restored.

There was a loud ovation as the crowd stood up, and hundreds called out the name of Victoria while she rose to her feet, smiling and waving with Vicky and Bertie sitting beside her.

When the crowd grew quiet and sat down, Albert spoke with conviction and told them that the queen had gained her wisdom from the God of heaven. He gave praise to the Lord Jesus Christ for providing salvation at Calvary for a lost humanity, then called on his pastor to come and lead in prayer.

The pastor prayed, in which he gave praise to Almighty God for the queen He had given Great Britain, and for the blessings the nation had received from His hand. After that the ceremonies began, led by Prince Albert.

Within an hour, the great crowd was passing through the bright displays which thirty-four nations had sent to show their friendship with the nation that was leading the world to maintain peace.

Less than a week after the Peace Festival, Queen Victoria gave birth to their seventh child, Arthur William Patrick.

In April of 1853, their eighth child was born: Leopold George

Duncan. In April of 1856, their ninth and final child was born: Beatrice, whom they dubbed Baby. With her satiny skin and big blue eyes, Beatrice was the darling of Windsor Castle.

Shortly after Victoria turned forty in 1859, their daughter Vicky—who was married to Prince Frederick William of Prussia—gave birth to a son, happily making Albert and Victoria grandparents. The following year, Vicky gave birth to a daughter.

In March of 1861, the Duchess of Kent died of a severe infection after having surgery on her arm to remove an ulcer. Victoria and the rest of her family grieved over Mary's death, especially because she died without ever having placed her faith in the Lord Jesus Christ for salvation.

Victoria placed Louise Lehzen at Buckingham Palace and gave her a permanent home, where she was given light responsibilities to keep her active. From time to time, Victoria had Louise come to Windsor Castle for meals, so they could spend some time together.

Later that year, Albert and Victoria's daughter Alice became engaged to Prince Louis of Hesse-Darmstadt, Germany. Albert, at forty years of age, had a severe attack of cholera, which put him down for a month. Shortly after this, he began to have frequent attacks of stomach pain.

In early December, Albert was stricken with gastric fever. The royal family's physician was now Dr. Walter James. Albert's gastric fever grew worse in spite of all Dr. James and the doctors and nurses who assisted him could do. Albert had insisted that he be kept in one of the castle's bedrooms near the master bedroom, so Victoria could rest well in her regular bed yet be close to him.

Vicky was at home in Prussia, and Bertie was on a trip to Germany, having left in late October.

On Monday morning, December 12, Victoria and Alice—who was now eighteen—were sitting together on a small sofa by the windows in the master bedroom. Alice was holding her mother's hand as they talked about her father's illness. Dr. James and his staff were in Albert's room, working to hold the fever down as much as possible.

It was just before ten o'clock when mother and daughter heard a light tap on the framework of the open bedroom door. They looked around to see Dr. Walter James, whose features were drawn and shoulders drooped.

"Please come in, Doctor," said Victoria.

Mother and daughter started to get up as he moved toward them, but he said, "Please…stay seated."

The doctor's lips quivered as he stood over them. "Your Majesty…Alice…at times like this I wish I had chosen another profession. I have to tell you that Prince Albert is not going to get better. He will not be with us much longer."

Alice squeezed her mother's hand.

Victoria swallowed hard. "How long, Doctor?"

"Maybe a day or two. Prince Albert knows his time is short. He asked me the same question, and I gave him the same answer."

Alice began to sniffle as tears welled up in her eyes.

Fighting her own tears, Victoria said, "May I have some time alone with him?"

"Of course. The nurses just finished bathing his face and wrists with cold water. It won't have to be done for another half hour. My staff and I will remain close, just out in the hall."

Victoria looked at her daughter. "Honey, you go to your brothers and sisters. Don't tell them that Dr. James says Daddy only has a day or two."

Alice sniffed, wiped tears from her cheeks, and nodded.

Dr. James excused himself, saying he would go and clear his staff out of the room.

Victoria hugged Alice, kissed her cheek, then went to a small table beside the bed and picked up her worn Bible.

As she moved toward the door, Victoria thought about how many royal families intermarried only for the sake of producing an heir for the throne. She and Albert had often talked about it, and rejoiced together in the deep and sweet love they had shared almost from the time they met.

Albert was lying on his back when Victoria entered his room. He looked up and smiled. "Dr. James cleared the place out so we could have some privacy," he said weakly.

Victoria sat down on the chair beside the bed and took hold of his hand. In her heart, she was asking the Lord to keep her from breaking down.

Albert licked his dry lips. "Dr. James said he told you. A day or two."

Victoria swallowed the hot lump that had risen in her throat. "Darling, it seems our time together has been so short."

"Yes, my love, but it has been so blessed of God. And together, we have accomplished much for His glory, as has been our greatest desire."

"That we have, sweetheart," she said, tears now misting her eyes and threatening to spill over. "And at this time, we must consider the great things the Lord has done for us."

Albert smiled again. "That's what Samuel told the people of Israel."

"Yes," she said. "I read it just this morning."

"I see you have your Bible. Would you read that passage to me?"

Victoria managed a smile. "That's exactly what I had planned to read to you."

She opened the Bible to 1 Samuel 12. Her eyes ran down the page to the portion where Samuel was addressing the discouraged people of Israel, telling them not to turn aside from following the Lord, but to serve Him with all their heart. Picking it up in verse 22, she read to Albert Samuel's words:

"'For the LORD will not forsake his people for his great name's sake: because it hath pleased the LORD to make you his people. Moreover as for me, God forbid that I should sin against the LORD in ceasing to pray for you: but I will teach you the good and right way: Only fear the LORD, and serve him with all your heart: for consider how great things he hath done for you.'"

Both were silent for a moment when Victoria finished.

Albert moistened his lips again. "How could we help but consider the great things our Lord has done for us, Victoria? He has been so good."

"Yes, darling," she said, her voice thick with unshed tears.

With what strength he had, Albert squeezed her hand. "We must always remember, my sweet, that our heavenly Father only does good things for us, even though some are difficult for us to accept. Our finite minds cannot comprehend it at times. But when we give our lives, hearts, and souls to Him, whatever He chooses in His matchless wisdom to bring our way is right and good for us. And sweetheart, He will bless us with grace for every trial."

Victoria blinked at the excess moisture in her eyes. "Darling," she said hesitantly, "in…in my mind, I realize all of this, but right now, my heart is having a hard time coping with it. I don't know how I am going to bear up when—when—"

Albert squeezed her hand again. His voice was growing more tired with each word, but with supreme effort, he said, "Sweetheart, with God all things are possible. Even at a time like this."

Victoria had let her head lower a bit and was looking at the floor.

At those words, she raised her head and set her bleak eyes on her dying husband. "Thank you, darling. I cherish you with an endless love."

Droopy-eyed, Albert gave her a weary smile. "Me, too."

Victoria watched him close his eyes. She knew by his even breathing that he had drifted off to sleep.

Quietly, she rose to her feet. Softly kissing one cheek then the other, she left his side and walked to the window where a pale, wintry sun was striving to warm the December air.

Leaning her forehead against the cold window, Victoria said in a whisper, "Please forgive me, Lord, for my selfishness in wanting to keep Albert with me. Forgive my doubts and fears. I want Thy will to be done. I just ask that You will give me the grace to go through this ordeal."

Even as those last words were coming from her lips, a quiet peace stole over her soul, and she knew in her heart that Albert was right. Indeed, with God all things are possible.

Dr. Walter James and his small staff continued to do what they could to make Prince Albert comfortable through the rest of the day.

Late that night, Alice was with her mother when Dr. James came to them and said he doubted that the prince would make it through the night.

Victoria told him she would stay at Albert's side. The doctor assured her that he and his staff would be in their rooms if she needed them.

When Dr. James was gone, Alice asked if she could stay till the end.

Victoria said she could, but only her. The other children were too young.

Mother and daughter stayed with Albert all night as his face grew more ashen and his breathing became increasingly labored. At times, he awakened, talked to them briefly, then fell back into slumber. When morning came, Victoria and Alice were pleased to find their loved one still alive.

Outside, an exceptionally brilliant sun illuminated the warm brown stones of the castle and streamed through the windows.

Dr. James and his staff worked over Albert while the queen and Princess Alice ate a small breakfast and reported on Albert's condition to the castle servants and guards. They spent a few minutes with the other children, but did not reveal that their father was on the edge of eternity.

When they returned to Albert's room, Dr. Rice whispered to them, saying he was amazed that the prince was still alive. He then took his staff out of the room to give queen and princess time with him.

Albert was weaker than ever when Victoria moved up beside the bed and took his hand in hers; Alice stood at her side.

Albert looked up at them with dreary eyes and spoke in a whisper. "My precious ones…it is almost time for me to go to heaven."

Victoria bent her face low over his with tears streaming down her cheeks. She whispered, "I must have one last kiss."

Alice looked on, silently weeping.

Between rapid breaths, Albert's cool lips brushed Victoria's cheek.

She stood erect, face pinched, and mouthed to Alice, *Stay with him. I'll be back.*

Alice nodded, knowing her mother had to leave the room in order to bring her emotions under control. As her mother disappeared, she leaned over and kissed her father's damp forehead. "I love you, Daddy."

Albert was so weak he could only nod.

Soon Victoria returned, eyes red from weeping, and took up her customary position, holding Albert's hand in hers.

The day passed with Albert stirring periodically to look at his wife and daughter, but without sufficient strength to speak. From time to time, Dr. James came into the room to look at his patient. At six o'clock in the evening, he sent his staff home, and told the queen he would be in his room if she needed him.

A little before eleven o'clock that night, Victoria was seated beside the bed, holding Albert's hand. Alice was seated next to her.

Albert, eyes closed, suddenly drew several long breaths, lightly squeezing Victoria's hand. He opened his eyes, which were amazingly clear, and looked up toward the ceiling. A smile curved his lips, and he let out his last breath.

Victoria set her tear-dimmed eyes on his pulseless breast.

A hush fell in the candlelit room as Alice rose from the chair and put an arm around her mother's shoulders. Holding her tight, she said just above a whisper, "Mummy, I think he got a glimpse into heaven just before Jesus took him. Did you see him smile?"

"Yes, sweetheart," replied Victoria, whose heart was at perfect peace. "Daddy is with Jesus now. He has plenty to smile about."

Princess Alice married Prince Louis at St. James's Chapel in July 1862, and the happy young couple left for Germany the next day.

On the first anniversary of her widowhood—December 13, 1862— Queen Victoria was delighted when she was told that Alice Whitaker was at the castle, asking to see her.

After a long and tender embrace, the two women sat down in the parlor. Alice set her large purse on the floor next to the overstuffed chair, set bright eyes on the queen, and said, "Your Majesty, I have some good news."

Victoria smiled. "Yes?"

"I'm getting married in two weeks."

"Oh, wonderful! And who is this most fortunate man?"

"You've probably seen him before at church. His name is Douglas Kenton."

"Oh yes! He's one of the deacons. I didn't know you two were seeing each other. But then, of course, I always have to be surrounded by my guards coming and going from church, and I don't get to socialize much. Tell me about Mr. Kenton."

"Well, he's a widower. His wife died two years ago. He is partner in a very successful law firm here in London."

"I'm so happy for you."

"I knew you would be," said Alice. "I wanted to let you know about the wedding, so you'd be aware that I will no longer need money from you."

Victoria smiled and nodded. "I guess not, since you're marrying a successful lawyer."

"But I want to thank you once again for the way you have so kindly helped me all these years. And of course, more than anything, I want to thank you for leading me to Jesus."

"In both, the pleasure was mine, I assure you."

Alice reached into her purse and pulled out a brand-new leather-bound Bible. "I want to give you this Bible as a token of my love and appreciation for all you have done for me. There's a little note inside. You can read it later."

Victoria took the Bible and ran her gaze over the beautiful cover. "Thank you, Alice. I will treasure this Bible for the rest of my life."

Alice smiled. "We haven't been able to communicate a lot these past few years, Your Majesty, so I want to tell you that Edgar finally got married in 1859. His wife, Nora, just gave birth to their second daughter. Edgar is now a banker, like his father was. In fact, he is at Barings Bank, too. I'm very concerned for Edgar. He is still bitter toward you for what he figures you did to his father, and he still wants nothing to do with the Lord."

"Well, honey," said Victoria, "keep loving him and don't give up."

In March 1863, Bertie married Princess Alexandra of Denmark, and after the couple honeymooned in Ireland, they returned to London.

Knowing since his childhood that he was the heir to the British throne, Bertie had been preparing for the day that he would be called upon to assume the duties and obligations as king of England.

As time passed, his mother gave him more and more responsibilities that were related to royal things to help prepare him. He respected his mother and the memory of his father greatly, and was pleased and honored to accept this trust. Alexandra was also preparing as best she could for the duties that would fall on her when Bertie one day ascended the throne.

Alexandra dearly loved and admired her mother-in-law, and they spent many hours together, deeply enjoying one another's company. They often shared many of their burdens and desires together in prayer.

In January 1864, a son was born to Bertie and Alexandra, whom they named Albert Victor. He was dubbed Eddy. Bertie was especially proud of his little son who was destined to one day succeed his father as king of England.

In June 1865, a second son was born. Bertie and Alexandra named him George Frederick.

In the Edgar Whitaker home, Edgar continued to nurse his hatred for the queen openly, doing his best to make his wife and daughters feel the same way.

In September of 1865, Nora divorced Edgar because of his consuming hatred toward Queen Victoria, telling the judge that he was permanently damaging the girls with his vehement tirades against the queen and attempts to bend their young minds to his way of thinking.

Nora left London and took her daughters with her.

Three months later, Edgar married a young woman from one of the poorer sections of London, whose parents had taught her to dislike the queen. With Florence as an ally against the queen, Edgar was superbly happy.

Alice Whitaker Kenton seldom ever saw her son and new daughter-in-law. Since they both knew how Alice felt about the queen—as did her husband—Edgar and Florence only came around the Kenton home once in a great while and never stayed very long. Another problem for Edgar and Florence was that the Kentons prayed before every meal and sometimes witnessed to them of their need to know Jesus Christ as Saviour.

Victoria's reign continued to be blessed of God as time rolled by.

In 1868, a son was born in the Edgar Whitaker home, whom they named Nigel.

Florence knew that Nigel was destined to be brought up learning to hate the queen, also. Even as much as Florence disliked Queen Victoria, she found herself becoming weary of hearing about the "wicked woman" from Edgar, and how much he wanted her to suffer for what she did to his father. She really didn't want little Nigel to grow up with this in his ears every day.

One evening after supper when the baby was asleep in bed, the Whitakers sat down in their parlor and Edgar got on his favorite theme, denouncing Queen Victoria. This time it was for influencing Parliament to make British chancellor of the exchequer, Benjamin Disraeli, prime minister of England in the place of Lord Derby, who had to resign the position because of ill health. Edgar had despised Derby's conservatism, and despised Disraeli the more because he was even more conservative.

In the middle of his tirade, Florence raised a palm toward him. "Edgar, this has got to stop!"

Anger seemed to crawl through Edgar Whitaker like a fever. All the bitterness he felt toward Queen Victoria congealed as a hard lump in his chest. Setting his jaw, he glared at Florence with blazing eyes. "What do you mean it's got to stop?"

"You know Victoria is not my favorite person by a long shot, but I'm sick and tired of having to listen to what's wrong with her every day of my life. I don't want Nigel growing up having to listen to it either. It's time you let it go."

"Let it go? I have a right to feel this way about that wicked witch of a woman! It's gonna be in my system until I come up with a way to make her suffer for what she did to my father. If she wasn't so well protected, it would be easy. But I have hopes that one day there will be a proverbial 'crack in the armor,' and I can have my vengeance without having to suffer the consequences like my father did. Understand?"

Florence sighed. "All right. I understand." She knew there was nothing she could do about her husband's deep-rooted bitterness against the queen. Nigel would just have to hear the hatred being spewed out by his father until Edgar could somehow get satisfaction.

Seventeen

In April of 1873, when Nigel Whitaker was five years old, his mother's heart was heavy because the child was already picking up on his father's ingrained bitterness toward Queen Victoria.

Florence remained silent in front of Edgar, but took advantage of private moments with her son to take the edge off the image his father had implanted in his mind about the queen. Nigel seemed confused, but managed to satisfy both parents by his comments when alone with one or the other.

On Friday, April 4, the newspapers came out with the story of a new park that was being opened in the section of London called Hackney. The park was being named Victoria Park in honor of the queen, and the papers reported that she would be on hand when the park would be dedicated on Tuesday, April 8.

Edgar Whitaker read the article in the first edition of the *London Monitor* at his desk before starting his day's work. "So the wicked witch is gonna be there for the dedication, eh?" he said to himself in a low whisper. "Well, maybe that will be my day!"

Edgar's mind went to Derek Smith, a man of the slums whom he had met recently. He had become acquainted with Derek just after the young man had been released from jail after serving a sentence for beating up an elderly man in the slums. This had not been Derek's first time to be arrested for an act of violence. Derek had come into the bank a few days ago to cash his first week's paycheck after landing a laborer's job the first day out of jail.

The teller recognized his face from the newspapers and was hesitant to cash the check. Edgar, who was a bank officer, happened to come behind the tellers' cages, and overheard the teller refusing to cash the check. Edgar had stepped up and told the teller that the account the check was drawn on was good, and he had no reason to refuse to cash it.

When Derek Smith left the teller's window, money in hand, he had come to Edgar's desk and thanked him, saying if he could ever do anything for him to let him know. He even wrote his address on a sheet.

Edgar ran into Derek on the street a couple of days after the check cashing incident, and while they were in conversation, Edgar made a disparaging comment about the queen. Derek let it be known that he also held discontent and agitation toward Queen Victoria—as did many in the slums, who blamed her for their impoverished state of life. Before they parted, Derek had once again told Edgar if he could ever do anything for him, to let him know.

Edgar laid the newspaper down on his desk and chuckled to himself. "You have violence in your blood, Derek ol' boy. I indeed need a favor, and you're just the man to do it. Let's see if you'll keep your word."

That night after eating supper, Edgar told Florence he had to go out for a while. She was used to his doing things he never explained and quietly watched him go out the door.

Thirty minutes later, Edgar approached the run-down flat where Derek Smith lived and climbed the rickety stairs to the third floor. As he drew up to the door of flat 310, he heard a baby crying inside.

He tapped on the door. When the door swung open, Derek smiled broadly.

"Well, I declare! It's banker Whitaker. What can I do for you?"

"Derek, who is it?" came a feminine voice from the rear of the flat, above the crying of the baby.

"I need to talk to you in private!" whispered Edgar. "It's about that favor you said you'd do for me. Something important, but very private."

Derek turned and called over his shoulder. "It's a friend, honey. We have some private business. I'll be back in a few minutes."

There was only the baby's crying. Derek's wife did not respond.

Stepping into the hall and closing the door behind him, Derek kept his voice low. "Never can be sure of privacy in here. Let's go outside."

They went down the stairs then out the front door of the building. Derek led Edgar around the corner of the building into the shadows between it and the next flat. A nearby street lamp provided enough light for them to see each other as they talked.

Speaking in a low tone, Derek said, "So what's this very important favor you need me to perform?"

"It has to do with the queen," said Edgar. "She needs to learn a lesson, and I've got a way to do it. It'll make you happy, I guarantee it. And it'll make me happy."

Derek grinned. "I'm listening."

Edgar brought up the new park in Hackney that was to be named after Queen Victoria and dedicated in her honor on the following Tuesday. As he was explaining his plan, neither man was aware of a middle-aged couple who were watching them from their window on the second floor of Derek's flat.

"There'll be a huge crowd there, Derek," said Edgar. "A smart guy like you could put a bullet in Victoria and get away before anybody could catch you."

A grin spread over Derek's mouth. "It could be done. And she deserves it."

"You know how to use a revolver?"

"Does the Thames River run through London?"

"I guess I've got my answer." As he spoke, he pulled a .45 caliber military officer's revolver from his hip pocket. "Here. It's fully loaded. In addition to the joy you'll have doing this, I'll pay you a hundred pounds."

Derek took the gun, and Edgar pulled a folded wad of bills from his shirt pocket. Slipping it into his other hand, he said, "When you've gotten away, toss the gun into the Thames."

"All right. A hundred pounds. Wow! That's more than I make in a month on my job. I can really use the money. I don't know how to thank you!"

"Putting the wicked witch in her grave will be thanks enough for me." With that, Edgar wheeled, hurried to the sidewalk, and disappeared into the night.

On the second floor, Arthur and Alfreda Downing watched Derek slip the revolver under his belt at the center of his back and round the corner of the building.

"I wish we had been able to hear what Derek and the other man were saying, Arthur," said Alfreda.

"Me, too," said Arthur. "For sure, they're up to no good. But since we don't know what, I guess we'd better stay out of it. One thing we don't want to do is get Derek mad at us. You know what's happened to other people who irritated him."

"Yes. We'd better just leave it alone."

On April 8, a huge crowd was gathered along the streets of Hackney and inside the park, as the royal carriage drew near. Victoria was seated on the rear seat with Bertie and Alexandra, waving at the cheering people.

It had been over eleven years since Albert had died, and Victoria had missed him every day. She especially missed him when she attended some public function. Even though she was always surrounded by her guards, there was a small feeling of insecurity.

Nearing the entrance to the park, Victoria thought about the times that Albert protected her, putting his own life at risk. Having him sit or stand beside her at events like the one about to take place always caused her heart to swell with pride and thanksgiving to the

Lord for the husband He had chosen for her.

Inside the park, Derek Smith was in the crowd, as close as possible to the spot where the dedication ceremony would be conducted by Hackney's mayor, Melvin Faber.

Derek had put a bandage on his face, making it look like he had been badly burned. Barely more than his eyes and mouth were showing. On his head was a hat that would make his appearance even more obscure. He did his best to keep from looking straight at anyone. From the corner of his eye, he watched a mother with a small child in her arms. She was no more than three steps from him. He figured the little girl was about a year old.

Derek noted the queen's carriage as it was pulling into the park, sided by her guards. The revolver was tucked under his belt and covered with a light sweater. When he saw that the queen was most vulnerable, he would shoot her then grab the baby girl from the mother's arms, put the gun to her head, and make the guards and everybody else understand that he would kill the baby if anybody followed him. He would then make his getaway with the queen lying dead behind him.

When he had reached the spot in an alley in the slums where he had stashed another set of clothes, he would take off the bandage, make the change, leave the baby, and run down the alley. Carrying the clothes and bandage with the gun hidden in his belt under the sweater, he would make his way to the Thames River. There, when no one was looking, he would throw it all in the river. He would be a free man, the queen would be dead, many of the people in the slums would rejoice, and his banker friend would be happy.

As the carriage drew up to the roped-off spot where the ceremony was to take place, Victoria saw Mayor Melvin Faber and his staff waiting for her. A small brass band was there. It was a beautiful April afternoon, and the crowd was welcoming her enthusiastically, but Victoria felt an uneasiness, though she knew not why. When the carriage drew to a stop and the mayor was walking toward her, she glanced at Bertie and Alexandra in the seat beside her, then ran her gaze over the guards, checking their positions.

Relieved that all seemed well, Victoria silently chided herself for being a worrywart. *God has always taken care of you, Victoria, and He is still in control.*

People in the crowd were shouting, "God bless you!" to their queen, and the band struck up a lively tune.

Bertie stepped out of the carriage, and when Victoria stood up to take his hand, Derek Smith saw her as a perfect target. Just as he was about to speedily pull the gun from under his belt, two young boys were playfully chasing each other through the crowd. Derek did not see them, but when he whipped out the revolver and eared back the hammer, he took aim at the queen's heart, and one of the boys bumped into him.

The gun fired, sending the bullet harmlessly into a tree, splattering bark in every direction.

Men in the crowd pounced on Derek, taking the gun from his grasp and pinning him to the ground. The queen's guards were there in a flash and cuffed his hands behind his back.

Everyone heard the chief guard tell two of his men to take the gunman to police headquarters. The guard then hurried to Victoria, who now was seated on one of the chairs taken from the dedication spot. Bertie was on one side of her, and the mayor on the other. The chief guard made sure the queen knew the would-be assassin was on his way to jail.

Leaning down and putting an arm around his mother's shoulder, Bertie said, "I'm sorry about this, Mother. We'll take you home."

"Oh no," said the queen. "I'm all right. Strange, but I have to say this attempt on my life is almost not a surprise. I…I had an inkling of some kind that all was not right. But, praise the Lord, He took care of me once again." Then she said to the mayor, "As far as I'm concerned, we can go on with the ceremony."

The dedication ceremony proceeded, with many in the crowd thanking God their queen was spared once again from an assassination attempt.

At police headquarters, Derek Smith sat in a small room with Chief of Police Silas Altman and Captain Frank Blume grilling him.

Though he tried to make them believe he had done it on his own, they were finally able to break him down and make him admit he was paid to do it.

When Altman offered to see to it that the judge would go easier on him—even with his police record—if he would give them the name of the man who paid him to shoot the queen, he gave in and named Edgar Whitaker.

It was late afternoon. Edgar Whitaker was seated at his desk in Barings Bank, talking with a customer. Edgar noticed two policemen enter the bank and enter the office of bank president, Lester Stockman.

Minutes later as his customer was leaving, Edgar saw the two police officers come out of the president's office with Lester Stockman behind them. They were headed straight toward Edgar, and Stockman stepped ahead of the officers, arriving at Edgar's desk a few steps ahead of them.

"Edgar," said Stockman, "these officers want to talk to you in my office."

Edgar frowned. "What about?"

"We'll explain that in Mr. Stockman's office, sir," said Officer Earl Shevlin.

Edgar's stomach went sour as he walked into the president's office with Lester Stockman at his side, preceded by Officer Wade Kirtland and followed by Officer Earl Shevlin.

When Shevlin closed the door, Kirtland set steady eyes on Edgar and said crisply, "You are under arrest for conspiracy to assassinate Queen Victoria."

Before Edgar could find his voice, Shevlin said, "Your accomplice tried to shoot the queen, but he missed. We've got him in jail. With a little persuasive bargaining, he confessed that he was hired by you to kill the queen and that you even supplied the revolver."

Horror washed over Edgar Whitaker. His face contorted as he batted his eyes in a gesture of innocence. "I have no idea what you're talking about. Who is this liar?"

"You know it's Derek Smith," said Kirtland.

Edgar shook his head. "I don't know any Derek Smith."

"He says different. Let's go."

Edgar was taken to police headquarters and questioned by Chief Altman but still denied he knew Derek Smith, and that he had hired him to kill the queen.

Derek was brought in to face Edgar, but even though Derek told his story in front of Edgar while looking him in the eye, still Edgar denied the charges.

Derek was taken back to his cell. The grilling continued by Altman, Shevlin, and Kirtland, and when an older officer was brought in and told them that Edgar was the son of the infamous Gordon Whitaker, they put him in a cell. The police talked to people in London who knew Edgar and learned of the hatred he had displayed openly toward Queen Victoria since he was a child.

The story of the assassination attempt came out in the newspapers the next day, telling of Smith's being subdued on the spot and of his indicating Edgar Whitaker as the man who hired him and supplied the revolver. The photographs of both men were on the front page of every newspaper. The story went on to tell that Whitaker was flatly denying the accusation.

Arthur and Alfreda Downing sat at their kitchen table and read the story in the *London Times*. The photograph of Edgar Whitaker confirmed to them that he was indeed the man they saw give Derek the revolver. They left their flat, went to police headquarters, and asked to see Chief Altman.

Ten days later in court, the Downings testified of what they saw in the alley that night, and pointed out Edgar Whitaker as the man they had seen give Derek Smith the revolver.

Both men were convicted in separate trials. Edgar was sentenced to life in prison with no possibility of parole. Derek was also sentenced to life, but for cooperating with the police, had a possibility for parole in twenty-five years if he proved to be a model prisoner.

The day after Edgar was locked up in Newgate Prison, Florence went to visit him. As she sat down and looked at him through the barred window, she saw deep despair on his face.

"Edgar," she said, "I'm not going to scold you for what you did. It won't accomplish anything. I want you to know that I still love you and always will."

Edgar closed his eyes, bit down hard on his lower lip, then opened them. "Where's Nigel?"

"He's home. Your cousin Abigail is staying with him."

"Oh. Well, I appreciate Abigail doing this so you could come and see me."

They talked about Abigail for a moment. She was his father's sister's daughter. That side of the family had suffered a great deal over Gordon's death. Abigail loved her Uncle Gordon and seemed to take it the hardest. She, also, had a burning hatred for Queen Victoria.

Tears filled Florence's eyes as she said, "Edgar, I can't bear the thought of you being in here for the rest of your life. Nigel cried himself to sleep last night wanting to be with you. He can't even comprehend what it means when I try to tell him you won't ever be coming home again."

Edgar's brow puckered and he put trembling fingers to his temples. He was in a cold sweat. "Florence, I wish…I wish they had executed me. I would rather die than be locked up for the rest of my life."

Florence broke down and sobbed, unable to speak. After a few minutes, a guard came and told her that her time was up. She was still weeping when the guard escorted her through the door.

When Florence arrived home, Abigail Clarendon saw the terrible condition she was in and folded her in her arms. While she held her with Nigel looking on, she said, "That wicked queen. She's been the source of pain and misery to this family ever since she took the throne and failed to keep the promises her mother had made to Uncle Gordon. Because of her, Uncle Gordon died in prison and so will Edgar. I hate her!"

As Florence continued to weep, Nigel wrapped his arms around her legs and said, "I hate her, too, Cousin Abigail! I wish I could kill Queen Victoria myself!"

With tears coursing down her cheeks, Florence let go of Abigail, bent down, and took hold of Nigel's shoulders. "Honey, listen to me. Don't talk that way. The queen is a bad woman, but you mustn't ever think about killing her."

Near Cardiff, Wales, fifty-five-year-old John Barlow came home to the Barlow Stables—which he had owned since purchasing it from his parents some twenty years ago.

When he entered the house, carrying the day's edition of the *Cardiff Sentinel,* Amanda was sitting at the kitchen table, holding their little one-year-old grandson Jeremy. The baby clapped his chubby hands together and made a sound with his mouth, smiling at John.

Amanda giggled. "You know, honey, that almost sounded like 'Grandpa.'"

John bent over, kissed Amanda's cheek, and affectionately tousled Jeremy's hair. "Oh, it definitely was Grandpa, wasn't it, little guy?"

Jeremy gurgled.

"See there? He just confirmed it."

"Why, of course," Amanda said, bending over to kiss the top of the baby's head. "And one of these days, you'll learn to say 'Grandma,' won't you, sweetie pie?"

John and Amanda adored little Jeremy. They had legal custody of him because their son Stephen and his wife had died in a boating accident six months ago.

"Did you get everything done in town you needed to?" queried Amanda.

"Yes," he said, then held up the folded newspaper in his hand. "Those two men who conspired to kill Queen Victoria in Hackney were both sentenced to life in prison. Smith has the possibility of parole in twenty-five years if he's a good boy. He cooperated with the police to help them nail Edgar Whitaker."

"Whitaker," Amanda said, shaking her head. "From following the news over the years, I'm really not surprised that Gordon Whitaker's son would carry a grudge against the queen. The family blamed her for Gordon's going bad years ago."

"Mm-hmm. I hope this conviction of Edgar will be the end of it. Well, what's for supper?"

Over supper, John and Amanda discussed once more the day he accompanied the sixteen-year-old Princess Victoria on a horseback ride. Then they talked about the day some thirty years ago when John saved little Vicky's life in Hyde Park and how Queen Victoria had so honored him for it.

They talked about how wonderful it was to have a born-again queen who had done so much to help spread the gospel all over the British Isles, and agreed that they must continue to pray daily asking God to keep her safe from her enemies.

That night, they knelt beside their bed and prayed earnestly for the Lord's protection on the queen. They praised Him for their own salvation in Jesus Christ and thanked Him for a queen who stood so firmly on the Word of God, the truth of the gospel, and the principles of morality.

As the months passed into years, Edgar Whitaker languished in prison, and each time Florence visited him, he seemed more despondent. Florence carried this burden with her, and Nigel saw what it was doing to his mother. This upset the boy deeply, and his hatred toward Queen Victoria grew stronger.

On Thursday, May 3, 1877, nine-year-old Nigel Whitaker stood behind his mother when she answered a knock at the door just before leaving for work that morning. Two prison officials entered at her invitation.

As they removed their caps, one of them said, "Mrs. Whitaker, we come with bad news. Your husband hanged himself last night in his cell. The guards found him dead at dawn this morning."

Both men helped Florence to a chair and stayed with her until her emotions had settled down. When the men left, Nigel stood behind the chair and put his arms around her neck.

While his mother clung to him and sobbed again, Nigel thought of how she had worked so hard to provide for them ever since his father had gone to prison. She had done housework for wealthy people all these years, and on her one day off a week, she had gone to the prison to see his father. He had very little time with her, and this—along with all he had learned about what the queen had done to his grandfather—put even more frustration in his mind.

The boy told himself that someday, some way, Queen Victoria would pay dearly for all the pain she had inflicted on his family.

As the years continued to pass in the following decade, Victoria's other children married and gave her more grandchildren, whom she loved dearly.

In June 1887, Victoria, for the time being, was living at Buckingham Palace.

At the first pink flush of dawn on Monday, June 20, uniformed troops were assembling on the palace grounds and in the adjacent streets. The clopping of cavalry horses' hooves and the scraping of carriage wheels created a ceaseless din.

By six o'clock, a military band was forming, and the soldiers were taking their positions for the great parade that would mark Queen Victoria's Jubilee, the fiftieth anniversary of her accession to the throne.

Over a half-million people were lining the streets to witness the events of the day. Most of them had spent the entire night in the streets in order to be in position to have a good view of the queen's carriage as it made its way from the palace to Westminster Abbey.

In the crowd was nineteen-year-old Nigel Whitaker, with a revolver in his pocket and murder in his heart. He found, however, that security was exceptionally tight. All along the parade route, police scrutinized the crowds, watchful for foreign-looking faces, sullen expressions, or any evidence of dark intent.

During her fifty years on the throne, the queen had escaped the hands of assassins six times. The police who patrolled the streets and the palace guards who flanked the royal carriage were in firm agreement that there must be no incidents.

It was just after ten o'clock when the queen's royal carriage came through the gate with her mounted guards surrounding her. In the carriage with her were Vicky and Helena and three grandchildren.

Just as the carriage turned onto the street, Victoria saw two familiar faces on the edge of the crowd. John and Amanda Barlow smiled and waved to her. Victoria called for the driver to stop the carriage and motioned for the Barlows to come to her. With them was fifteen-year-old Jeremy. When they drew up to the side of the carriage, John and Jeremy bowed in respect to their queen, and Amanda made a deep curtsy.

"Your Majesty," said John, "it is so nice to see you again. We weren't sure you would recognize us after all these years. This is our grandson, Jeremy."

Victoria greeted Jeremy warmly, saying what a fine looking boy he was. "John, Amanda, neither of you have changed much. I would know you anywhere." She turned to her oldest daughter. "Vicky, this is John Barlow. Does that name mean anything to you?"

Vicky's eyes misted. "Oh, my! John Barlow! You saved my life. Thank you."

As she spoke, Vicky leaned toward John, opened her arms, and hugged him. John patted her back, then said, "You don't remember her, but this is my wife, Amanda."

After Vicky had hugged Amanda, she introduced them to her sister. Helena greeted them and said, "I want to thank you, too, Mr. Barlow, for saving Vicky's life. My mother often mentions you and Mrs. Barlow."

"John and Amanda," said the queen, "we have to get the parade under way. It has been far too long since we have had a chance to visit. Could you come to Buckingham Palace tomorrow evening for dinner? And Jeremy, too, of course."

John and Amanda, a bit taken aback by the invitation, nodded at each other. "Your Majesty, we would love to."

"Good," said the queen, a smile creasing her round and wrinkled face. I will alert the guards at the gate and have the cooks prepare a very special meal. Dinner will be at eight."

"We will be there, Your Majesty," said John. "We are deeply honored."

"My children and I will be there, too, Mr. Barlow," said Vicky. "We are here from Prussia for the big celebration, and are staying at the palace. It will be nice to get to know you better."

"We'll look forward to it, dear," said Amanda.

Victoria smiled at the Barlows again. "Until then." She motioned to the driver, and the smile lingered on her face as the carriage pulled away.

Flanked by the guards, the carriage quickly met up with the marching band, and soon the parade was underway.

Soon the marching band reached the spot where Nigel Whitaker stood in the crowd. He ran his eyes over the beefed-up unit of guards around the queen's carriage and decided this was not the time. He would not chance it today. But someday he would make her pay for what she had done to the Whitaker family—especially his father and grandfather.

Eighteen

Five years later.

On January 14, 1892, Albert Victor, Bertie's oldest son— called Eddy—died at the age of twenty-eight. Queen Victoria's grief was heavy and the story of her grief, along with that of Eddy's parents and the rest of the family, was reported in the newspapers.

Eddy's death put Bertie and Alexandra's second son, George Frederick, in line for the throne after his father. They talked about when he became king, he would be known as King George V.

On July 6, 1893, George Frederick married Princess Victoria Mary of Teck.

Thirty-two years had passed since the queen's beloved Albert had gone home to be with the Lord. The years had been kind to her, and she enjoyed her large family. Now living most of the time at Buckingham Palace, Victoria kept a sizable painting of Albert above the fireplace in her private quarters. Daily, as her gaze rested on his handsome face, she still felt the tug of love in her heart.

Since becoming queen of England, Victoria had been extremely involved in other people's lives and even more so since Albert's death.

Yet deep in her innermost being, she had lived each day since Albert had been taken from her with a yawning void in her life. Her days and most nights were filled with activities of various kinds, as well as meetings with Parliament, discussing subjects of national import, and making consequential decisions that affected the nation. But when she pillowed her head each night, a loneliness engulfed her. Albert, indeed, had been the love of her life.

On July 23, 1894, Prince Edward Albert was born to George Frederick and Mary, and they dubbed him "David." When the news came to great-grandmother Victoria, she was elated. It especially meant a lot because the "Albert" in his name was after his great-grandfather.

A few days after David's birth, the royal carriage pulled up in front of George and Mary's home, and while the chief guard helped Victoria down, Mary stood at the window. The great-grandmother had asked if she might come and see David before Mary's physician would allow him to be taken from the house. Mary met Victoria at the door, and welcomed her warmly with a hug and a kiss on the cheek.

"Oh, I can hardly wait to see him!"

Mary put an arm around her. "Well, let's go. He's in his cradle in the nursery."

When they entered the nursery, the baby's governess was there. She curtsied to the queen, and excused herself saying she knew Her Majesty would like to see David for the first time with just his mother.

The baby was asleep in his white cradle that was draped with gossamer curtains. Quietly, Victoria approached the cradle and looked on the sleeping infant. A sharp gasp escaped her lips, and she quickly raised a hand to her mouth.

"What is it, Mother?" asked Mary, moving up beside her and laying a hand on her shoulder. "Are you all right?"

The queen turned misty eyes toward Mary. "Yes, dear. I'm fine. I was just so startled to see how very much he resembles his great-grandfather." Victoria gently ran a finger over David's downy head. "I love you, little man. We'll have many wonderful times together."

⤞⤝

Another year passed, and early on a warm June evening in 1895, in Cardiff, Wales, nineteen-year-old Cecelia Parker was in her second-floor bedroom of the fashionable Parker home.

There was a tap on her door. She recognized the maid's knock, and said, "Yes, Angie?"

The door came open. "Mr. Gibson is here, mum."

"Thank you. Tell him I'll be right down."

Cecelia rushed to the mirror and checked her hair. She and Royce Gibson had been dating for over a year, and both had declared their love for each other. She was expecting him to propose soon and had her "yes" ready.

Often of late, she had practiced in front of the mirror, the way she would make her facial expression when Royce proposed, and exactly how she would say yes.

Cecelia descended the winding staircase almost as if she had wings, with a smile on her face. Her parents looked on with joy as their daughter and her suitor embraced discreetly. They were going out to dinner, then to a concert.

"You children have a wonderful time," said Alvera, waving as they headed for the door.

"We will," said Royce, holding Cecelia's hand.

"But please be home by midnight, honey," said Donald.

"I'll have her home by then, I promise, sir," Royce said as he opened the door.

Both parents waved, and the happy couple were out the door.

Donald and Alvera Parker walked to the vestibule window and watched Royce help Cecelia into his carriage. As they drove away, Alvera said, "Papa, I'm sure that young man is going to propose soon."

"Maybe even tonight," said Donald.

That evening after the concert, which had taken place in the open air at a large park, Royce pulled his pocket watch from his vest and looked at it by the light of a nearby lantern. "It's a quarter after ten, pretty lady. Could we take a stroll down the path that leads through the park? I can still have you home easily before midnight."

"Sounds good to me," she said, showing her beautiful set of snow white teeth in a warm smile.

Arm in arm, they moved down the path, and soon they were away from the crowd that was still milling about the orchestra pavilion. Moments later, they sat down on a bench in the moonlight.

Cecelia noticed Royce become a bit nervous as he looked into her eyes and said, "Darling, I love you with all of my heart."

"And I you," she cooed with a dreamy look in her violet eyes.

He took hold of her hand. "I can't wait any longer. Cecelia, will you marry me?"

Thrilled that the moment had finally come, Cecelia completely forgot the facial expression and vocal tone she had rehearsed. Tears moistened her eyes. "Oh, Royce, my love, yes I will marry you!"

Royce produced an engagement ring from his shirt pocket and slipped it on the third finger of her left hand. "Then it is official. The beautiful Miss Cecelia Parker will become Mrs. Royce Gibson."

They kissed tenderly.

Royce caressed her cheek. "I think we should set a wedding date within a couple of weeks."

"I agree," she breathed.

"As you know, I am my parents' only son and the only one who can carry on the family name. Since Dad owns a string of department stores all over Wales, which he inherited from my Grandfather Gibson, and since I am vice president of the corporation, my parents want me to produce a son who can carry on the Gibson family tradition."

"Of course," said Cecelia. "I understand, and I will be proud to bear you children. And especially a son who can carry on the Gibson family tradition."

Cecelia's parents were ecstatic when she returned home, ran up the stairs, told them that Royce had proposed, and showed them the engagement ring.

Royce's parents and the Donald Parkers had dinner together two nights later to celebrate the engagement. Two weeks later, the young couple set their wedding date for Saturday, September 14.

One evening the next week, when Royce and Cecelia were riding around Cardiff in his carriage, he smiled at her and said, "You know that little favor I've been asking of you?"

"Oh. You mean about learning to ride a horse?"

"Mm-hmm."

Royce was an ardent horseman and had been trying to get Cecelia to learn to ride so they could go riding together, but she had held back because she had never been on a horse and was a bit intimidated by them.

By the light of a street lamp they were passing, Cecelia looked at the diamond sparkling on her left hand, then set her eyes on Royce. "Well, since you love horseback riding so very much, and we are soon to be husband and wife, I guess I'd better give in. All right, darling, I'll go riding with you."

"Good! How about on Saturday?"

"Saturday it is."

On Saturday morning, August 10, Royce and Cecelia were in his carriage, heading out of the city into the beautiful countryside.

"So, this Barlow's Stables is where you always go riding, Royce?" said Cecelia.

"Yes. It's the best in Wales. It's only about ten miles out of Cardiff. Fellow named John Barlow owns the place. His grandson, Jeremy, works with him. Actually, Jeremy's parents died when he was just a baby and his paternal grandparents adopted him. Nice family."

Secretly, Cecelia was feeling fear, but she told herself she would have to get over it. Since Royce loved horses so much, she would have to conquer her fear of them.

Soon they pulled onto the Barlow property and headed for the barn and stables. Seventy-seven-year-old John Barlow and Jeremy Barlow, who was twenty-three, welcomed them. Royce introduced his bride-to-be to both men and explained that he wanted her to learn to ride so they could spend much time riding together.

Cecelia stood in dread as she watched the three men saddle the horses.

Jeremy said, "Royce, usually when more than one person goes riding, I go along as an escort. Would you like me to ride with you and Miss Cecelia?"

Cinching up Cecelia's sidesaddle, Royce said, "That won't be necessary. Even though she has never ridden a horse before, I'm quite well experienced, as you know. I can take care of her."

"All right," said Jeremy, smiling.

Royce checked the sidesaddle and found it secured tightly to the mare's body. He turned to Cecelia. "Okay, future Mrs. Gibson, let's go."

Royce hoisted Cecelia into the saddle, showed her how to sit and how to hold the reins. He explained how to start and stop the mare and how to steer with the reins.

Royce swung aboard the black gelding, and he saw that Cecelia was nervous. "Now, sweetie, you just relax. You'll be fine."

As Royce and Cecelia trotted out of the corral onto the open fields, Jeremy said, "Grandpa, I hope he keeps a close watch on her. She's really scared."

Less than a half hour later, John and Jeremy were working on one of the corral gates when Jeremy looked up and said, "Uh-oh."

John's head came up. They saw Royce riding in, holding Cecelia in his arms, the mare trailing behind.

"She's hurt, Grandpa."

"Looks like it."

As Royce reined his horse to a stop with Cecelia in his arms, it was evident that she was in extreme pain.

"What happened?" asked John.

"Her horse shied at a fox that sprang out from behind a tree, and she fell out of the saddle. Her left leg is hurting her."

Jeremy stepped up and said, "Would you like me to take her down for you?"

"Sure."

Raising his arms, Jeremy said, "I'll be careful, Miss Cecelia. Just lean toward me."

Gritting her teeth from the pain, Cecelia did as she was told, and found herself resting in Jeremy's strong arms.

Dismounting, Royce said, "Let's put her in the carriage. I'll take her to St. John's Hospital."

Royce and John followed as Jeremy carried the lovely young woman to the carriage. Jeremy eased her onto the seat, then turned to Royce. "If you don't mind, I'll follow along on my horse. I'd like to know the extent of the damage."

"Of course," said Royce, climbing in beside Cecelia, who was gripping her left leg with both hands. "I appreciate your concern."

At the hospital, Royce and Jeremy jumped to their feet in the waiting room when Dr. Paul Ralston came in, wearing the customary white frock.

"I'm glad to tell you, Mr. Gibson, that your young lady's leg is not broken."

"Oh good," said Royce.

"God be praised," said Jeremy.

Ralston rubbed the back of his neck. "However, the fall might have done some damage to her internal organs. I want to keep her here a couple of days for observation."

"Could this be serious, Doctor?" asked Royce.

"Well, yes, it could. There are two other doctors here who will keep an eye on her as well as myself."

Royce nodded solemnly. "All right, Doctor. I'll go inform her parents that she's in here."

"I'll come and check on her tomorrow, Royce," said Jeremy.

When he arrived at the hospital the next morning, Royce sought out Dr. Ralston immediately. He found him in his office with another physician, whom he introduced as Dr. Shelby Evans, a prominent gynecologist. In a grave tone, he explained that Dr. Evans had just examined Cecelia.

A worried look captured Royce's face. "What's wrong?"

Evans set solemn eyes on Royce. "Dr. Ralston tells me you and Miss Parker are getting married next month."

"Yes, sir. What's wrong?"

"Cecelia was awake most of the night with pain in her midsection," said Ralston. "I sent for Dr. Evans at dawn. He did an examination and found that she indeed has been injured internally."

Royce looked at Evans. "To what extent, Doctor?"

Evans took a deep breath. "It's not good news, Mr. Gibson. Miss Parker may never be able to give birth to children as a result of this injury. There could be a slim chance, but I seriously doubt it. Dr. Ralston and another physician here in the hospital concur."

Royce put a hand to his forehead.

"Miss Parker's parents are with her right now, Mr. Gibson," said Dr. Ralston. "They're trying to comfort her. She's very upset."

Royce nodded, his features displaying the mental agony he was experiencing.

"We'll have to keep her here a few more days for treatment," Dr. Evans said. "I'm sure she needs comfort from you, too. She's in room 212."

"I'll go up right now."

Royce was drawing up to room 212 as the door opened and Donald and Alvera Parker came out, closing the door behind them. Alvera's eyes were red and swollen from weeping. Donald had an arm around her. They stopped as they saw Royce coming toward them.

"I just talked to Drs. Ralston and Evans," said Royce. "They told me the bad news. How's she doing?"

"Not very well," said Donald. "She really needs to see you. She's afraid now that you won't want to marry her."

Royce gave them a grim smile. "I'll talk to her."

"We'll be back to see her this evening," said Alvera, and with Donald's arm still around her, they went away.

Royce looked at the door, and wished he didn't have to go in. He stood there, berating himself for pressuring her into going horseback riding.

He braced himself for what he knew he had to do. He could not disappoint his parents and family. He must produce an heir to carry on the Gibson name and family tradition in the department store business.

It would have been a good marriage, he thought. *Even though I don't love her as I have said to her, I could have grown quite fond of her. But my reason for wanting to marry her was because she is beautiful, comes from a wealthy family, and could bear me sons and daughters.*

Royce knew what he had to do would not be easy, and he really disliked hurting Cecelia. With a deep sigh, he pushed the door open and entered the room.

Cecelia was lying flat on her back in the bed, and when she saw Royce, tears flooded her eyes and she reached for him.

Unable to touch her, Royce stopped short of the bed. "Cecelia, I'm sorry this has happened to you, but I have to be honest. I can't marry you now. My family would never forgive me if I didn't produce a son to carry on the Gibson name and tradition."

Cecelia stared at him in disbelief. "But…but you love me. How can you just dump me like this?"

There was a brief moment of silence as Royce stared at the floor. Then looking at her again, he said, "I can't do this to my family."

With that, he wheeled and headed for the door.

Suddenly the engagement ring he had given Cecelia sailed past him, struck the wall, and clattered to the floor. He stopped, squaring his shoulders and facing the door.

"You heartless beast! I never want to lay eyes on you again! Since you can so easily dump me, I know now that you really didn't love me! You just wanted the children I could give you."

Royce pulled the door open and walked out of the room without looking back.

Early that afternoon, Jeremy Barlow entered Cecelia's room and stepped up to the bed. "So how's the patient doing?"

Cecelia's lower lip quivered. "Not so good."

A frowned creased Jeremy's brow. "I'm sorry. You're hurt worse than we thought? Is it the internal organ damage that Dr. Ralston spoke of?"

"Yes, but I'm hurting worse in my heart than my body."

"What do you mean? That is, if it's any of my business. I realize you don't know me."

"I know you well enough."

Jeremy listened intently as Cecelia explained the doctors' diagnosis concerning her ever being able to bear children, then told him what had happened when Royce learned of it.

"He…he called off the wedding because it's doubtful you can give him the son he and his family say they can't live without?"

"Yes," she said, tears filming her eyes.

Laying a hand on her forearm, Jeremy said, "Miss Cecelia, I'm so sorry you've had your heart broken like this. But if Royce could throw you away on that account, he really didn't love you. It's better that you found out now, than after you were married."

"You're right about that," she agreed. "But it hurts to know that he really didn't love me."

"Of course. You were prepared to live your whole life with him. Since you found out in time that he didn't love you, now you can find that young man who will really love you and make you a good husband."

Cecelia's lip stopped quivering. "You really think so?"

"Sure. A young lady as lovely and charming as you are isn't going to be an old maid."

She let her lips make a smile. "Thank you, Jeremy. You are a real encouragement."

"I certainly want to be. How much longer will you be in the hospital?"

"I'm not sure. It will be up to Drs. Ralston and Evans."

Jeremy bent a little lower over her. "Would it be all right if I pray for you before I go?"

Cecelia was a bit surprised at this. "Why, yes. I would appreciate it."

Jeremy bowed his head, closed his eyes, and prayed earnestly for Cecelia, asking God to heal the injuries she had sustained in the fall from the horse, and asked Him to encourage her in this time of heartache brought on by the jolt of being forsaken by Royce Gibson.

He closed his prayer in Jesus' name and was pleased to see that she was smiling at him.

"That was very kind of you, Jeremy," she said. "I've never had anybody pray for me before. In fact, except for a funeral I attended once, I've never heard anyone pray."

"Really? You and your family don't attend church anywhere?"

"No."

"Do you understand that God's only begotten Son, the Lord Jesus Christ, came into the world to save sinners?"

"Well, I've heard that. Usually at Christmastime."

"But that's as far as you've gone with it?"

"I guess you'd say that."

"Would you like to hear more about Jesus?"

"Yes, I would."

"All right. I have to meet my dad at the saddle and harness shop in a few minutes, but I'll be back to see you tomorrow. I'll bring my Bible and show you things you really need to know."

Feeling more at ease with Jeremy than she ever had with Royce, Cecelia said, "I'll look forward to it."

As he walked out of the hospital, Jeremy was happy that though Cecelia was not a Christian, she was not antagonistic toward the things of the Lord. In his heart, he asked the Lord to give him wisdom as he presented the gospel to her the next day.

Cecelia was in the hospital for five more days. Jeremy visited her every day for approximately an hour, giving her the gospel and reading Scriptures to her. On the second day, he brought her a small bouquet of wild flowers. On the third day, he brought her a box of cookies that his grandmother had baked, and on the fourth day, he presented her with a book of poems. She was delighted with each gift and thanked him with deep appreciation.

Each day, Cecelia had looked forward to Jeremy's visits, and was glad to be learning more about the Son of God and what He had done for her at Calvary.

On the last day, Cecelia's parents arrived to take her home just after Jeremy had spent his hour with her. They told him how much they appreciated the way he had encouraged their daughter, and told him he was welcome to come by the house anytime. Cecelia asked him to come soon.

The very next day, Jeremy showed up at the Parker home in midafternoon and was warmly welcomed. Cecelia told Jeremy right in front of her parents that she had shared with them some of the things about Jesus Christ that he had taught her, and they also had shown interest and wanted to know more.

Jeremy told her he just happened to have his Bible out in the buggy and hurried out to get it. The Parkers listened closely as Jeremy gave them passage after passage that dealt with sin, salvation, heaven, and hell, then took them to the cross and made clear exactly why God had sent His Son into the world.

Within another week, Jeremy led Cecelia to the Lord, and three days later, he had the joy of leading her parents.

The Parkers were baptized in the Bible-believing church where the Barlows were members, and soon became close friends with John and Amanda.

Jeremy and Cecelia began to feel an attraction for each other and were together much of the time.

As time passed, Jeremy knew in his heart that he had fallen in love with Cecelia, and felt that she was also in love with him. Wanting to be perfectly honest with her, on a cool night in late September, he took her for a carriage ride into the country after they had dined together in a Cardiff restaurant.

A crystal-clear full moon was spraying silver light on the land from the star-bedecked sky, and Jeremy pulled the carriage to a halt beside a small, gurgling stream. Turning to her as she tugged her collar up close around her neck, he used the pet name he now called her. "Celie, there is something I have been wanting to tell you. I've been waiting for just the right time, and this is it."

Moonlight danced in her eyes. "Yes, Jeremy?"

"Well, you see, I have an uncle in America who owns a stable just like my grandfather's. Uncle Jack Barlow. Actually, he is my great-uncle. He is my grandfather's younger brother."

"Uh-huh."

"Uncle Jack plans to retire when he turns seventy in early 1897."

"I see," said Cecelia. She had hoped Jeremy was going to tell her he was in love with her.

"Uncle Jack and his wife, Dorine, are sweet Christian people, Celie. You see…I—" He cleared his throat nervously. "I am already slated to go to America and take over the stable for him. It's located just outside Philadelphia, Pennsylvania, and is doing quite well. The plan is that one day, I will own it."

A cold hand seemed to squeeze Cecelia's backbone. "I…I see."

As a new Christian, Cecelia wasn't sure what she should do or say. She knew she had fallen in love with Jeremy, but told herself that she must have misread the signals she thought he was giving her. In her sore heart, she said, *Dear Lord, please help me.*

"Yes," Jeremy went on, "Uncle Jack has done very well there, and I figure the stable will only do better as—" He noted the strange look on her face, and it dawned on him that she was not showing interest at all. He looked closely at her. Tears were brimming in her violet eyes and her lips were quivering.

"Wh-what's wrong, Celie? Why are you crying?"

She looked at him, love shining through the mist of tears.

"Oh, my. Oh, my," he said. "I'm so dumb. I'm getting the cart before the horse. I didn't mean that I am going off to America and leave you." He took her hands in his. "I want you to go with me to America as my wife. I—I—oh, I am so dumb! Celie, I had this all planned and scripted in my mind. Boy, have I messed up. Precious lady, I am head over heels in love with you, and I'm asking you to marry me and go with me to America when the time is right for Uncle Jack's retirement. Will you?"

While tears spilled down her cheeks, Cecelia said, "Oh, my darling Jeremy, I'm head over heels in love with you, too…but—"

"But what?"

"Are you sure you really want me? I won't be able to give you any children."

"Sweetheart, I love children, but that doesn't make any difference. I'm in love with you, and I want you to be my wife. Maybe we can adopt a child once we are settled in Pennsylvania."

A glowing smile caressed her face. "That would be wonderful. I do want children in our home."

"Great! Will it…will it bother you to go to America with me? I mean, leaving your parents and friends?"

She squeezed his hands. "Jeremy, won't I say in the wedding vow, 'Whither thou goest, I will go'?"

"Well, ah…yes. You will say that."

"Then I'm saying it now. Whither thou goest, I will go. Even to Philadelphia, Pennsylvania, U.S.A."

They enjoyed their first sweet, tender kiss.

Jeremy surprised her by taking an engagement ring from his pocket and placing it on her finger. He kissed her again, then said, "All right. It's official. We are engaged."

On Sunday afternoon, June 7, 1896, Jeremy and Cecelia were married, and plans were that they would take a ship for America in February 1897.

Nineteen

On September 23, 1896, Queen Victoria reached a milestone. She noted in her journal: "Today is the day on which I have reigned longer, by a day, than any English sovereign."

She now had her mantelpiece in the drawing room at Buckingham Palace crowded with photographs of grandchildren and great-grandchildren.

Though Victoria dearly loved all of her grandchildren and great-grandchildren, there was one great-grandchild who was the apple of her eye: little David—Prince Edward. She doted on the child, spending as much time with him as his parents would allow.

When newspaper reporters came to Buckingham Palace on September 24 for an interview with the queen concerning the milestone she had passed the day before, she managed to bring up little David, saying he was "a most attractive little boy, and so forward and clever for a two-year-old child."

On September 25, Nigel Whitaker—now twenty-eight—read the milestone article in the *London Times* to his wife, Portia, whom he had married the previous year.

Portia's father owned a large manufacturing plant in New York City, and had offered his son-in-law a good job. They were planning to leave for America aboard the British ocean liner *Victoria* on Wednesday, February 10, 1897. They had not purchased their tickets, but were planning to do so in the next few days. They were looking forward to their new life in America.

Portia had been persuaded by Nigel that Queen Victoria was a wicked, heartless woman, and the proof was what she did to his father and grandfather.

After he had read the article to Portia, Nigel laid down the paper. "I had about given up on getting even with the queen before we left for America, but there's a chance that I can do it."

"And how is that?" queried Portia.

"You will remember that my twenty-five-year-old second cousin Effie Clarendon came to England from Scotland back in June. You met her."

"Yes."

"Well, Effie is employed at King George Hospital, if you recall."

"Mm-hmm."

"And you will remember I told you that Effie is my grandfather's sister's daughter, and used to live in London, but the family moved to Scotland fifteen years ago."

"Yes. So what is all this leading up to, and how is it going to help you get your vengeance on the queen?"

Nigel grinned. "Just pay attention now. I didn't think to tell you that I ran into Effie day before yesterday, downtown. But she just came to mind as I read you this article. The part about Victoria's adoration for Prince David, her great-grandson."

"I don't understand."

"Hang on. You will. Effie told me she had heard that Prince of Wales George Frederick and his wife are looking for a new governess for their son, Prince David. The governess they had got married and moved away. Effie said George and Mary had looked for a governess at London Orphanage where the royal family usually obtains governesses for their children. But George and Mary had not found one they liked."

"Well, this is interesting, honeylamb. Go on."

"Effie has it in for the queen just like I do, Portia, for what she did to the Whitaker family. She saw how her mother suffered severely, almost losing her mind when her cousin Edgar committed suicide in prison."

"I can understand that. And it was all Victoria's fault."

"Exactly. Well, my plan jelled when I read in the article about Victoria's love for her great-grandson, David."

"Okay. Let's hear it."

"Tell you what," he said, rising from his chair. "I've got to go see Effie. I'll tell you the whole thing once I've talked to her. Be back in a little while."

Two hours later, Nigel returned to an inquisitive Portia, who asked, "So how'd it go with Effie?"

"Excellently, my dear. Come. Sit down, and I'll tell you all about it."

Portia poured tea for both of them then set eager eyes on her husband.

Nigel took a sip of tea. "Effie loved my plan. Believe me, she wants to have revenge on Victoria every bit as much as I do. So here's what's happening. She is going to apply at Prince George's house yet today for the governess job. You see, she has it over most women who work as governesses."

"How's that?"

"She's a certified medical nurse. Most governesses are not qualified nurses. Effie graduated from Florence Nightingale's nursing school at St. Thomas's Hospital here in London in 1893. Since royal governesses get better pay than hospital nurses, Effie will tell George and Mary she wants the job because she needs the extra money. Since they didn't find a suitable governess at London Orphanage, Effie's chances of getting the job are excellent. And there is no way she can be connected to the Whitaker family, because there is no one in London who knows she is related to me."

"That's good."

"Right. And though Effie is a dedicated nurse, her hatred for Victoria and her desire to get even are stronger than her dedication to nursing. If she gets the job, she will be in a perfect position to help you and me carry out my plan, Portia, which is for us to kidnap David."

Portia's eyes widened. "Kidnap Victoria's great-grandson?"

"Yes, indeed! We'll use false names when we purchase our ship tickets and take David aboard as if he is our own son. We'll take him to America with us!"

Portia's mouth was wide open. "Honey, that's brilliant!"

"Thank you," said Nigel. "Since Victoria loves David so much, his disappearance—never to see him again—will deal her misery, sorrow, and heartache which she deserves. She'll finally get her payback for what she did to my father and my grandfather."

"Good! Very good! So what will we do with David when we get him to America? You certainly don't want to keep him with us."

"Oh, of course not. We'll leave him on a doorstep somewhere so he'll have a home. Since he's only two years old, he won't be able to tell them who he is. Victoria says he's clever, but he's not that clever."

Portia laughed. "Hardly. I sure hope Effie gets the governess job. This will be true revenge for you and your family."

That evening, as Nigel and Portia were just sitting down to eat, there was a knock at the door.

"I'll get it," said Nigel, rising from the table.

Seconds later, Portia heard her husband speak Effie's name, followed by happy chatter. She dashed to the front of the house, and as she arrived, Nigel had an arm around his cousin's shoulder.

"Honey, she got the job!" Nigel said excitedly.

"Great!" said Portia, and quickly embraced Effie. "I'm so glad you got the job, Effie. We were just starting to eat supper. How about eating with us? There's plenty."

"I'll just do that," said the tall, slender nurse. "Thank you."

While eating supper, they discussed the queen's feelings toward Prince David, agreeing that to make him disappear and never know whether he was dead or alive would crush her. Effie added that after all she had done to the Whitaker family, it would finally bring at least a measure of justice. When supper was over, they sat down in the parlor to make plans.

After they had gone over what was planned already, Nigel said, "Since the ship leaves on February 10, Effie, you will need to find a way to get David into our hands just before we board the ship."

"Don't you worry," said Effie. "I'll have some time to work on it, and you'll have him at the exact moment you need him."

The next day, Nigel went to the docks and purchased the tickets for New York under the names Scott and Elsa Meador.

On the first day of the new job, Effie Clarendon found herself in a Christian home, which made her quite uncomfortable. But she told herself she could endure it, knowing it would only be until February.

Once David had been kidnapped and taken across the Atlantic Ocean by Nigel and Portia, George and Mary would no longer need a governess. She would go back to work at the hospital, which was always short of nurses.

George and Mary were pleased to see that before Effie put little David to bed on the very first night, he had already attached himself to his new governess. After observing Effie with their son for two weeks, George and Mary sat down with her one night after David was in bed.

"Effie," said George, "Mary and I want you to know how very pleased we are with your work. Our little boy really loves you and this makes us very happy."

"You take such good care of him," said Mary. "Much better than his previous governess. She only took him to Dothan Park once or twice a week in his little wagon. You have taken him every day, and he loves it."

"Was it the distance, mum?" asked Effie. "I mean, the park is only a little more than two blocks from here."

"That may have been it, I'm not sure. Anyway, we're glad you don't mind taking him. He loves to ride in that little four-wheeled wagon, and it's evident he enjoys being with you. We appreciate you very much. And we especially like it that you are a nurse and can effectively treat him whenever he gets a cold, a stomachache, runs a fever, or has other problems that naturally come to children his age."

Effie smiled. "I'm thrilled that you feel this way. I'll do my best to take care of that sweet little boy. I can sure understand why Queen Victoria loves him so much."

"Oh, and speaking of the queen," said Mary, "she has asked to meet you. We have let her know how David has responded to you, and how much we appreciate your work. How about tomorrow?"

Effie knew the day would come when she would have to meet the queen, which to her would be a drudge. But she put on as if she would be honored, and made it appear that she was a bit intimidated by the prospect of being in the queen's presence.

"Don't you let it frighten you, dear," said Mary. "You will find her very sweet and easy to get to know."

Batting her eyes in her pretense, Effie said, "This is what I've been told, mum. But she is the queen. I'll do my best to hold myself together."

"You'll do fine, Effie," said George. "My grandmother really wants to meet you."

Late the next morning, Effie Clarendon was escorted into Buckingham Palace by Prince George and Mary and introduced to the queen.

Effie was carrying David, and after Victoria had welcomed her, she took David from his governess, sat down, and put him on her lap. Even though the queen was very kind to her, Effie felt the hatred burn inside her. As she watched Victoria dote on David, she saw that Nigel was right. When the little prince disappeared, the queen was going to suffer severely.

After kissing her great-grandson, Victoria set her eyes on Effie. "As you know, Effie, George and Mary go to a different church than I do. I haven't had opportunity to visit their church since the new pastor came. Do you like his preaching?"

Effie felt her blood heat up. Sundays were especially difficult for her, since she had to attend church services with George and Mary in order to watch over David. The gospel of Jesus Christ was preached and Effie was miserable during the preaching. She also had a hard time during prayer and Bible reading time in the prince's home.

Putting on a false smile, she said, "Pastor Beemer is a fine preacher, Your Majesty."

"Do you know the Lord Jesus as your Saviour, Effie?" asked the queen.

Effie worked hard to keep her face from flushing, and she was miffed that the queen would have the gall to ask such a question. Forcing a sweetness into her voice, she replied, "No, ma'am, but these kind people have talked to me and explained about salvation. I've been thinking about it."

"Good," said Victoria. "The greatest need in your life is to have Jesus in your heart."

"Yes, ma'am," said Effie, wishing they would leave her alone about it.

The months passed with Effie keeping a guard on her heart against the gospel. As January 1897 came, she and Nigel made their final plans.

On Wednesday morning, February 10, the sky was clear and the air was cold.

Effie's stomach was churning as she was dressing the fair-haired little two-and-a-half-year-old prince in the nursery. She was glad that George and Mary were leaving before she would take David for his wagon ride in the park. They were going to attend a wedding in the city of Stansted, some thirty-five miles north of London.

As she was buttoning David's shirt, she heard footsteps, and the parents came in, already clad in their coats and hats.

"Well," said George, "looks like our big boy is almost dressed."

"Papa!" cried the little prince, smiling at his father.

"And doesn't he look handsome!" said Mary.

"Mama!" cried David, raising his arms to her.

Effie stepped aside, allowing Mary to pick him up.

When Mary kissed his cheek, she frowned and pressed her own cheek to his. "Effie, he feels a little warm. He may be coming down with a cold. Perhaps he should stay in today and not go to the park."

Effie's heart slammed against her ribs. The plan to abduct David wouldn't work if she didn't take him to the park. Nigel was expecting her to have him there. Her mind awhirl, she laid a hand on David's brow. "Oh, mum, I'm sure it's nothing. He is a little warm, but it's probably no more than just one of those things that come and go at his age. I'll keep a close watch on him for the next couple of hours. If he is still warm by then, I won't take him out. He just so much enjoys his rides in the park."

Mary frowned and cocked her head. "Are you all right, dear? You seem a bit nervous."

Effie's heart pounded harder. "Oh yes, mum. I'm just fine."

"Well, all right, but remember if Prince David is still running a fever at all, you are not to take him out today."

"Yes, mum. I'll watch him closely."

Mary kissed David's cheek again. "Be a good boy for your nanny, sweet one. Mama loves you."

George took the child from his mother's arms, nibbled on his ear as he often did, and said, "Papa loves his boy. You and Miss Effie have a nice day together." He nibbled on the ear again.

David giggled at the nibbling, and George handed him to Effie.

The parents walked to the door, turned and looked back, then were gone.

"Whew!" Effie murmured to herself, shaking her head. "That was a close one!"

Effie had given David a small dose of salicylic acid shortly after she fed him breakfast, and by ten o'clock the slight fever was gone.

Her heart was throbbing again as she bundled him up at eleven-thirty, put him in his wagon, and headed down the street. She met and chatted with neighbors, who took the time to pat the little prince's capped head and speak to him.

Effie and Nigel had agreed that they would meet in Dothan Park at a certain spot at noon. They also had agreed what they would do if there were people in that area of the park at that time. But being February and quite cold, they felt there wouldn't be very many people anywhere in the park.

As Effie reached the park, pulling the wagon behind her, she saw a few people walking about, but when she reached the appointed spot, she smiled to herself. No one in sight.

She hauled up beside a large tree and picked David up. "Well, little man, you're about to go on a nice long trip."

At that moment, she saw movement among the trees, and smiled as Nigel came into view. David spotted him and looked a bit apprehensive.

Holding the child tight, Effie said, "David, this nice man is going to take you for a walk. He loves little boys like you."

Her words had the designed effect on the little blond prince, and as a smiling Nigel held out his arms to him, he smiled back and said, "Nice man."

"Thanks, Effie," Nigel said, looking around to make sure no one was near. "We'll finally get our revenge. Portia's waiting at the docks. I don't know if I'll ever see you again. Take care of yourself."

Nigel hurried away with the child in his arms and soon disappeared amid the trees.

Running a panorama of the area to make sure she was alone, Effie stepped up to the big tree, took a deep breath, and began slamming her face against the trunk. After a few seconds, she felt her face to see if blood was running. There was a little, but not enough. She banged her face against the rough bark repeatedly until the blood was flowing freely.

With pain throbbing in her jaws, cheeks, and forehead, she dropped to the ground beside the little wagon and began crawling across the tawny grass toward the street.

Moments later, when she crawled onto the sidewalk at the curb, a man spotted her and came running. Kneeling down, he said, "Ma'am, what happened to you?"

Acting dazed, Effie put a wheeze in her voice. "Police…I need the police."

"You stay right here, ma'am," said the man, rising to his feet. "I'll find a bobby."

Effie saw both men and women looking on, and two of the women came and bent over her.

"What happened to you dear?" queried one.

"Police," gasped Effie. "Th-that man is…going after a police-man."

"She's in shock, Esther," said the other.

Suddenly they heard galloping hooves on the paved street. Esther looked up and said, "Here's your policeman, dear."

The man who had gone after the bobby was running toward the scene as the officer dismounted and knelt beside Effie.

"Oh, my," he said as he focused on her bleeding face. "Somebody really worked you over, ma'am. I sent another officer to get a police wagon so we can take you to the hospital. Who are you? Who did this to you?"

"My…name…is Effie Clarendon, sir. I am…governess of Prince George of Wales' two-year-old son, David."

"Prince David!" gasped the officer.

"Yes. I…regularly take him for a…ride in his little wagon here in the park. Prince David and I were back there in the trees…and a man suddenly came up…behind me and slammed my face hard against a tree. He did it…several times. I must have gone uncon-scious. When I woke up…the wagon was still there, but Prince David was gone. Oh, what am I going to do?"

"We'll take you to King George Hospital, Miss Clarendon, and we'll send an officer to advise Prince George and his wife what's hap-pened."

Effie swallowed hard. "Prince George and Mary aren't home, sir. They are in Stansted for the day."

"I see. Do you know what time they will be home?"

"It will be late, sir. Probably at least nine o'clock."

"Well, here comes the police wagon, miss. First thing is to get you to the hospital."

❧

When the cuts and bruises had been treated on Effie's face and she was ready to leave the hospital, two bobbies helped her into another police wagon and took her to police headquarters. Scotland Yard had been notified of the kidnapping, and Chief Inspector Hoyt Monroe was there with one of his men.

London's new police chief, Hiram Berry, made sure Effie had water to drink, then as he, one of his men, and the two Scotland Yard men sat in a semicircle around her, Chief Inspector Monroe said, "We know you're not feeling too well, Miss Clarendon, but you understand it is essential we get some vital information from you."

Effie took a sip of water. "I understand, sir. I want to do all I can to help you find Prince David, and to make that kidnapper pay to the fullest extent of the law."

"Can you give us a description of the man who assaulted you and took little David?"

"Not much, sir. As I've told the police, he came up from behind me and started banging my face into the tree. From the angle he took hold of me, I would say he was exceptionally tall. Well over six feet." She gloated inside. Her cousin Nigel was barely taller than herself, and Effie was five feet nine.

"Well, we appreciate this much, Miss Clarendon," said Monroe. "Is there any way that you could tell how he might be built?"

"I would say he's quite husky. With his height, he no doubt weighs a good two-hundred-twenty or thirty pounds. Maybe more."

Nigel would tip the scales at no more than a hundred and fifty pounds.

"Anything else at all you can think of to help us find this man?" asked Monroe.

"No, sir. I'm sorry. I just didn't get a real good look at him."

"Well, we appreciate what you have told us. At least we know we're looking for a tall, husky man."

"All right, Miss Clarendon," said Chief Berry, "we need to take you home."

"May I suggest, Chief," said Monroe, "that you take her to

Buckingham Palace? I think Queen Victoria should be notified about little David's abduction even before Prince George and his wife return."

"Good idea," said Berry. "We'll take you to the palace right now, Miss Clarendon. And in the meantime, I'll have a couple hundred officers searching the city for this big man who has Prince David."

"Actually, Chief," said the Scotland Yard chief inspector, "I think you and I should both go with Miss Clarendon and tell Queen Victoria what's happened, and what we're doing about it."

"Of course," said the new chief, "I was about to suggest that."

When Queen Victoria heard the story from Monroe and Berry, she was terribly upset, and in no uncertain terms told the two law officers they must find her great-grandson.

"I feel quite certain David is being kept somewhere here in London, Your Majesty," said Monroe. "A ransom note will be forthcoming."

"No doubt," said Victoria. "We will just have to handle it as we see fit once we have the ransom note in our hands."

"Believe me, Your Majesty," said Berry, "we'll get your great-grandson back and see that this big man dangles at the end of a rope."

When the law officers were gone, the queen called a meeting of all the available palace servants. They had prayer for little David, asking God to bring him back to his parents and the rest of the family safely.

Twenty

Portia Whitaker was waiting nervously on the docks, her eyes scanning the milling crowd of people to catch sight of her husband with little Prince David.

She whispered, "Come on, Nigel. Come on."

Suddenly she caught a glimpse of a man with a child in his arms moving amid the crowd, then lost sight of them. Craning her neck, she fixed her eyes on the spot. When the two came into view again, clearly it was Nigel with a small boy in his arms. The child's cap was pulled so low she could hardly see his face.

Portia moved toward them as they drew near, and as they met, Nigel said, "This is her, David. She's my wife, and she loves little boys."

Portia leaned close. "Hello, David. I sure do love little boys."

David stared at her blankly.

Frowning, Portia said, "Honey, why do you have his cap pulled down so low?"

"I want to cover as much of his face as possible," came the reply. "Though relatively few people in London have ever gotten a close look at him, you remember that the photograph with him sitting on

Victoria's lap was on the front page of the *London Times* less than two weeks ago. We can't take any chances."

"Oh. Sure."

"Well, let's get our tickets."

Soon Nigel and Portia were standing in line inside the ticket office. Nigel still had the boy in his arms, and he was trying to pull his cap off.

"Better lift it some," said Portia. "I think it's uncomfortable for him."

Nigel nodded and raised the cap to a place where David seemed satisfied.

The lines were moving tediously slow.

After several minutes, the Whitakers noticed that a middle-aged woman in an adjacent line kept looking at David. She was with a man about her age, whom they assumed was her husband. The woman studied Portia's face, then Nigel's, making them quite nervous. When both of them looked at her at the same time, she smiled and said, "Hello. That's a handsome little boy you have there."

"Thank you," said Nigel.

"He looks familiar to me," said the woman.

Nigel's heart thumped his ribs as did Portia's.

"You folks Londoners?"

"Ah…yes," said Nigel.

"What are your names?"

"I'm Scott Meador and this is my wife, Elsa," Nigel said.

The woman's husband was now looking on.

She shook her head. "Well, Mr. and Mrs. Meador, your faces aren't familiar to me, but your son's face is quite familiar. I just can't think of where I've seen him before."

Cold chills were darting down the spines of the Whitakers.

"Avery," said the woman to her husband, "don't you think this handsome little fellow looks familiar?"

The man looked at David and squinted. "He sure does." Then to the Whitakers: "I heard you say, sir, that your name is Meador. I'm Avery Pollock. And this lovely lady with me is my wife, Corrine. We are Londoners, on our way to visit our daughter and her husband in Brooklyn, New York. They went there as immigrants two years ago. Our son-in-law works at the Flatbush Shoe Factory."

Queasy of stomach, Nigel smiled in a tight way. "Nice to meet you."

Portia felt her stomach muscles drawing taut, then her heart almost stopped when Avery said, "I know why this little fellow looks familiar, dear. His picture was in one of the newspapers recently."

While his own heart turned to ice, an unpleasant picture formed in Nigel's mind. He saw himself standing on a gallows with a noose around his neck. Queen Victoria was in the crowd who were there to see him hanged and was pointing an accusing finger at him while holding David in one arm.

"Oh yes," said Corrine. "It was in the *London Times.* Remember?"

The guilty pair exchanged frightened glances. Portia was asking with her eyes, *What shall we do?*

And then Corrine said, "It was that advertisement last week. The one about children's clothing at Harrington's Department Store. They had him dressed in a cute little suit with vest and jacket."

Avery looked at David again. "Sure! That's it."

"My, you must be proud to have your little boy model for Harrington's," said Corrine.

"We sure are," said Portia, willing to leave it right there.

"Indeed," said Nigel.

Another twenty minutes brought the Whitakers to the ticket counter, and while the agent was taking care of them he made light conversation, informing them that some two-thirds of the passengers were going to America as immigrants to start a new life.

As the Whitakers left the ticket office and headed across the docks, David began whimpering, wanting his mother. Portia took him in her arms and worked at consoling him, but as they threaded their way through the milling crowd, his whimpering became louder, and soon was a full-fledged wail as he cried, "Mama! Want Mama!"

Nigel guided Portia up beside a small supply shack. "We've got to get him quiet. People are staring."

Trying to soothe the child's fears, Portia spoke in soft tones. She gently pushed his face against her shoulder, muffled his cries, and patted his back.

Smiling nervously at the people moving by who were staring at the wailing child, Nigel said in a whisper, "Hurry, Portia! Get him quiet!"

Portia's voice and words of reassurance soon had David quiet.

They turned and looked at the huge ship. The *HMS Victoria* was sleek and black on the hull, and the cabins and deckhouses on the upper decks were white. The majestic vessel's name was emblazoned in gold on both sides, near the bow. British flags flapped in the breeze at both bow and stern and a red stripe ran the length of the hull on both sides, just below the main deck. The three massive smokestacks rose skyward, and though black in color, had wide red stripes.

Hurriedly, the Whitakers made their way across the dock and moved up the gangplank. Nigel handed the tickets to the agent on deck, who gave them directions to their second-class cabin on the second deck.

When they entered the cabin, Portia plunked down on one of the beds and immediately David began to squirm and wriggle, trying to get out of her arms.

None too gently, she put him down, and he dashed toward the door, crying, "Mama! Want Mama!"

Nigel grabbed him and deposited him on the bed beside Portia. "Do something with him," he said in a frustrated voice above the child's crying. "If he keeps up these outbursts, somebody's gonna wonder why he's wanting his mother when it's supposed to be you."

Portia gave her husband a frown, opened her shoulder bag, and took out a sack of goodies. Quickly, she pulled out a sugar cookie and held it so he could see it. The cookie caught David's attention immediately and his crying was reduced to sniffles. He raised his tear-filled eyes to her questioningly.

"You may have this cookie, David," she said sternly, "if you stop that bawling."

His lower lip quivered at the sharp sound of her voice, but the desire for the cookie won out. He rubbed his chubby hand over his eyes and nose, then reached for it. He took a bite, and while he was chewing it, the tension of the day caught up with him. His eyes began to grow heavy. He took another bite, chewed it, and his head bobbed like it was on a rubber neck.

Portia stood up and said, "Here, David. Lie down." She helped him lie down, then stepped back.

The child was still chewing on his second bite of cookie as Portia moved to a chair. Nigel sat down in another chair, facing her. They both rubbed their necks and temples without a word.

"I'm sorry I was a little short with you, honey," said Nigel. "I know your nerves are as shaky as mine."

Portia nodded, then turned her head to check on David. He was fast asleep, the partial cookie still in his hand.

"Well, at least he's quiet," said Nigel. "We're going to have to convince him that everything is all right, or he will bring us the wrong kind of attention."

"Yes," said Portia. "We had best keep him here in the cabin most of the time, the two of us taking turns going out on deck. And when we do take him out, we need to ply him with goodies and promises of more if he will be good and not cry for his mother."

"Okay," said Nigel. "We've got to make this look as normal as possible and always stay alert for any problem that comes along."

Portia sighed. "Of course. But I don't mind telling you that I'll be glad when this whole thing is over."

"Me, too, believe me. I thought of something right after we had that incident with the Pollocks. It would be best if we tell anyone who asks that his name is something other than David."

"Oh yes. He should have another name. How about Michael?"

"Okay. Michael it is."

Suddenly there was a vibration that made the cabin tremble.

Portia looked at her husband with puzzlement.

Nigel grinned. "They just started up the engines. I've done some reading about this ship, even though I don't like the person they named it after. It has six steam engines with pistons that travel ten feet on each stroke. I guarantee you, there are clouds of smoke billowing out of those big smokestacks right now."

Several minutes passed, then the sound of the ship's bell resounded across the harbor. The captain was heard commanding his men to weigh anchor, and five minutes later the *HMS Victoria* began to back away from the docks.

When the ship was far enough from the docks, the engines were reversed and it began heading south in the English Channel, the propellers churning dual bubbly, white streams behind. Coal smoke and ashes rose from the three smokestacks, roiling into the air.

Three hours later, as the *Victoria* left the English Channel, turned west, and headed out into the open sea, Nigel and Portia found the little prince once again crying and asking for his mother. Portia gave him another cookie, and both of them talked sweetly to him. Finally, they were able to convince him that all was well.

As the sun was setting, painting the calm surface of the waters a reddish gold, Nigel and Portia took the boy to one of the ship's dining rooms for dinner. When they were led to a table by the waiter, they found a young couple at the next table looking at David as Nigel was putting him in a booster chair. The Whitakers exchanged nervous glances as they sat down.

As the meal progressed, the young woman kept smiling and winking at David. Soon she had him giggling. Setting her violet eyes on the Whitakers, she said, "What's your darling little boy's name?"

Both said "Michael" simultaneously.

But the child, who would be three years old in June, looked at the young woman and said, "My name David."

Nigel, his scalp tingling, chuckled hollowly and cleared his throat. "Actually his name is Michael David. All our relatives and friends call him David, so he calls himself by the same name."

"Well, David," said the young woman, "you sure are a handsome boy. I love those big blue eyes."

David giggled.

The young man smiled and said, "My name is Jeremy Barlow. This is my wife, Cecelia. We're from Cardiff, Wales."

Nigel returned the smile. "I'm Scott Meador and this is my wife, Elsa. We're from London."

"Cecelia and I are going as immigrants to America," said Jeremy. "My uncle owns a riding stable just outside of Philadelphia, Pennsylvania. Uncle Jack will soon be retiring, and I'm taking the business over for him. My father owns a stable just outside of Cardiff. It's been my life since the day I was born."

"Sounds interesting," said the man posing as Scott Meador.

"I love it. Cecelia and I are excited about living in America. We're finding this voyage very enjoyable. We can hardly wait to see the Statue of Liberty in New York Harbor."

"Us, too," said a still shaky Nigel. "Quite a feat, the French erecting that statue, then dismantling it and shipping it to America."

"I'll say. Are you folks going to America for a visit or are you immigrants?"

"Full-fledged immigrants," replied Nigel. "I have a job waiting for me in Portland, Maine."

"Well, hello!" came a familiar masculine voice.

The Meadors looked up to see Avery and Corrine Pollock smiling down at them.

"Hello, yourself," said Nigel. "Nice to see you."

After Corrine and Portia had exchanged greetings, Corrine laid a hand on the little prince's head. "Hello to you, too, little sweetie pie. What's his name?"

"David!" came the reply from the two-year-old.

"Well, it's actually Michael David," said Nigel, "but everyone in the family calls him David. Let me introduce you to these folks, whom we just met ourselves. Avery and Corrine Pollock, this is Jeremy and Cecelia Barlow from Cardiff, Wales. They're immigrating to Philadelphia, Pennsylvania. The Pollocks are going to America for a visit with their daughter and son-in-law in Brooklyn, New York."

Avery and Jeremy shook hands, and the proper amenities were exchanged between the couples.

"Honey, our waiter wants us at our table," said Corrine. "We'd better go."

Avery excused himself and Corrine, and they hurried off to their table.

When the Barlows had finished eating, they rose from their table, and Cecelia found David eyeing her. She stepped to him and chucked him under the chin. "See you later, David."

The child reached up to her.

Cecelia looked at Elsa. "May I pick him up?"

"Of course," said Portia, using a napkin to wipe food from the child's face.

Cecelia held him close for a long moment, and Jeremy could see it in her eyes. She wanted to be a mother in the worst way. She kissed little David's cheek, thanked him for letting her hold him, and started to put him back in the booster chair.

Quickly, he reached for her face, and she brought him back in her arms once more. He wrapped his arms around her neck and laid his head against her cheek.

"I think you've found a friend, Cecelia," said Portia.

Cecelia smiled, held him where she could see in his eyes, and said, "That goes two ways."

David patted her face lovingly.

This time, he let her put him in the chair, and the Barlows excused themselves, saying they would see the Meadors later.

That night, after David had been put to bed and was asleep, Nigel and Portia sat facing each other.

"David has really taken to Cecelia," Portia said quietly.

"For sure," said Nigel. "I think because she has the same black hair as his mother. And I think she even looks a bit like Mary."

"I was thinking that, too. Add that to the fact that Cecelia paid so much attention to him this evening. He really took to her, all right."

When Prince George and Mary drove up to their house, the carriage lanterns shining, it was almost ten o'clock. They were surprised to find Police Chief Hiram Berry, Scotland Yard Chief Inspector Hoyt Monroe, and two police officers waiting for them.

They were told the story of little David's abduction and panic set in. Monroe and Berry told them they were doing everything possible, and that the queen wanted them to come to Buckingham Palace, where she had Effie Clarendon.

At the palace, Queen Victoria had gathered all the relatives who lived in and around London. Bursting into tears when she saw George and Mary, Victoria rushed to them and embraced them. The three of them clung to each other.

There were four pastors present, from the different churches where the family members attended. Victoria explained to George and Mary that they had been praying for David's safe return. She then called for prayer again, now that David's parents were there.

While one of the pastors was praying, Victoria was so overcome with grief that some of the servants took her to her room.

When all four pastors had prayed again, George and Mary talked to Effie, wanting to hear the story firsthand. Effie made them believe she was terribly sorry for allowing David to be kidnapped.

Mary asked if David's fever had gone down. While sniffling, Effie told her it did, or she would not have taken him out. Again, she told Mary how sorry she was for allowing David to be taken by the big man. Patting her hand, Mary told her it was not her fault. She must not blame herself.

George told Mary the police were right. Soon a ransom note would be delivered. They would pay the ransom and get David back. Hopefully the guilty man would be apprehended.

Keeping up the act, Effie sobbed uncontrollably.

The next evening at sea the Barlows entered the same dining room, and while they were standing just inside the door, the Pollocks came in. Jeremy explained that they were waiting for the Meadors and asked Avery and Corrine to join them.

Soon the Meadors arrived with Elsa carrying David. Corrine was first to step up to the child and call him her little sweetie pie. David allowed her to hug him, but when he saw Cecelia, he reached for her. After the two new friends had a moment together, Cecelia kissed David's cheek and relinquished him to his mother.

The conversation at dinner covered several subjects, but soon the Pollocks learned that the Barlows were born-again people, and when the subject went to spiritual things, the Meadors found themselves quite uncomfortable.

When the meal was over, Nigel and Portia excused themselves and left, under the pretense of needing to get David to bed.

The Barlows and the Pollocks stayed together for almost another hour, enjoying the fellowship that being Christians gave them.

In the days that followed on the Atlantic Ocean, the Barlows and the Meadors spent much time together, eating, chatting, and playing games on deck. Cecelia often held David and played little games with him. Sometimes the Pollocks were with them and it was apparent to all that David had especially attached himself to Cecelia and vice versa.

On an exceptionally warm day for February, Cecelia was holding David on her lap while sitting on a deck chair. The bright sun was glistening off the dancing waves of the deep blue water. Jeremy and the Meadors were standing close by at the railing in conversation with a middle-aged couple from Scotland's Shepherd Islands, who had introduced themselves as Andrew and Fiona Naysmith.

The Naysmiths were explaining that they were on their way to America to join Andrew's younger brother Paul and his wife in Wilmette, Illinois. Paul owned a thriving restaurant there and had asked Andrew to come into partnership with him.

The ocean breeze blew a wisp of hair across Fiona's face. She brushed it away and said, "Andrew and I are so excited about our new life in America."

Even as she spoke, Fiona's eyes fell on little David. She stepped away from the others and approached Cecelia. "Your little son is such a handsome boy. What's his name?"

Just the thought of having her own child put a warmth in

Cecelia's heart and a lump in her throat. Swallowing the lump, she smiled and said, "His name is David, ma'am. But he isn't my son. Elsa Meador is his mother."

"Oh. I'm sorry."

"Please don't be. How would you know? David and I have become best friends since we met on the first day at sea."

Fiona caressed the child's blond head. "Well, you sure are a fine little boy, David Meador."

At that moment, the Pollocks drew up. Corrine said hello to Fiona, bent down, and looked David in the eye. "Well, how's my little sweetie pie today?"

David reached for her and Cecelia relinquished him to her arms.

Scott introduced the Pollocks to the Naysmiths.

Fiona and Andrew made over David a few minutes, then Fiona kissed the boy's cheek and gave him back to Cecelia. He smiled at Cecelia and lovingly patted her face. Cecelia hugged him, kissed an ear, and once again sat him on her lap.

That night, Jeremy Barlow had been asleep an hour or so when he awakened at the sound of Cecelia weeping. Pale moonlight was streaming in through the cabin's two portholes.

Already knowing in his heart what was troubling his wife, Jeremy whispered, "Lord, help me to be a comfort to her."

He rolled over and laid a hand on her shoulder.

Cecelia drew a shuddering breath, looked into his eyes, and said, "I'm sorry I awakened you, sweetheart. I'm just having a difficult time with my emotions tonight."

"Maybe it would help to talk about it," Jeremy said softly. "You know we can always share everything."

Cecelia sat up. Taking her corner of the sheet, she dabbed at the tears in her eyes and took a deep breath. "Yes. I know it will help."

She propped her pillow up against the head of the bed and scooted up against it. Jeremy sat up and positioned himself so he could see her face by the dim light in the room. Taking her hands in his, he waited patiently, looking into her eyes.

"Today…today, when Fiona Naysmith called David my son, it…it really did something to me, Jeremy."

She rubbed her thumbs nervously over his hands. "I…I know God never makes mistakes. And…and I know if I hadn't fallen off that horse, I would no doubt be miserable in a loveless marriage to Royce Gibson. Even though I could have given him the children he wanted, my life would have been unfulfilled. And besides that, I would still be unsaved because it was you who led me to the Lord."

"So you can see God's hand in your life from the moment you fell off that horse."

"Oh yes. It's just—"

Cecelia burst into tears again, sobbing as if her heart would break into a million pieces. Jeremy folded her into his arms.

She sobbed for a moment, then gulping back a fresh onslaught of tears, she said, "Oh, Jeremy…I want a baby of our own so desperately that sometimes it just simply overwhelms me. I…I'm so thankful that you are my husband, and that you wanted me even though you knew I couldn't give you children."

Jeremy squeezed her tight, then eased back, took her hands into his once more, and looked into her tear-dimmed eyes. "I love you, my precious one, and nothing will ever change that."

Cecelia lowered her head. Tears splashed on their clasped hands as she spoke in a choked voice. "I love you, darling, with an abiding love. And I always will. But…but I just don't understand why God took away my ability to have children. He took away the ability, but not the desire. Darling, I don't mean to sound like I'm questioning God's right to do as He sees best. But, being human, I…I just don't understand. I trust the Lord to do what is right and best for us, but getting close to little David since we started on this journey has very much aroused my maternal instincts and made me long more than ever for a child of my own."

Jeremy loosened one of his hands from her tight grasp and placing it under her chin, gently raised her head.

As her eyes met his, he said, "Sweetheart, I don't have the answer to your question. I don't know why the Lord took away your ability to bear children but left the desire. But I know this…in His time,

AL AND JOANNA LACY

and in His wisdom, He will reveal the answer. All He asks of us is that we be faithful to Him and trust in His divine sovereignty to provide what is best for us. Maybe there is an orphan child in America who needs a loving Christian home, and God is just waiting for us to get there so He can bring us together."

Suddenly there was a touch of excitement on her tear-ravaged face. Her eyes lit up. "Oh, darling, do you really think so?"

"Yes, I do. I really do. You can't bear a child yourself, but you still have the desire to be a mother. Well, I believe the Lord left the desire there because He is going to give you a child. Maybe more than one as time passes."

Cecelia closed her eyes, trying to picture herself holding a little adopted son or daughter in her arms. This calmed her.

She opened her eyes. "What a joy it will be, darling, when the Lord makes it a reality!"

"Think you can sleep now, sweetheart?" asked Jeremy.

"Yes. But before we go back to sleep, let's talk to Jesus, thank Him for His blessings on us, and tell Him we are entrusting everything into His hands."

And they did just that.

Twenty-one

On the evening of the tenth day at sea, the Barlows and the Meadors ate dinner at a table next to the Pollocks and the Naysmiths. When the meal was over, the Naysmiths took the Pollocks to their cabin and the Barlows took Nigel, Portia, and little David to their cabin.

In the Barlow cabin, they sat and talked, with David on Cecelia's lap.

The conversation soon led to their talking about the past. Nigel and Portia lied about their past lives for some time, then asked to hear about Jeremy and Cecelia.

Cecelia went first, telling them that her maiden name was Parker and told of growing up in the home of a wealthy family. She told about meeting Royce Gibson, and how after dating for a year, he asked her to marry him. She went on to give the details about the ride on horseback and the fall that injured her. She fought tears as she told them the diagnosis of the gynecologist Dr. Shelby Evans concerning her chance of ever bearing children.

A smile creased Cecelia's lovely features as her story brought her to how Jeremy had stood by her when Royce had called off the wedding and walked out of her life, and how they subsequently had fallen in love and married. There were more tears when she told what it meant to her that Jeremy would marry her even though the prospect of her ever bearing him children was all but impossible.

Portia smiled. "This helps me to understand better why you have so attached yourself to David. I'm glad he has given you some happiness."

"Thank you, Elsa," said Cecelia, wiping tears from her cheeks. She then told how Jeremy had led her to the Lord and her parents, also. The Meadors sat in silence.

It was Jeremy's turn to tell of his past. He happily told of growing up in the home of his paternal grandparents and the joy of working with horses. He paused to interject the story of when at seventeen, his grandfather had the privilege of taking sixteen-year-old Princess Victoria on a horseback ride. Both Nigel and Portia stiffened at the mention of Victoria. Further mention of Queen Victoria as Jeremy told about his grandfather saving Vicky's life and the honor bestowed on him by the queen put cramps in their stomachs.

Jeremy went on with his life story and wove in how he and his grandparents had come to the Lord. Again, the Meadors sat silently, making no comments.

Jeremy went on to give his side of the story concerning how he met Cecelia and fell in love with her. The Barlows then brought up Queen Victoria and how much they appreciated her Christian principles.

Inwardly, Nigel and Portia squirmed as Jeremy took it from there and witnessed to them of their need to know the Lord Jesus Christ as their Saviour.

Nigel nervously adjusted himself on his chair and said, "I don't mean to offend you, Jeremy, but Elsa and I believe as long as a person lives the best he or she can, they will go to heaven when they die."

Jeremy smiled. "I mean no offense, either, Scott. If what you just said is true, then tell me why Jesus went to the cross. If we could make it to heaven by our good works, why did He purposely come to earth, go through all that He suffered, and die on the cross?"

Dead silence.

Portia put fingers to her temple and said, "Scott, darling, I hate to shorten our visit this evening, but I've had a headache coming on for about an hour, and it's getting unbearable. I really need to go to the cabin and lie down."

Cecelia gave David a hug and kiss, and relinquished him to Scott. The Meadors said good night and left.

The next morning, there were dark clouds covering the sky and the wind was picking up.

The *HMS Victoria*'s captain, Duane Redmond, called all the passengers together on deck before they went to breakfast. Standing on the bridge and using a megaphone while the wind plucked at his cap and clothing, he said, "Folks, I don't know how many of you have been on ocean voyages before, nor how many have been at sea when a storm came, but we have a big one on its way. Our barometer indicates it is quite fierce.

"We expect the brunt of it to hit us in about two hours. I want you to get your breakfast eaten and go to your quarters. Please stay there until you are notified it is safe to come out. Some of you are going to get sick. Those of you in steerage can go to the sick bay. As you know, it is down on your level at the bow of the ship. Those of you in staterooms will have to stay there, no matter how sick you are.

"Now, please eat your breakfast, then go to your quarters immediately."

The Barlows and the Meadors ate breakfast together in their favorite dining room, with David sitting in his booster chair next to Cecelia.

While they were eating, the high seas broke over the bow, sprayed across the decks, and splashed against the staterooms. The ship was beginning to toss and heave on the angry sea. A concerned Jeremy Barlow tactfully brought up salvation to the Meadors again, and while he was explaining the gospel, a mixture of snow and ice began to pour out of the dark clouds.

"I think the brunt of that storm is going to hit us sooner than

Captain Redmond thought," said Nigel, wanting to change the subject.

"You're right, honey," said Portia. "And I have another headache coming on. Could we cut breakfast a little short and go to the cabin?"

"Of course," said Nigel, wiping his mouth with a napkin and placing it next to his plate. He stood up. "Let's go."

As Portia rose to her feet, so did Jeremy.

Cecelia left her chair and picked up David.

When Nigel reached for the child, he shook his head and wrapped his arms around Cecelia's neck. "Wanna stay wif her."

"You can't, son," said Nigel. "We have to take you with us."

Holding David close, Cecelia shifted her feet to keep her balance in the rocking, swaying ship, and said, "Since Elsa has another headache, Scott, if it's all right with you, Jeremy and I will take him to our cabin. We'll keep him till the storm is over and she is feeling better."

The sea was getting rougher rapidly. Passengers were hurrying out of the dining room.

Nigel and Portia looked at each other. Nigel started to speak, but suddenly the ship took a deep dip on the rough sea, and passengers all over the dining room who were on their feet had to grab on to a chair or table to keep from falling. Jeremy swung his arms around Cecelia and David, spreading his feet to maintain his balance.

Nigel said, "Elsa, I think that's a good idea. With your headache, it's going to make caring for David a real strain on you. Let's go."

"All right," said Portia. Then to Cecelia: "Thank you."

Before Cecelia could respond, the ship rose up suddenly, rebounding from the downward pitch a moment before. Chairs slid across the floor, and what was left of the meals slid off the tables, which were anchored to the floor. Plates, bowls, and coffee cups were shattering on the floor all over the dining room.

Nigel and Portia rushed out the door with other people who were wanting to get to their quarters immediately. They glanced at each other while struggling to keep from falling, both knowing what the other was thinking. Getting away from David would give them a break from having him in their cabin, needing almost constant attention.

Jeremy and Cecelia watched them go, and Jeremy—still holding her and David—said, "Honey, it already looks dangerous out there. Let's sit back down here and hold on to the table."

"I agree," said Cecelia.

A few other passengers already had the same idea, but most were vacating the dining room. The ship pitched heavily again just after the Barlows had gotten seated with David still in Cecelia's arms, and a half dozen people fell to the floor.

There was a scramble to get to their feet, and the women told their husbands they wanted to stay in the dining room until the worst of the storm was over.

Outside, as the two impostors stepped onto the rocking, bouncing deck, Nigel got a good hold on Portia to keep her from slipping on the wet surface. Others were doing the same thing all around them. Some were falling while others who had done so were struggling to get up.

Nigel caught a glimpse of Captain Duane Redmond on the bridge, flanked by two crewmen. They were gripping the rail and looking down at the frightened passengers.

The howling wind was fierce, and the ship was pitching so hard, each time it went downward, big waves were washing on to the deck with a loud roar.

Nigel gripped Portia as the ship lifted upward from a downward plunge, fighting to keep them both on their feet. They found that they were amid a small group of passengers, who like themselves, were struggling to get across the deck to the stairs that led to the second level. Wind-whipped ice and snow struck their faces, the ice particles stinging painfully, causing them to close their eyes and turn away.

Suddenly the giant vessel plunged downward and a massive wave roared like a wild monster as it hit the deck. It caught the small group who were almost to the stairs and swept them across the deck, over the side railing, and into the angry sea.

Up on the bridge, the captain and his pair of crewmen stood transfixed in horror at the sight of it.

After Jeremy and Cecelia and the other passengers who had chosen to remain in the dining room had been there an hour, the storm began to abate. Three hours after that, the wild pitching of the ship was over, and though walking on the deck was still difficult, the people in the dining room began discussing whether or not to make an effort to get to their cabins.

While the discussions were going on, a crewman was coming across the deck, opened the door, and stepped in. Jeremy was holding a sleeping David in his arms.

The crewman wiped water from his face. "Folks, we've had a real tragedy. During the early part of the storm, there was a group of passengers who were trying to get to their staterooms. They were caught in a huge wave that rolled over the deck. It swept them overboard."

There were gasps and moans.

"We haven't been able to identify who they were," the crewman went on. "We won't be able to do that until we identify those who are still with us. A process of elimination will tell us who we lost." He took a deep breath. "You can go to your quarters now if you wish. Just be very careful. The decks are still wet, and as you can tell, the ship is still pitching some."

Ten minutes later, Jeremy and Cecelia entered their cabin with David. Jeremy laid him on the bed. Both of them watched him drop off to sleep, then Jeremy said, "Honey, I'm going to Scott and Elsa's cabin. I want to make sure they're all right."

Cecelia sagged onto a chair. "Hurry back, won't you?"

"Just be a few minutes."

When Jeremy was gone, Cecelia sighed and said, "Thank You, Lord, for keeping the ship from going to the bottom of the ocean."

Twenty minutes later, a droop-shouldered Jeremy came in, his face ashen. Cecelia rose from her chair, a frown knitting her brows together.

"Honey, what's wrong?"

Jeremy ran his tongue over dry lips. "Scott and Elsa were in the group that went into the ocean."

"Oh no!"

"They weren't in their stateroom, so I went to see the captain. He had already written their names and David's as having gone overboard because the Pollocks caught a glimpse of Scott and Elsa from the second level just before the wave took the group over the rail. They went to Captain Redmond and reported it just a few minutes ago. They had only gotten a brief glimpse, so they assumed Scott and Elsa had David with them. The captain was very glad to hear from me that we have David, and so were the Pollocks. I stopped at their cabin to let them know."

Cecelia was stunned. "Jeremy, what will happen to David?"

"The authorities will have to make contact with his relatives back in England. They'll have to come to America to get him. He'll be in our care until then."

David stirred and opened his eyes. Cecelia picked him up off the bed and held him in her arms. "Poor little boy," she said, kissing his forehead. "You won't understand what's going on, but we'll take good care of you."

David asked for a drink of water. While she was pouring water from a pitcher into a cup that sat on a small table, there was a knock at the door.

Jeremy opened it, and found Avery and Corrine Pollock huddling together against the cold wind.

"We just wanted to come and see how David is doing," said Avery.

Jeremy invited them in, and while they were removing their coats and hats, Corrine said, "Cecelia, Jeremy explained why the two of you had David when his parents were on deck and went to their deaths in the ocean. He told us you would probably be taking care of this little sweetie pie for the rest of the voyage. If you need our help in any way, we'll be glad to do anything we can."

"Thank you, Corrine," said Cecelia. "We'll keep that in mind."

Little David smiled at Corrine and reached for her. Cecelia

handed him to her. Corrine kissed his cheek, called him her sweetie pie again, and pressed him to her breast.

"He has really taken to you, Corrine," Cecelia said with a smile.

Corrine kissed his cheek again. "It's the grandmother in me. Avery and I have six grandchildren. But, Cecelia, David really has taken to you. It's obvious that he loves you very much."

"We haven't told you, but I can't have children. David's attraction to me must be that he senses how very much I would love to be a mother."

Avery and Corrine were surprised to hear that. Avery said, "That may very well be part of it, dear, but you show him so much love. He just naturally responds to it."

Tears misted Cecelia's eyes. "I do love him very much. It's going to be hard to let him go whenever he is taken from us. I'm sure the authorities will find his relatives, and of course, they will want him. Maybe we can keep him for a while in America till they come to get him."

"Well, I'm glad he has you and Jeremy to look after him until then," said Avery.

There was a knock at the door. Jeremy opened it and found one of the crewmen there.

"Mr. Barlow," said the crewman, "Captain Redmond asked me to let you know that we have changed course. We are heading for St. John's, Newfoundland. When we reach St. John's, the captain will send a wire through transatlantic cable to our office in London and tell them what has happened. We now know the names of every person who was washed overboard. Captain Redmond will ask our people in London to make contact with their families and let them know they are dead. The Meadors's relatives will, of course, be told that little David is alive. We'll let you know what the relatives say about coming to America to get him."

"Fine," said Jeremy. "How long will it take us to get to Newfoundland?"

"Six or seven days, unless we have some more rough weather."

Jeremy nodded. "Thank you for letting us know."

The next morning there was a strong wind blowing across the Atlantic. The waves were rising in dark mounds, but were chopping up into little white crests that rose and fell. The ship was pitching to and fro.

Jeremy and Cecelia were about to rise for the day when suddenly, Cecelia jumped out of bed and hurried to the bathroom. Jeremy heard her gagging, and when she came out, she was white as a sheet.

"Honey, did I hear what I thought I heard?"

"Yes," she said, easing back onto the bed and lying down. "It has to be seasickness, the way the ship is bouncing around."

Jeremy raised up on his elbow. "Strange it would happen now. When the ocean was much rougher than this, it didn't upset your stomach."

"Well, people's bodies react differently at some times than others."

"That may be," said Jeremy, leaving the bed, "but I'm going to go get the ship's doctor."

Cecelia smiled in spite of her nausea. "Why? It sure can't be morning sickness, though I wish it were. It'll pass. Don't bother the doctor. He's probably quite busy right now."

The waters stayed choppy for another two days, and Cecelia continued having nausea periodically. During this time, the Pollocks took little David to their stateroom to help out. The child proved to be perfectly content staying with the older couple.

On the morning of the third day, the ocean was clear and sapphire blue, and the surface was smooth.

But Cecelia's nausea remained.

The Pollocks still had David.

At midafternoon, warm sunshine was coming through the portholes, brightening the Barlow stateroom. Cecelia was feeling better. While dressing, she told Jeremy she would like to eat a little, then go to the Pollocks' cabin and get David. They had some snack items in the cabin, so Jeremy put them on the table, saying he was glad she finally felt like eating.

At the same time Cecelia was eating her snack, the Pollocks were on the main deck, sitting near the railing and talking to two other couples. David was on Corrine's lap. The air was warm and many passengers were outside enjoying it. A small group of children were playing near the spot where the Pollocks were sitting.

David began to squirm, wanting to get off Corrine's lap. While she was saying something to the two women, Corrine put him down and kept an eye on him while he moved from one adult to the other.

The conversation went on.

At one point in time—between visits to adults—David's attention went to the sounds of the children. Unnoticed by the chatting adults, he toddled his way to the place where the children were playing. They were somewhat older than David and paid him no mind.

David decided to do a little exploring on his own. His attention went to the railing along the edge of the deck. Beneath the top rail were two more, but there was room under the bottom rail for a small child to crawl through the space.

The glistening blue surface of the ocean was fascinating, and David decided to take a closer look.

Jeremy and Cecelia had gone to the Pollocks' cabin, and getting no answer to their knock, decided they must be on the main deck somewhere.

Jeremy had an arm around Cecelia as they went down the stairs, since she was still a bit unsteady on her feet. Jeremy turned his head both ways when they reached the main deck, trying to spot the Pollocks.

"Don't see them, honey," he said. "Let's just move toward the bow. If we don't find them in that direction, we'll head for the stern."

They had gone about fifty feet when Cecelia pointed ahead. "There they are."

"Where?"

"Right over there. Close by where those children are playing."

Suddenly they heard a girl's voice, pitched high and strained as she screamed repeatedly that a little boy had just fallen into the ocean.

The Barlows suddenly saw Corrine jump from her chair, followed by Avery. When Corrine reached the railing she cried, "Avery! It's David! He's in the water!"

Cecelia's heart froze, as did her feet.

In a flash, Jeremy was bolting toward the spot at the railing where people were gathering.

When he reached the railing, Jeremy drew up between two men, and set his fearful gaze down on the water. He saw a writhing, terrified little David bob to the surface below at the side of the ship. Instantly he hopped the rail and dived into the ocean.

Crewmen arrived having heard the screaming, and spotting the man and the boy in the water, tossed a life preserver toward them.

Moments later, with a coughing, squirming David in his arms, Jeremy was pulled aboard the ship while people cheered. Cecelia, the Pollocks, Captain Duane Redmond, and the rest of the passengers who knew what had happened, crowded close.

Cecelia was first to reach the dripping pair. She wrapped her arms around them, weeping with relief. Corrine was standing close, sobbing, and asking Cecelia to forgive her for letting David get out of her sight. The ship's doctor arrived, pushing his way through the crowd, and put his attention quickly on the boy.

While Jeremy held David and the doctor examined him, Cecelia wrapped her arms around Corrine and said, "It's all right, honey. I forgive you. The main thing is that Jeremy rescued him. He's breathing and conscious. Praise the Lord, he'll be all right."

It took the doctor only a minute to smile and say, "He's fine, Mr. Barlow. He must have held his breath most of the time, as children will sometimes do. You got to him before he inhaled very much water. He's more frightened than anything."

A crewman showed up at that moment with towels. While Cecelia and Corrine were wrapping David in one of them and Jeremy was draping one over his shoulders, Captain Redmond stepped up, laid a hand on his shoulder, and said loudly so the large crowd which had now gathered could hear: "Mr. Barlow, you are to be commended for such an heroic deed! You went after little David at the risk of your own life!"

There was applause and cheering.

Redmond then explained to the crowd about David's parents having been washed overboard in the recent storm.

Four days later, the *HMS Victoria* pulled into St. John's Harbor. The passengers were asked to stay on board.

Two days after docking in the harbor, the Pollocks were visiting the Barlows in their stateroom when Captain Duane Redmond appeared at the door.

Redmond said, "Folks, I just heard back from our home office in London. They have been able to contact the families of every one of the fourteen people who were washed overboard—except the Meadors. They can find no one named Meador living in or near London who were related to Scott and Elsa, nor anyone else who even knew them."

Puzzlement showed on Jeremy and Cecelia's faces.

"That's strange," said Jeremy. "They told us they were from London."

"Strange, indeed," said Redmond. "They gave London as their home when they purchased the tickets. But as you know, no local address is given at our ticket desk when the passengers are going to America as immigrants. The wire said our people have turned it over to Scotland Yard, who are now doing further investigation. But they won't be able to let me know of any results until we dock in New York."

"There has to be some relatives somewhere," said Avery. "Uncles, aunts, grandparents."

"You'd think so," said Redmond, "but since our people haven't found them, as thorough as they've already been, I'm not too sure Scotland Yard will find them, either."

Keeping her thoughts to herself, Cecelia held David close to her heart. *Oh, David, could you possibly be the child God has for us?*

Still stunned at the sudden death of David's parents, Cecelia told herself that maybe the Lord knew there were no relatives to take David and raise him, and had chosen Jeremy and her. This hope was trying to take root in her heart, but she knew it was probably unrealistic.

Captain Redmond returned to the pilot's cabin on the bridge, and soon the *Victoria* was steaming her way toward America.

As time moved on and the ship left its dual white trails on the sea behind it, Jeremy Barlow became quite concerned with the obvious obsession Cecelia had with David. He had overheard her talking to him when she thought Jeremy couldn't hear, saying that maybe David was going to get to be her little boy.

One morning as she was dressing David, Jeremy came from the deck and drew up to the door of the stateroom, which stood open. Once again, she was telling David that maybe she would get to be his mother.

Even as she spoke, Cecelia saw the shadow on the floor that came from the open door. "Oh, you're back already, darling."

Jeremy stepped in and kissed her cheek. "Honey, we need to talk."

She smiled. "All right. Let me finish dressing our boy and we'll go out and sit on the deck. It's nice out there today."

Moments later, when they sat down on deck chairs a few feet from the door of their stateroom, Cecelia had David on her lap.

"Sweetheart," Jeremy said in a loving tone, "I'm concerned that you are letting yourself get too close to David. I've heard you tell him more than once that maybe you would get to be his mother— or put it the other way—that he might get to be your little boy."

Cecelia's face crimsoned. Tears filmed her eyes. "Jeremy, I admit that nothing would make me happier, and I guess I'm selfish, but it wouldn't make me upset if Scotland Yard never did find any relatives and we could keep him."

"Honey, you mustn't let yourself cling to such a hope. It will just hurt you more when David is given to his relatives."

Cecelia blinked at her tears. She caressed David's blond head and said, "I'm also aware that this precious baby lost his parents a few days ago. He must be very confused, even at his young age. He needs a lot of love and attention to help him feel secure."

"I suppose you're right about that," said Jeremy, "but be careful with your heart, honey. I don't want to see it broken."

Cecelia let a weak smile lift her lips. "I'll be just fine, darling. I promise."

Twenty-two

As they sat down in one of the receiving rooms at Buckingham Palace, Queen Victoria, Prince George, and Mary set weary eyes on Scotland Yard's chief inspector, Hoyt Monroe.

Victoria sighed and said, "Chief, we are absolutely baffled. It has been over three weeks, and we have received no ransom note yet."

"I understand, Your Majesty," said Monroe. "We are baffled, too. We can't figure out why the kidnapper took David, if it wasn't for money. I assure you, we are working day and night to find some clue as to David's whereabouts. Every newspaper in the British Isles is carrying the story daily, with the latest photograph of David on the front page. That's the one with you and him together."

Tears rushed to Victoria's eyes. "Yes."

"We'll just have to keep praying, Grandmother," said George. "God knows where David is, and only He can bring him back to us."

"That is true, Prince George," said Monroe. "And we at Scotland Yard will continue to do our job as God would have us do. If He chooses to use the Yard to locate and return your little son, then praise be to His name. If not…at least we'll know we did everything we could."

"We appreciate your attitude, Chief Monroe," said Mary.

"Yes," said Victoria. "It is so wonderful to have the chief inspector of Scotland Yard a spiritual man who loves the Lord and acknowledges His hand in human affairs."

Monroe smiled. "And may I say, Your Majesty…it is even more wonderful to have the queen of this great nation a spiritual lady who loves the Lord and acknowledges His hand in human affairs."

Prayer meetings were being held daily at Buckingham Palace, led by the queen's pastor, Adam Norden. George and Mary were staying at the palace for the time being and were in on every prayer meeting. As was the queen.

Having placed as many of her normal responsibilities as possible on the men of Parliament, Victoria concentrated most of her energies and resources to bringing about the safe return of her much adored great-grandson. When she went about the daily tasks that only she could handle, there was always a prayer in her heart.

Friday, March 19, had been a particularly long and taxing day, with several important decisions having to be made for Parliament that only the queen could make. Late that afternoon, the weary seventy-seven-year-old queen went to her bedroom with her long-time personal maid, Emily, at her side. Only upon the insistence of her doctor and her family had she consented to lie down for a while before dinner. Emily kept a hand on Victoria's elbow as she guided her to the bed and quickly fluffed up two pillows, positioning them where the queen's head would lie.

Easing on to the bed in a sitting position, Victoria said, "Will you help me remove these shoes, dear? My feet and ankles are quite swollen today."

"Of course, mum," Emily responded, dropping to her knees.

Once the shoes were off, the maid rose to her feet and swung Her Majesty's swollen legs up on the bed. Victoria sighed in relief as she lowered her head to the pillows.

"Now you take a good nap, mum. You'll feel better for it."

Victoria smiled up at her. "Kind of bossy, aren't you?"

Emily chuckled. "Yes, mum. After all, how many people in Great Britain get to boss the queen around?"

The queen smiled at Emily again as she placed a light coverlet over her and started to turn away. Victoria grasped her hand and Emily turned back around.

Looking her maid square in the eye, the aging queen said, "George and Mary have promised that should any word come about David, they will apprise me at once, even if I am asleep. I want that same promise from you."

"You have my word, mum."

"Thank you, dear," she said, releasing Emily's hand. "That's good enough for me."

She then closed her weary, red-rimmed eyes and let a smile form on her lips.

Emily bent down and kissed her forehead, and with that, left the room, closing the door behind her.

The smile was still on Victoria's round face as she opened her eyes and looked at the closed door. She closed her eyes once more and said, "Dear Lord, Your Word says the effectual fervent prayer of a righteous man availeth much. I am righteous because I am cleansed by Your precious blood. I am claiming this promise. As fervently as I know how, I am begging You to bring my sweet little David back to us. Thank You, Lord, that we can always trust Your promises."

On Saturday morning, March 27, the *HMS Victoria* left the Atlantic Ocean and swung into New York Harbor. The sun was shining brightly, its reflection twinkling in magnificent splendor on the water as the ship passed through the narrows between Brooklyn and Staten Island.

Great excitement and expectation filled the throng of passengers as they crowded onto the port side of the main deck to get their first glimpse of the Statue of Liberty. Many had dreamed, planned, and waited for this day for years. And now that it had finally come, a feeling of trepidation mixed with their elation. As Lady Liberty came into view, holding her torch high, a hush fell over the crowd. The immigrants were contemplating their future in the strange and wondrous new land.

The Barlows were standing at the railing between the Pollocks and the Naysmiths. Jeremy was holding little David in his arms. The child's eyes were wide as he beheld the sights around him. When the ship arrived at its closest point to the magnificent statue as it beelined for Ellis Island, Cecelia gripped her husband's arm. "Oh, Jeremy! It's all like a dream. I just know we have a wonderful future in America."

"Yes, we do, sweetheart."

"Makes me almost wish we were moving here, Corrine," said Avery Pollock.

Andrew Naysmith chuckled. "Well, I imagine your daughter and son-in-law would be very happy if you were."

"Yes, they would," said Corrine. "Who knows? Maybe we will move here someday."

Little David finally spotted the massive, towering statue. Pointing while he tugged at Cecelia's sleeve, he cried excitedly, "Mama! Look!"

Cecelia was so overjoyed to hear the child address her as "Mama" she could hardly speak. It did not escape Jeremy's notice, but he remained silent. Cecelia finally found her voice and said, "Oh yes, David! She's beautiful, isn't she?"

"Beeyoodifil, Mama," he said, nodding.

Cecelia knew the child was desperately missing his mother, and felt honored that he cared enough for her to adopt her.

Moments later, the crewmen of the *Victoria* dropped anchor near Ellis Island, and a host of ferryboats drew up beside the ship. They would carry all the passengers to the island, where the visitors would pass through customs and be checked through by the United States immigration authorities.

Captain Duane Redmond approached the Barlows while the ferryboats were getting in line at the gangplanks and told them he would accompany them, since arrangements had to be made for them to legally take David to Pennsylvania with them.

The Barlows, Pollocks, and Naysmiths said their good-byes, realizing they might not see each other again once they were on Ellis Island.

Soon the Barlows and little David were on a ferryboat with Captain Duane Redmond, and after the short trip of some 800 yards, were on solid land. Both Jeremy and Cecelia had trouble walking, and the captain explained that after so many weeks aboard ship, they had developed sea legs. It would take a little time to get their land legs back.

Redmond stayed with them while they had their medical examinations and met with the immigration officials to answer the usual questions.

As soon as they were approved to enter the country, Captain Redmond took them to the port authority office. There he explained to Richard Kogler, the agent in charge, what had happened to little Michael David Meador's parents, and that he had sent a wire from St. John's, Newfoundland, to the shipping company's offices in London, giving the names of the fourteen people who had been washed overboard in the storm. He went on to explain that in the company's return wire, they had located relatives of everyone but little Michael David's parents, Scott and Elsa Meador, and that Jeremy and Cecelia Barlow were willing to take the child with them to their destination in Philadelphia, Pennsylvania, and take care of him until Scotland Yard—who were now on the case—could find some of David's relatives and he could be returned to England.

Kogler immediately sent a wire to Scotland Yard to see if they had located little Michael's relatives by then. He told Jeremy and Cecelia that he would put them in a waiting room where they could stay until he received a return wire from Scotland Yard. Captain Redmond bid the Barlows good-bye, saying he must get back to his ship. They thanked him for his help and were taken to the waiting room.

Nearly three hours had passed when Richard Kogler came in. Jeremy saw his wife tense up.

"Well, folks," said Kogler, sitting down and facing them, "I just received the return wire from Scotland Yard. They say they have been unable to find anyone in the British Isles who were related to the Meadors or who even knew them. Chief Inspector Hoyt Monroe asks if you are willing, that you take Michael with you to Pennsylvania and keep him until further notice."

Cecelia's face brightened. "Of course we will! Jeremy and I will keep him as long as is necessary, Mr. Kogler, and you can rest assured he will have a good home."

"All right. If you will give me the address in Pennsylvania where Scotland Yard can make contact with you, I'll wire Chief Monroe, tell him you are willing to keep the child, and give him the address."

Holding David close to her heart, Cecelia dropped a kiss on his blond head. Raising her eyes, she caught Jeremy watching her and sent a bright smile to him. Jeremy gave Kogler his uncle's address, and soon they were on a ferryboat to Manhattan Island where they would catch their train to Philadelphia.

As they sat on a bench inside the boat, Cecelia was holding David on her lap. "Darling, maybe our prayers are answered. Maybe God is giving David to us."

Not desiring to dampen her joy, yet wanting to be realistic, Jeremy said, "Honey, please don't forget that as of now, this is not a permanent arrangement."

The smile left Cecelia's face and she drew David more snugly in her arms.

The next day, Jeremy and Cecelia arrived in the Philadelphia depot and took a hired buggy to Jack and Dorine Barlow's home in the country.

When Dorine opened the front door of the large house, a smile spread over her face, followed by a stunned look as she saw the lovely brunette holding the little blond boy.

"Jeremy! It's so good to see you! And Cecelia, you are even more beautiful than Jeremy's letters described you!" Dorine's eyes then were fixed on the child. "But—but—"

"We'll explain little David, Aunt Dorine," said Jeremy, embracing her.

Jeremy then took David so Cecelia and Dorine could embrace.

At that moment, Jack came in from the rear of the house and showed the same surprise at the presence of the child. Jeremy took care of the introductions, then Dorine said, "Come sit down, so you can tell us about this darling little boy and your trip."

"I have to help the driver bring our luggage and trunks in, Aunt Dorine. Then we can sit down and talk."

"I'll help, Jeremy," said Jack. His shoulders were stooped more than they had been the last time Jeremy saw him.

"No need, Uncle Jack," said Jeremy. "I'll take care of it."

When the luggage and the two trunks had been placed in the vestibule, Jeremy entered the parlor, only to find that his aunt was holding David on her lap.

"He's such a sweetie, Jeremy," said Dorine.

Jeremy sat down beside Cecelia. "Did you tell them, honey?"

"No. I thought we should tell them together."

When Jack and Dorine heard the story, they were sympathetic with little David, but already having been advised in a letter from Jeremy that Cecelia couldn't bear children, they expressed their joy that she could be a mother to David, at least for a while.

Cecelia then told them of Jeremy's diving into the ocean to save little David from drowning. Jack and Dorine commended him. Jack took David from Dorine, sat the boy on his lap, and said, "Little guy, this temporary papa of yours risked his life to save you. I hope someday when you grow up, you two can get together so you can thank him."

David didn't understand what Jack was saying, but smiled and nodded.

The conversation then went to Jack's upcoming retirement. Jack brought up the small house on the property where Jeremy and Cecelia would be living until he and Dorine would leave, saying he hoped they would find it comfortable.

Jeremy suggested they go see it now, and he would take the trunks and luggage. Using a small wagon that Jeremy could pull by himself, they went to the cottage with Jack carrying David.

When they stepped inside, Cecelia said, "Oh, it's lovely!"

The cottage was clean and shiny. A warm late-afternoon sun pushed its way through the sparkling windows; in the cherry trees in the back yard, the early spring birds raised their voices in a song of welcome to the new tenants.

Jack said, "Jeremy, there are some things I need to talk to you about right away, concerning your taking over."

"Sure, Uncle Jack. I'll unload these trunks for Cecelia, then we can go wherever you want and talk."

"Well, I'll go start supper," said Dorine.

When Jeremy had unloaded the trunks and put them on the back porch, he and Jack walked away together.

Cecelia immediately busied herself putting things away, and at the same time, keeping a eye on David as he played near the hearth. Humming a nameless tune, she gave competition to the birds as she arranged their belongings and made the little house into a warm home for her husband and little David.

For a moment, a wave of homesickness assailed her, and she missed her parents. But this was eased when she spoke from a thankful heart to the Lord for His numerous blessings.

The next morning, Jeremy was awakened when he felt Cecelia leave the bed in a hurry and opened his eyes to see his wife dart into the water closet. He heard gagging and coughing, and when she came out, her face was sheet white.

As Cecelia lay back down beside him, Jeremy said, "Honey, I'm taking you to a doctor. Uncle Jack and Aunt Dorine can recommend one to us, I'm sure."

She patted his arm. "No, no. It will pass. I'll be fine."

Jeremy raised up on his elbow and frowned. "Honey, aboard ship, we assumed it was seasickness. But we're on land now, so it can't be that."

"I know, honey. If the nausea doesn't go away real soon, I'll let you take me to a doctor."

In London, Effie Clarendon put on a facade of grief over the kidnapping of little Prince David, acting like she would never get over it. She returned to work at King George Hospital, and since everyone knew the story, she kept up the act of grieving.

To keep her act looking genuine, Effie often stopped by the palace and spoke to Prince George and Mary, asking if there had been any word from Scotland Yard. Each time, when told there had not been, she spoke in tender tones, trying to comfort them.

Often at night, when Effie was trying to get to sleep, she was haunted by the gospel sermons she had heard at church during the time she was David's governess. She was also haunted by the Scriptures she had heard on the subject of salvation, heaven, and hell from Queen Victoria, Prince George, and Mary. Sleep often eluded her as she thought about spending eternity in hell, and each time as she lay awake, she found herself in a cold sweat.

One day in the first week of April, Effie was crossing a busy street in London while walking home from the hospital. Being in the city's busy business district, there was heavy traffic.

Effie made it to the middle of the street and waited for several buggies and carriages to pass before venturing to the other side.

Suddenly she was aware of a frightened horse hitched to a buggy, whinnying and bolting ahead of the rest of traffic with the wide-eyed driver doing his best to bring the horse to a stop.

Terror gripped Effie when she saw the speeding buggy heading straight for her as it threaded through slower-moving vehicles. Because of the steady traffic on both sides of her, there was nowhere to move to elude the charging horse and buggy.

She froze, her heart seemingly a dead thing in her chest.

Seeing the young woman ahead of him, the driver yanked the right rein with all his might, and the frightened horse veered to the right, sideswiping a bread wagon. The impact brought a loud bang with wheels and spokes shattering, and the charging buggy missed Effie by inches.

Traffic on both sides of the street came to a halt.

Further up the street both drivers were able to get their vehicles stopped. At the same time, a weak-kneed Effie Clarendon began staggering toward the sidewalk.

A young man who had seen it all, jumped out of his carriage and took her by the arm. "Here, miss. Let me help you."

People on the sidewalk who had seen it gathered close as the young man sat Effie down on a bench in front of the grocery store. "Miss, are you all right?"

"I—I'll be fine in a moment," said Effie, wiping sweat from her face with a hankie produced from her dress pocket. "That…that was close."

"It sure was," said the young man. "Fast as that horse and buggy were moving, if they'd hit you, you'd have been killed. You're fortunate to be alive. You can thank God for watching over you."

"Uh…yes. Thank God."

"Miss, you look a bit pale. Would you allow me the privilege of taking you wherever you are headed in my carriage?"

Effie took a deep breath, and mopped more sweat. "I'm heading home, sir. I would appreciate it."

"Come on. Let me help you to my carriage."

By the time the carriage pulled up in front of the boardinghouse where Effie lived, her nerves had settled down, and her color was back. As the young man was helping her out of the carriage, Effie's attention was drawn to a royal carriage parked just ahead of it, and she saw two uniformed palace guards leaving the porch of the boardinghouse.

The guards explained that Queen Victoria wanted her to come to dinner at the palace. Knowing it would be unwise to refuse, Effie thanked the young man who had been so kind to her, then was assisted into the royal carriage.

Soon Effie found herself at the queen's table in Buckingham Palace. While they dined alone together, Victoria said, "Effie, dear, the reason I wanted to have dinner with you this evening is to help you if I can. George and Mary have been telling me of the grief you are carrying over little David's kidnapping."

A bit surprised, Effie said, "Why, thank you, Your Majesty. I appreciate your concern and your kindness. It…it just has been so difficult for me because David's parents had trusted me to take care of him and I let them down."

"Honey, I know they have both told you, as I have, that there is no blame on your part. You were simply doing your job as governess. It was no fault of yours. You must stop blaming yourself. I'm just sorry you were beaten up so badly. I'm glad your face has healed so well."

Making all of it she could, Effie puckered her brow and said, "Thank you. But I still feel so guilty, and can't seem to get over the fact that little David is gone."

"Tell you what," said Victoria, "after dinner, I want to show you some things in the Bible. Maybe I can help you."

Effie nodded. "Yes, Your Majesty."

When they had finished eating, Victoria took Effie into her private receiving room. They sat down side by side on a small sofa, and Victoria picked up a Bible from the end table next to it.

Taking Effie from one Scripture passage to another, the queen showed her how God can give comfort to those who belong to Him.

"The greatest comfort in time of heartache on the face of this earth, dear," said Victoria, "is God's comfort. In fact the Bible calls the sweet Holy Spirit the Comforter. But He can only comfort those who have received the Lord Jesus into their heart as their personal Saviour.

"When I received Jesus as a girl, the Holy Spirit took up residence literally in my very body, which the Bible says is His temple. I have comfort that only a born-again child of God can have. But as far as I know, you have not yet opened your heart to Jesus, Effie."

"No—no, ma'am."

"May I show you some things you really need to know?"

Effie knew better than to refuse. "Of course."

Victoria opened the Bible, turning to the New Testament. "It all starts with the sin problem we all are born with, dear. You are aware, I'm sure, that the first man God put on this earth was Adam."

"Yes."

"Look what it says here in Romans 5:12: 'Wherefore, as by one man sin entered into the world, and death by sin; and so death passed upon all men, for that all have sinned.' It says that all have sinned. That includes me, Effie. The queen of England. And it means you, a nurse at King George Hospital. Right?"

"Y-yes."

"And all of us have to physically die, don't we?"

"Yes."

"From what we just read, death came to the world because of sin, right?"

"Yes."

"I used the words physically die, dear. There also is a spiritual death. Let me show you."

Victoria took Effie to Genesis chapter 1 and showed her that Adam and Eve were created in the image of God. She pointed out that in verse 26, God said, "Let us make man in our image, after our likeness…" And emphasized the plural: *us* and *our,* which coincides with other Scriptures, which say that God is a triune Being: Father, Son, and Spirit.

She then explained that man was created a triune being: body, soul, and spirit in the image of God. The body is man's earth contact, the soul is the person himself, and the spirit is the God contact, because as Jesus pointed out in John 4:24, "God is a Spirit: and they that worship him must worship him in spirit and in truth."

Victoria then showed Effie the command God made to Adam in Genesis chapter 2, concerning the tree of the knowledge of good and evil in the Garden of Eden: "And the LORD God commanded the man, saying, Of every tree of the garden thou mayest freely eat: But of the tree of the knowledge of good and evil, thou shalt not eat of it: for in the day that thou eatest thereof thou shalt surely die."

Effie was looking at the verses on the page.

Victoria said, "Please note these words, honey. 'In the day that thou eatest thereof thou shalt surely die.' The very day Adam ate of the forbidden fruit, he would die, correct?"

"That's what God said."

"Do you know the story? Adam and Eve both ate the forbidden fruit in the next chapter."

"Yes, I know it."

"Did God hold their funeral and bury them that day they took the fruit?"

"No. They lived a long time after that."

"Right. Physically. How, then, did they die that very day?"

"Well they must have died spiritually."

"Correct. They became depraved beings of only body and soul. They died spiritually that very day. The spirit—the God-contact—was dead and gone. They could not worship God in spirit because they were spiritually dead. Do you see that?"

"Yes."

"So that's spiritual death."

"Now, every person on earth comes to that day when they die physically, don't they?"

"Yes." Effie thought of how close she came to dying earlier that day.

"Now let me show you that there is also a death that God calls the second death."

Victoria then took Effie to Revelation chapter 20 and showed her that in verse 14, the lake of fire where all unbelievers will spend eternity, is called the second death. She showed it to her again in Revelation 21:8.

"When a person dies physically and they are not saved, Effie, they will die a second time. When they are cast into the lake of fire, which is hell in its final state. But did you know that when a person is born the second time, he cannot die a second time and spend eternity in hell?"

Effie frowned. "Born a second time?"

"Yes. Jesus told about it. Look what He said."

Victoria turned to John chapter 3 and read verse 3 to Effie, where Jesus said, "Except a man be born again, he cannot see the kingdom of God."

"We have to be born again," said the queen, "because we were born into this world in Adam's image, not God's. You and I were born body and soul, but dead spiritually. The spirit—the God-contact—must be brought to life. Look here at verse 6 at what Jesus said: 'That which is born of the flesh is flesh; and that which is born of the Spirit is spirit.' You were born of the flesh when you came into this world from your mother's womb. But in order to go to heaven, you must be born again…born of the Spirit."

Effie nodded slowly. "I see."

"Now, the Bible tells us in order to be saved, we must come to Jesus in repentance of our sin and put our faith in Him and Him alone to save us. Repentance simply means that you turn from your sin, acknowledge to God that you are a sinner deserving hell, but are asking Him to forgive you and save you. Look over here in John 1:12. It's speaking of Jesus when it says, 'But as many as received him, to them gave he power to become the sons of God, even to them that believe on his name.'

"Notice we have to become God's children, Effie. We are not God's children until we receive His Son into our heart as our Saviour. That's when we're born again. Nothing can save us from the second death unless we have been born the second time. Do your understand?"

Effie swallowed hard. "Yes."

"Honey, it was Jesus who hung on Calvary's cross, shed His precious blood, died for our sins, was buried, and rose from the dead three days later so He would be alive to save us. If you are willing to repent and receive Him into your heart, He will save you right now."

Suddenly, Effie Clarendon felt the guilt of what she did to help the Whitakers kidnap Prince David, and the weight of all her sins came down hard on her soul. "What do I do to receive Him?"

"Romans 10:13 says, 'For whosoever shall call upon the name of the Lord shall be saved.' Just call on Him. Acknowledge that you have been a wicked unbeliever, and ask Him to come into your heart and save you. I can help you to know what to say if you'd like."

Suddenly, Effie dropped to her knees and said, "Dear Lord Jesus, I am a guilty sinner. I have been a wicked unbeliever, but now I believe You died for me on the cross, and I'm asking You to come into my heart and save me. Make me a child of God."

The queen was wiping tears, and was stunned when Effie went on, saying, "And dear Lord, please bring little Prince David back to us. It's my fault he's gone! It was me who put him in Nigel Whitaker's hands that day in the park. I helped him and Portia do the kidnapping!"

With these words, Effie broke down and sobbed.

When Effie had stopped sobbing, Victoria told her to sit down again and to explain about David's kidnapping. Tearfully, Effie told her the whole story, including Nigel and Portia's destination in America. Victoria was elated, and praised the Lord that David was all right.

Effie asked if she was going to prison. Victoria embraced her, saying that no matter what—she was saved now, and would never see hell. She then said that she would speak to the judge who heard her case and ask him to go light on her since she had confessed.

Victoria then sent a palace servant to Scotland Yard, asking that Hoyt Monroe come to the palace immediately.

Another servant was sent upstairs to George and Mary's room, saying the queen wanted to see them right away. When George and Mary came down, Victoria told them in front of Effie about her just being saved and what she had confessed.

Chief Monroe came and when he heard Effie's story, he was sure they now had a lead on David's whereabouts. He would go to the office and wire the New York authorities, telling them the name of Portia's father and the name of the manufacturing company. He would take Effie with him and turn her over to the police. Victoria gave Effie a brand-new Bible before Monroe took her away, and told her to read it every day.

The next morning, Chief Monroe came to the palace and told the queen, George, and Mary, that Portia's parents had been in contact with the shipping company, trying to find out why she and Nigel were not on the *Victoria* as they were supposed to be.

Monroe went on to say that with the information Scotland Yard had gained from the shipping company, they figured out that Nigel and Portia used the names Scott and Elsa Meador when they bought their tickets and were swept overboard in the storm that took a total of fourteen people to their deaths in the ocean. Prince David, whom the Whitakers had called Michael, was safe in Philadelphia with Jeremy and Cecelia Barlow of Cardiff, Wales.

Victoria was elated to know that her little great-grandson was in the care of John Barlow's grandson. There were many tears of joy and relief at the good news, and while Victoria, Mary, and George wept and wiped tears, they talked about the situation.

After considering just how to bring David home, Victoria said, "Something just came to me."

George and Mary set curious eyes on her.

"I just remembered," said the queen. "Right now, Parliament member Horace Naylor is in Washington, D.C., visiting the president of the United States. We need to send Horace a message by transatlantic cable and see if he could make arrangements to bring him with him when he comes home. I think Mrs. Naylor might have gone with him."

Prince George stood up. "I'll take care of that right now, Grandmother."

Twenty-three

On Wednesday, April 14, Jack and Dorine Barlow sat down to breakfast with Jeremy, Cecelia, and little David, who was in a high chair.

Both Jack and Dorine observed with delight as Cecelia fussed over the child, making sure everything was just right for him. At the same time, Jeremy had a nagging dread in his mind, feeling quite sure that one day some of David's relatives would be found and he would be taken back to England. Cecelia was going to be crushed.

They were just finishing breakfast when they heard a knock at the front door of the house.

Leaving the others in the kitchen, Jack made his way to the front door and found Philadelphia County Sheriff Ned Prater on his porch. "Good morning, Jack. Am I here too early? Are you eating breakfast?"

"We're just finishing with breakfast, Sheriff. Please come in."

"Thank you," said Prater, stepping inside. He noted the quizzical look on the stable owner's face. "Jack, are Jeremy and Cecelia Barlow here?"

"Yes. Jeremy is my nephew. He is going to take over the place when I retire in a couple of months."

"Do they have a little fair-haired two-year-old boy with them?"

"They do, and somehow you must know the situation. Have the boy's relatives in England been located?"

"Yes, they have, and I need to talk to Jeremy and Cecelia."

"Of course. They're in the kitchen. Come on."

As Jack led the sheriff past the winding staircase and down the wide hall toward the kitchen, his heart was heavy for Cecelia.

When Jeremy and Cecelia saw the uniformed man with the sheriff's badge on his chest, they exchanged puzzled glances.

"Jeremy, Cecelia," said Jack, "this is our sheriff, Ned Prater."

Jeremy stood up and shook Prater's hand. "Nice to meet you, Sheriff."

Prater said the same, then greeted Cecelia and Dorine. He looked down at the boy in the high chair, laid a hand on his head, and said, "And this little fellow is David."

Immediately Jack said, "David's relatives have been located in England."

Cecelia's body stiffened.

Jeremy reached down and took hold of her hand. Setting steady eyes on Prater, he said, "Who are David's relatives, Sheriff?"

Prater took a shallow breath. "His father is Prince George Frederick."

The room was suddenly silent as a tomb.

Jeremy and Cecelia were stunned.

Dorine looked at her husband, who had his eyes on the young couple.

Cecelia worked her jaw loose, blinked, and said in a shaky voice, "We…we have actually been taking care of Prince David…the future king of England?"

"That's right, ma'am," said the sheriff.

Cecelia shook her head as if to clear away the effects of Prater's words. Tears flooded her eyes. "How can this be? Sheriff, are you sure? Could this be some mistake?"

"It's no mistake, ma'am. The Scotland Yard authorities know that this little lad is Prince Edward Albert, Queen Victoria's great-grandson, who one day will be Great Britain's King Edward VIII. He was kidnapped on February 10 by a Nigel and Portia Whitaker with the help of the boy's governess. The Whitakers took David aboard the *HMS Victoria* to bring him to America. They bought their tickets under the names of Scott and Elsa Meador."

"Whitaker," said Jeremy thoughtfully. "There's been a Whitaker family who has dealt Queen Victoria no end of heartaches for years."

"This is what the Scotland Yard people told me in their wire," said Prater. "The kidnapping wasn't for ransom, but simply another way of dealing misery to Queen Victoria. From what the wire said, the governess had broken down and confessed her part of the crime, and told the authorities the whole story. Because of this, Scotland Yard was able to learn that the Whitakers—posing as the Meadors—were swept overboard along with several other people in a storm at sea."

Jeremy shook his head in amazement. "And this is where we entered the picture, Sheriff. Cecelia and I had David with us in our stateroom when the Whitakers were on deck and were carried to their deaths in the ocean. We were given permission by both British and American authorities to bring David here and keep him until we heard differently."

"That's the way I understand it," said Prater. "It just so happens that Horace Naylor, a member of the British Parliament, and his wife are in Washington, D.C., visiting President William McKinley. In a wire from Prince George Frederick, Naylor has been instructed to pick up the little prince and bring him back to England. The Naylors will be here day after tomorrow to do so."

The stark reality that she was going to lose David washed over Cecelia like a giant ocean wave. She jumped up, lifted David out of the high chair, and held him tightly to her breast. Her grasp was so tight that the child grunted and squirmed in her arms, trying to free himself.

"Celie," said Jeremy, gently prying her arms from around David, "you're hurting him."

A grimace of utter devastation was on Cecelia's face, and as Jeremy's words made their way into her consciousness, her mouth fell open. "Oh, David, I'm sorry, honey. Mama didn't mean to hurt you."

Taking the boy from her, Jeremy set him back in the high chair. "Celie, you and I need to talk in private. Uncle Jack, Aunt Dorine, Sheriff Prater, please excuse us. We'll be back shortly." Putting an arm around Cecelia's waist, he led her from the room.

While the child looked on, confusion evident on his face, Dorine picked him up, held him close and said, "Sheriff, Cecelia has grown very close to David. He has even been calling her Mama. This is all very difficult for her. May I get you a cup of coffee while we wait for them to come back?"

In the parlor, Jeremy sat Cecelia down on the couch, then dropped to one knee in front of her. Tears were streaming down her cheeks as she stared at him stonily.

Praying earnestly in his heart for divine guidance, Jeremy pulled a handkerchief from his pocket and gently dried the tears from her ravaged face.

Before he could form his scattered thoughts into words, Cecelia spoke in a tiny, shaking voice. "Jeremy, I…I tried not to let myself count on the Lord letting us keep David. I really did." More tears welled up in her eyes. "But…but I love him so much. He calls me Mama."

"I know, sweetheart. And I know how much letting him go is going to hurt you. But listen to me. Can you, for a moment, put yourself in David's real mother's place? Can you imagine how she has suffered all this time? Think how she must have mourned and grieved for her son, not knowing where he was or if she would ever see him again."

Cecelia's eyelids fluttered. She thumbed tears from her eyes, and after a long moment, nodded her head. "Oh, Jeremy, how selfish I've been. Since…since Sheriff Prater told us who David really is, I haven't given a moment's thought to how his parents have been suffering. Dear Lord, please forgive me for putting my own feelings and desires above theirs!"

A fresh onslaught of tears overtook her, but God was making them cleansing, healing tears. When at last the weeping had passed, a look of sweet peace filled Cecelia's countenance.

Taking Jeremy's hand, she placed a kiss in his palm. "Thank you, my love, for being so patient with me. Let's go back to the others now. I'll be fine."

As they walked down the hall toward the kitchen, a silent prayer of thanksgiving wended its way heavenward from a very grateful young husband.

On Thursday, Jeremy stayed close to Cecelia in their cottage as she spent her last day with the little boy she had come to love so much.

While Cecelia sat on the floor with David, playing one of their little games with him and he was laughing happily, her eyes filled with tears. She looked up at Jeremy, who sat close by. "Honey, I just thought of a Scripture I read in my personal devotions a few days ago. I didn't realize how fitting it was then, but I want to show it to you."

"I'll get your Bible for you," he said, rising from the chair. "Be right back."

When Jeremy returned, he handed Cecelia her Bible, then picked David up and sat down, holding him lovingly on his lap.

Remaining on the floor, Cecelia opened her Bible to the book of Ezekiel. "This is what I read, honey. Ezekiel 34:23 and 24. 'And I will set up one shepherd over them, and he shall feed them, even my servant David; he shall feed them, and he shall be their shepherd.' Honey, this can't be the psalmist David, who was king of Israel centuries before. This is prophecy. It has to be speaking of the Lord Jesus, who was to come to earth and be the good Shepherd, the great Shepherd, and the chief Shepherd. Son of David, the Bible calls Him, because through His stepfather, Joseph, He was of the earthly family of David."

"You are so right, sweetheart," said Jeremy. "It's referring to the virgin-born Son of God, without question."

Cecelia smiled. "Now, listen to what the heavenly Father says in verse 24. 'And I the LORD will be their God, and my servant David a prince among them; I the LORD have spoken it.' Jeremy, did you catch those words? 'My servant David, a prince among them.' Do you see how fitting it is in this situation? David, a prince among them."

Jeremy was shaking his head in wonderment as Cecelia rose to her knees, tears in her eyes, and moved to where the child sat on his lap, looking at her with a smile. Cupping David's face in her hands, she said, "Precious little David, we didn't know you were a prince among us, but the Lord let us have you for a little while so you would always be a part of our lives, even though you won't remember us."

That night, Cecelia cried herself to sleep in Jeremy's arms.

It was late morning the next day when Horace Naylor and his wife, Nellie, arrived at the Barlow home. Naylor expressed the thanks of Prince George and Mary and Queen Victoria to Jeremy and Cecelia for so kindly and faithfully caring for little David through the entire ordeal.

Jack Barlow told the Naylors of the incident on the ship when David fell overboard by the negligence of someone who was supposed to be watching him, and how Jeremy came along seconds after the child hit the water, dived in, and saved him from drowning.

The Naylors looked at each other, wide-eyed, then Horace set admiring eyes on Jeremy. "Mr. Barlow, this is really something. Then, if it weren't for your unselfish deed of rescuing little David from the ocean, there would have been no good news for his family. He would have gone to a watery grave. I will most certainly see that David's parents and the queen learn of this!"

Cecelia set loving eyes on her husband and beamed with pride.

Horace rose to his feet and said, "Well, Nellie, we'd best be going. We have to catch that train in Philadelphia in just about an hour."

Everyone walked to the front door. Cecelia held David while Jack and Dorine kissed him good-bye. Jeremy took him long enough to hold him, hug him, kiss the top of his head, then gave him back to Cecelia. Struggling to keep her composure, Cecelia held the child close, kissed him several times, and with misty eyes, said, "Good-bye, sweetheart. I will never forget you. I love you."

David patted her face as he had done so many times. "Wuv Mama."

Cecelia gulped back the sob that was trying to escape from her throat and handed him to Nellie.

As the Naylors started out the door, David screamed and cried, reaching for Cecelia.

The scene touched Horace's heart. "Wait a minute," he said, halting and turning around. "Nellie, give the boy back to Cecelia. Let's you and I go have a private conversation. Where could we go, Mrs. Barlow?"

"Just go into the parlor, Mr. Naylor," said Dorine. "We'll wait right here."

David's wailing stopped the instant Nellie placed him in Cecelia's arms. He called her Mama and hugged her neck. Cecelia bit down on her lower lip and held him close.

Less than three minutes had passed when the Naylors returned, and Horace set his gaze on the young couple. "Would you two have the time to return to England with us? Nellie and I talked about it, and we agree that it would be much better for David if he could have both of you on the voyage. He's been through a lot for a little fellow his age. I can speak for Parliament. We will pay your round trip, and you will receive a generous check for your time and effort."

"Well, I can say they most certainly do have the time," said Jack. "I can hold off retiring until they get back."

"I agree," said Dorine. "It will help little David immensely, I'm sure."

"How about it?" Horace asked Jeremy and Cecelia.

"It's fine with me," said Jeremy.

Cecelia kissed the child in her arms. "Me, too!"

"Good!" said Horace. "We rented that horse and buggy outside in Philadelphia. We'll head on back right now. I'll send a wire to the palace in London and explain the situation to Prince George. I will let you know as soon as I hear back from him if our plan to take you to England with David and us is all right with him and his wife. It may take a day or two."

Cecelia stroked the little prince's blond hair. "Won't David's parents be happy to see him!"

Jeremy chuckled. "They won't be any happier than his great-grandmother will be, I guarantee you!"

At dawn the next morning, Jeremy was sitting up in the bed when Cecelia came out of the water closet.

"That settles it, sweetheart," he said. "I'm taking you to a doctor today."

Cecelia sat down on the edge of the bed. "There's no need, honey. It's just my nerves bringing the nausea on. Giving David up when I thought maybe I would get to be his mother has had me strung pretty tight. There is nothing a doctor could do. I'll be all right once my nerves aren't strung so tight."

Jeremy shook his head stubbornly. "No, Celie. You can't put it off anymore. I'm taking you to a doctor. You'll need some kind of medicine, anyway, to keep you from getting seasick when we traverse the Atlantic two more times."

Cecelia leaned toward him and stroked his cheek tenderly. "You are a stubborn man, Mr. Barlow."

"Hah!" He laughed. "Look who's talking about being stubborn!"

Jeremy was in the waiting room at Dr. Preston Hailey's office late that morning when Cecelia came out of the examining room after being in there exceptionally long. The doctor, in his white frock, was on her heels.

Before the doctor had taken Cecelia into the examining room, they had told him the story about little Prince David, and Cecelia's attachment to him.

The first thing Jeremy noticed was the look of shocked disbelief that was on his wife's pale face. *Oh no,* he thought. *It must be something terrible. Lord, help me to handle whatever it is.*

Knowing her husband so well, and seeing the look of utter terror on his face as he rose from the chair, Cecelia knew he was thinking the worst. Wanting to relieve his tortured mind, she gave him the most beautiful smile he had ever seen.

Unable to reconcile his dark thoughts with Cecelia's happy countenance as she drew up, Jeremy stuttered, "Wha-what i-is it?"

Still smiling, Cecelia said, "First, let me tell you that Dr. Hailey says everything is going to be fine. He sees no reason why I should have any problems at all."

"That's right," said the physician, who had halted one step behind Cecelia.

Jeremy frowned. "Honey, what is it?"

Cecelia's smile broadened. Her voice was low and musical. "Morning sickness."

Cecelia's reply sent slivers of shock through Jeremy's brain. Slowly he mastered his thoughts, then worked at getting control of his speech mechanism.

While he was doing so, Dr. Hailey said, "Your little son or daughter will be born in early October, Mr. Barlow."

Jeremy gasped to get a breath, then took Cecelia in his arms. "Praise the Lord! It's a miracle! Hallelujah!"

The doctor turned and smiled at his nurse, who was giggling, then turned back to Jeremy, smiling.

"Well, doctor," Jeremy said, a lilt in his voice, "if it's a boy, in my eyes, he will be a prince! And if it's a girl, she will be a princess!"

Cecelia laughed. "Sweetheart, I've already got the names picked out. If it's a boy, we'll call him David, and if it's a girl, we'll call her Victoria."

Jeremy kissed her cheek. "I couldn't have thought of more appropriate names myself! Oh, praise the Lord, we're going to have a baby!"

Cecelia laid her head on his chest and wrapped her arms around him. "It is truly a miracle from our Lord, honey. Oh, He has been so good to us!"

Jeremy nodded his agreement, then looked at Hailey and said, "Doctor, when we explained about little Prince David a while ago, we didn't tell you that we may have to travel to England, stay a few days, then come right back. Will this be a problem for Cecelia?"

"I don't see why it would," said Hailey. "She's just about past morning sickness time. The sea voyages this early in her pregnancy will put neither mother nor baby in any danger."

When Jeremy and Cecelia pulled onto Barlow Stables property, they saw Jack at the barn, sending a group of men and women off for a ride. As they trotted away toward the open fields, Jack turned and waved at Jeremy and Cecelia.

They waved back. "Look, honey," Jeremy said. "There's the Naylors with Aunt Dorine and David on the front porch."

"Let's tell them all at the same time," said Cecelia.

Jeremy drew rein and called to his uncle, "Head on over to the porch. We've some marvelous news!"

Jack arrived at the porch at the same moment Jeremy was helping Cecelia out of the buggy. "So what's this marvelous news?"

"You'll know in a minute," said Jeremy, planting the expectant mother's feet on the ground.

The three of them climbed the porch steps together, and Dorine said, "What's this about marvelous news?"

"We'll tell you after we learn from Mr. Naylor if we have news from England."

David slipped off Dorine's lap and ran toward Cecelia. "Mama!"

Horace rose to his feet. His face was beaming. "Good news from England. Queen Victoria, herself, had the return wire sent. She wants both of you to come with us, and has personally authorized Parliament to cover all your travel expenses. She also said to tell you that you will be paid handsomely for escorting her great-grandson home."

"Wonderful!" said Cecelia, picking David up.

Jeremy frowned. "Honey, should you be doing that?"

Smiling at him, she said, "At this point, it's all right, darling."

"At this point in what?" asked Jack.

"My pregnancy," came Cecelia's quick reply.

Everyone stared in awe as Jeremy spoke up and told them of God's miracle in their lives.

Congratulations were quickly passed around, and then Horace Naylor had a disparaging thought. "Tell me," he said nervously, "will this mean you can't make the voyage to England?"

"We already talked to the doctor about that, Mr. Naylor," said Jeremy. "He said it will be no problem."

"Wonderful!" said Naylor. "I know the queen and David's parents would be terribly disappointed if you couldn't come."

Cecelia laughed happily. "Then they won't be disappointed, because we're going!"

Twenty-four

On Tuesday, May 18, 1897, as the ship swung into London's harbor, the Naylors and the Barlows stood at the starboard railing near the bow with the breeze caressing their faces. Little David was in Jeremy's arms.

Other passengers were at the railings on both sides of the deck, eager to catch a glimpse of the docks. The sun was shining brightly out of a partly cloudy sky, its beams kissing the surface of the water. Seagulls flew around the ship, squawking and squealing.

Jeremy pointed to them and said, "See, David, even the birds are welcoming you home!"

"I'm sure they are," said Horace, "but they're not the only ones. Look up there!"

Horace was pointing to the dock where the ship was headed.

"Oh, my!" said Nellie.

Jeremy and Cecelia saw it at the same instant. There was a massive crowd gathered on the dock waving British flags and banners, and a brass band was playing. They could barely hear the band, but as the ship carried them closer, the music became louder.

Squinting to focus on the banners, Jeremy said, "Can you see what's on those banners? They say, 'Welcome home, Prince David'!"

A lump rose in Cecelia's throat. "Jeremy, I think I see Queen Victoria and David's parents near the gangplank. See them? They're surrounded by a phalanx of palace guards."

"Sure enough," said Jeremy.

"I figured they would be at the dock," said Horace.

"I would if I were in their place," said Cecelia.

Soon the ship came to a halt at the dock and the crew dropped anchor. The gangplank was attached to the side of the ship, and the captain signaled for the Naylors and the Barlows to leave the ship ahead of the rest of the passengers.

Standing at the foot of the gangplank as the two couples came toward them, Queen Victoria, Prince George, and Mary had tears shining on their cheeks.

When they reached the bottom of the gangplank, Mary dashed up, arms open wide, and Jeremy placed the child in her arms. George moved up close, and David's eyes widened. He looked back at Cecelia, puzzlement on his features, then looked back at his parents and cried, "Mama! Papa!"

At first, Cecelia felt a pang strike her heart, then as she dropped her hand to her midsection, the pain went away. The baby who one day would call her Mama was growing in her womb.

When George and Mary had hugged and kissed their little boy, David was placed in Victoria's arms. As she kissed him repeatedly, he said, "I wuv you, Granmama!"

There were more tears shed as David's parents and his great-grandmother welcomed Jeremy and Cecelia with sincere hugs, expressing their appreciation for all that they had done for the little prince.

During a gala celebration at Buckingham Palace that evening, the Barlows and the Naylors, along with Scotland Yard's chief inspector and his wife, and Pastor Adam Norden and his wife, were seated at the table of honor with Queen Victoria, Prince George, Mary, and little David. Some two hundred British dignitaries were present, including the men of Parliament. A small orchestra was also there, positioned near the podium. They played soft music during the meal.

When dinner was finished, the queen stepped to the podium and made comments about the reason they were gathered there, and asked her pastor to come and offer thanks to God for little Prince David's safe return. After Pastor Norden's prayer, the small orchestra played a heart-touching rendition of "Amazing Grace."

The queen then asked Scotland Yard's chief inspector to come to the podium and relate little David's story to everyone. Hoyt Monroe stood before the crowd and told the entire story of the kidnapping, giving every sordid detail. He closed off by telling how Effie Clarendon had told Queen Victoria all about how Nigel and Portia Whitaker had planned the abduction, and why…even though it exposed her own guilt. Monroe added a light note to the story by saying that because of Effie's honesty and the fact that it was her confession that had eventually led them to David's whereabouts, Queen Victoria had seen to it that she was given a full pardon for her part in the crime.

Then at the queen's bidding, Horace Naylor told what he knew about the Barlows and their care of Prince David. He emphatically added the story of Jeremy's heroism in rescuing David from certain death in the ocean at the risk of his own life.

The orchestra played a rousing piece, and the crowd applauded and cheered.

Once again the queen stood regally at the podium, and when all was quiet, she gave God the glory for keeping His mighty hand on Prince David.

Then a look of anguish filled her eyes as she said, "The sorrowful part of this otherwise wondrously happy event is the loss of two lives: Nigel and Portia Whitaker. Through many decades the Whitaker family was full of bitterness and hatred toward me. They sought vengeance by kidnapping this precious little child.

"I feel so sorry about Nigel and Portia. To my knowledge they died without the Saviour. And let me say to those of you within the sound of my voice, don't let this happen to you. Don't wait until it's too late."

Victoria let her gaze move over the crowd with a prayer in her heart for each of them, then a smile graced her lined face as she said, "Now, I would like to call Jeremy and Cecelia Barlow to the podium."

The Barlows looked at each other, wondering what the queen was going to do. Jeremy pushed his chair back, helped his wife to her feet, and they held hands as they moved to the podium. There was sudden applause as they stepped up beside Queen Victoria.

Victoria choked up a bit as she embraced them both, then faced the crowd. "Ladies and gentlemen, you have heard of the marvelous manner in which this precious young couple cared for my two-year-old great-grandson, who will one day be king of England. Prince David's parents and I have agreed that Jeremy Barlow should be made an honorary knight of Great Britain and that Cecelia Barlow be made an honorary dame to show our appreciation for their unselfish deeds."

Even as the queen spoke and the crowd broke into applause, a uniformed palace guard appeared, carrying a silver sword.

Jeremy and Cecelia were quickly told by the guard that they should kneel before the queen. Victoria took the silver sword and tapped the shoulders of the kneeling pair, officially making them knight and dame. Asking them then to rise, she stood beside them and said, "Ladies and gentlemen, I present unto you Sir Jeremy Barlow and Dame Cecelia Barlow."

The next day, Queen Victoria spent the day with Jeremy and Cecelia and a large portion of the time she talked to Jeremy about his grandfather, and the blessing he had been to her personally.

The next morning, it was time for the Barlows to board a ship and head back to America. Jeremy had a check in his wallet, written in an amount that staggered him and Cecelia. A special royal carriage pulled up in front of Buckingham Palace as Jeremy and Cecelia stood on the veranda with the queen, George, Mary, and little David. It was a bittersweet moment as the Barlows bid the royal family good-bye.

When Cecelia held the little prince and kissed his cheek, another lump rose in her throat. But it dissolved when she reminded herself of the new life that was growing in her womb.

Tears were on everybody's cheeks when Jeremy and Cecelia boarded the coach, which would carry them to the docks. As the coach pulled away and the Barlows waved at the little group on the veranda, Cecelia said, "Darling, that little boy doesn't even know it, but he has taught us some valuable lessons that will make us better parents to our own children."

"That he has, sweetheart," said Jeremy. "We've gone through a valley with him, and I'm grateful to the Lord that we are now about to pass out of that valley. We must fasten our eyes on the mountain-top ahead."

Cecelia took hold of his hand and squeezed it. "Yes! The mountaintop ahead."

Soon the carriage moved out of the city and headed toward the harbor where they would board the ship and cross the Atlantic to their new home.

Jeremy squeezed Cecelia's hand and smiled. "What an honor Queen Victoria bestowed on us, sweetheart."

"Yes. I never dreamed of being a dame."

Jeremy chuckled. "When our little David or Victoria is born, will he or she call you 'Dame Mama'?"

Cecelia laughed. "Certainly! And he or she will call you 'Sir Papa'!"

Epilogue

The mighty hand of God was evident on Queen Victoria during her reign, sparing her from death in six assassination attempts. On January 22, 1901, in His perfect plan, God allowed her to die at nearly eighty-two years of age of a stroke, and took her home to be with Him.

Upon Victoria's death, Prince Albert Edward—known as "Bertie"—became king of England as Edward VII. He reigned until May 6, 1910, when he died at the age of sixty-eight. He was succeeded by his son, George Frederick, who became King George V. Considered to have been one of England's greatest kings, George reined until his death at seventy years of age on January 20, 1936.

On that day, his son Prince Edward Albert known as "David" became King Edward VIII. However, David's reign lasted less than a year. In 1934, as Prince of Wales, he had met a twice-divorced American woman named Wallis Simpson, and was infatuated with her.

Rumors had been circulating in British society ever since the pair first met. After becoming king in January 1936, David began seeing Mrs. Simpson even more than he had as Prince of Wales. The rumors became more malicious when the king and Mrs. Simpson went on a cruise down the Dalmatian Coast together in the summer of 1936.

The rumors were disturbing to the royal cabinet. They expressed their feelings about the relationship to the king, telling him that respectable people recoiled at the thought of a twice-divorced American adventuress sitting on the British throne.

David told them he was deeply in love with the lady and was considering asking for her hand in marriage. The cabinet pled with him to think about what it would do to the country. He told them he would give it careful consideration, which he did for six months. Mrs. Simpson, loving Edward VIII very much, offered to step out of his life and return to America if it would help him put his duty to England before his love for her.

On December 8, David told her he loved her too much to let her go. He would abdicate the throne and they would marry. The next day he announced this to his cabinet, who pleaded with him to reconsider.

On December 10, King Edward VIII signed the instrument of abdication, and the next day Parliament passed the bill of abdication, which ended his reign. David's younger brother, George, ascended the throne as George VI.

In March of 1937, David was named Duke of Windsor by British royalty, but kept a low profile before the people of England until his death from lung cancer on May 28, 1972. He left behind his loving wife of thirty-five years.

George VI reigned for sixteen years until he died after four years of illness brought on by arteriosclerosis on February 6, 1952. He was deeply and genuinely mourned as a monarch who, like his father, had put duty to his country before everything. He was succeeded by his oldest daughter, who reigns to this present day as Elizabeth II.

The publisher and author would love to hear your comments about this book. *Please contact us at:* www.allacy.com

An Exciting New Series by Bestselling Fiction Authors

Let Freedom Ring
#1 in the Shadow of Liberty series

Young Russian Vladimir Petrovna is always minutes away from disaster. He is a Christian in a pagan country that exacts extreme penalties from believers. His farm is nearly destroyed by blight and he cannot pay the taxes he owes. He is a husband and father whose daughter is secretly in love with a Cossack—one of the very soldiers who persecute families like Vladimir's. Though he may lose everything he loves, Vladimir must trust God as he navigates his river of trouble. When he finally arrives in the "land of the free and the home of the brave," his destiny—and faith—are changed forever.

ISBN 1-57673-756-X

The Secret Place
#2 in the Shadow of Liberty series

Handsome, accomplished Dr. Erik Linden veers between heroism and accolades, failure and despair in this fascinating new historical novel. A recent medical graduate in nineteenth-century Switzerland, Erik finds himself in a crisis of faith after his former fiancée dies on his operating table. Should he give up performing surgery? Should he abandon his homeland and seek a better life in a freer place? Meanwhile, lovely young Dova, a friend in Erik's hometown, faces murderous avengers after identifying them to the authorities, even as she struggles with an affection that she must keep quiet. As the two young people cope with love's longings on opposite shores, can they find the serenity of God's covering in *The Secret Place?*

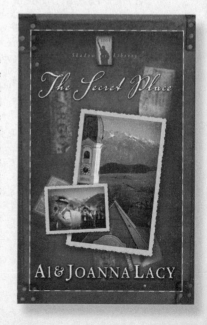

ISBN 1-57673-800-0

Mail Order Bride Series

Desperate men who settled the West resorted to unconventional measures in their quest for companionship, advertising for and marrying women they'd never even met! Read about a unique and adventurous period in the history of romance.

Hannah of Fort Bridger series

Hannah Cooper's husband dies on the dusty Oregon Trail, leaving her in charge of five children and a general store in Fort Bridger. Dependence on God fortifies her against grueling challenges and bitter tragedies.

Angel of Mercy series

Post-Civil War nurse Breanna Baylor uses her professional skill to bring healing to the body, and her faith in the Redeemer to bring comfort to thirsty souls, valiantly serving God on the dangerous frontier.